Things We Could Design

Design Thinking, Design Theory

Ken Friedman and Erik Stolterman, editors

Design Things, A. Telier (Thomas Binder, Pelle Ehn, Giorgio De Michelis, Giulio Jacucci, Per Linde, and Ina Wagner), 2011

China's Design Revolution, Lorraine Justice, 2012

Adversarial Design, Carl DiSalvo, 2012

The Aesthetics of Imagination in Design, Mads Nygaard Folkmann, 2013

Linkography: Unfolding the Design Process, Gabriela Goldschmidt, 2014

Situated Design Methods, edited by Jesper Simonsen, Connie Svabo, Sara Malou Strandvad, Kristine Samson, Morten Hertzum, and Ole Erik Hansen, 2014

Taking [A]part: The Politics and Aesthetics of Participation in Experience-Centered Design, John McCarthy and Peter Wright, 2015

Design, When Everybody Designs: An Introduction to Design for Social Innovation, Ezio Manzini, 2015

Frame Innovation: Creating New Thinking by Design, Kees Dorst, 2015

Designing Publics, Christopher A. Le Dantec, 2016

Overcrowded: Designing Meaningful Products in a World Awash with Ideas, Roberto Verganti, 2016

FireSigns: A Semiotic Theory for Graphic Design, Steven Skaggs, 2017

Making Design Theory, Johan Redström, 2017

Critical Fabulations: Reworking the Methods and Margins of Design, Daniela Rosner, 2018

Designing with the Body: Somaesthetic Interaction Design, Kristina Höök, 2018

Discursive Design: Critical, Speculative, and Alternative Things, Bruce M. Tharp and Stephanie M. Tharp, 2018

Pretense Design: Surface over Substance, Per Mollerup, 2019

Being and the Screen: How the Digital Changes Perception, Stéphane Vial, 2019

How Artifacts Afford: The Power and Politics of Everyday Things, Jenny L. Davis, 2020

Meaningful Stuff: Design That Lasts, Jonathan Chapman, 2021

Things We Could Design: For More Than Human-Centered Worlds, Ron Wakkary, 2021

Things We Could Design

For More Than Human-Centered Worlds

Ron Wakkary

The MIT Press
Cambridge, Massachusetts
London, England

© 2021 Massachusetts Institute of Technology

All rights reserved. No part of this book may be reproduced in any form by any electronic or mechanical means (including photocopying, recording, or information storage and retrieval) without permission in writing from the publisher.

This book was set in Stone Serif and Stone Sans by Westchester Publishing Services. Printed and bound in the United States of America.

Library of Congress Cataloging-in-Publication Data

Names: Wakkary, Ronald, 1964- author.
Title: Things we could design : for more than human-centered worlds / Ron Wakkary.
Description: Cambridge, Massachusetts : The MIT Press, [2021] | Series: Design thinking, design theory | Includes bibliographical references and index.
Identifiers: LCCN 2020050508 | ISBN 9780262542999 (paperback)
Subjects: LCSH: Design--Philosophy.
Classification: LCC NK1505 .W34 2021 | DDC 745.4--dc23
LC record available at https://lccn.loc.gov/2020050508

10 9 8 7 6 5 4

Contents

Series Foreword   vii
Acknowledgments   xiii

    Chapter 1: Introduction   1

Part I: Design

    Chapter 2 Prologue: Photobox, Long-Living Chair, and Olly   31
    Chapter 2: Nomadic Practices   35
    Chapter 3 Prologue: Fairphone, Pocket Receivers, and Kar-a-Sutra   57
    Chapter 3: Designing Artifacts, Objects, and Products   65

Part II: Things

    Chapter 4 Prologue: Phototrope, +Lichtlijn, New Faces, New Identities, Prayer Companion, and the Great Pacific Garbage Patch   87
    Chapter 4: Things Are Interconnected and Transformative   95
    Chapter 5 Prologue: Tilting Bowl, Being the Machine, Obscura 1C Digital Camera, Morse Things, Burgundian Black Collaboratory, and Mineral Accretion Factory: Underwater Table   121
    Chapter 5: Things Are Relational and Vital   135

Part III: Designer

    Chapter 6 Prologue: Living in a Prototype, Greenscreen Dress, Supersurface, and Children Village   163

Chapter 6: The Designer as Biography 173
Chapter 7 Prologue: Anti-biographies and Lifepatch 193
Chapter 7: The Constituency of the Designer 201

Conclusion

Chapter 8: Designing-with 233

Notes 253
References 257
Index 279

Series Foreword

As professions go, design is relatively young. The practice of design predates professions. In fact, the practice of design—making things to serve a useful goal, making tools—predates the human race. Making tools is one of the attributes that made us human in the first place.

Design, in the most generic sense of the word, began two and a half million years ago when *Homo habilis* manufactured the first tools. Human beings were designing well before we began to walk upright. Four hundred thousand years ago, we began to manufacture spears. Forty thousand years ago, we moved up to specialized tools.

Urban design and architecture came along ten thousand years ago in Mesopotamia. Interior architecture and furniture design probably emerged with them. It was another five thousand years before graphic design and typography got their start in Sumeria with the development of cuneiform. After that, things picked up speed.

All goods and services are designed. The urge to design—to consider a situation, imagine a better situation, and act to create that improved situation—goes back to our prehuman ancestors. Making tools helped us to become what we are: design helped to make us human.

Today, the word *design* means many things. The common factor linking them is service, and designers are engaged in a service profession in which the results of their work meet human needs.

Design is first of all a process. The word *design* entered the English language in the 1500s as a verb, with the first written citation of the verb dated to the year 1548. *Merriam-Webster's Collegiate Dictionary* defines the verb *design* as "to conceive and plan out in the mind; to have as a specific purpose; to devise for a specific function or end." Related to design is the act of drawing, with an emphasis on the nature of the drawing as a plan or map, as well as "to draw plans for; to create, fashion, execute, or construct according to plan."

Half a century later, the word began to be used as a noun, with the first cited use of the noun *design* occurring in 1588. *Merriam-Webster's* defines the noun as "a particular purpose held in view by an individual or group; deliberate, purposive planning; a mental project or scheme in which means to an end are laid down." Here, too, purpose and planning toward desired outcomes are central. Among these outcomes are "a preliminary sketch or outline showing the main features of something to be executed; an underlying scheme that governs functioning, developing, or unfolding; a plan or protocol for carrying out or accomplishing something; the arrangement of elements or details in a product or work of art." Today we design large, complex processes, systems, and services, and we design organizations and structures to produce them. Design has changed considerably since our remote ancestors made the first stone tools.

At a highly abstract level, Herbert Simon's definition covers nearly all imaginable instances of design. To design, Simon writes, is to "[devise] courses of action aimed at changing existing situations into preferred ones" (Simon 1981, 129). Design, properly defined, is the entire process across the full range of domains required for any given outcome.

But the design process is always more than a general, abstract way of working. Design takes concrete form in the work of the service professions that meet human needs, a broad range of making and planning disciplines. These include industrial design, graphic design, textile design, furniture design, information design, process design, product design, interaction design, transportation design, educational design, systems design, urban design, design leadership, and design management, as well as architecture, engineering, information technology, and computer science.

These fields focus on different subjects and objects. They have distinct traditions, methods, and vocabularies that are used and put into practice by distinct and often dissimilar professional groups. Although the traditions dividing these groups are distinct, common boundaries sometimes form a border. Where this happens, they serve as meeting points where common concerns build bridges. Today, ten challenges uniting the design professions form such a set of common concerns.

These challenges—three performance challenges, four substantive challenges, and three contextual challenges—bind the design disciplines and professions together as a common field. The performance challenges arise because all design professions

1. act on the physical world,
2. address human needs, and
3. generate the built environment.

In the past, these common attributes were not sufficient to transcend the boundaries of tradition. Today, objective changes in the larger world give rise to four substantive challenges that are driving convergence in design practice and research. These substantive challenges are

1. the increasingly ambiguous boundaries between artifacts, structure, and process;
2. the increasingly large-scale social, economic, and industrial frames;
3. an increasingly complex environment of needs, requirements, and constraints; and
4. information content that often exceeds the value of physical substance.

These challenges require new frameworks of theory and research to address contemporary problem areas while solving specific cases and problems. In professional design practice, we often find that solving design problems requires interdisciplinary teams with a transdisciplinary focus. Fifty years ago, a sole practitioner and an assistant or two might have solved most design problems. Today, we need groups of people with skills across several disciplines and the additional skills that enable professionals to work with, listen to, and learn from each other as they solve problems.

Three contextual challenges define the nature of many design problems today. While many design problems function at a simpler level, these issues affect many of the major design problems that challenge us, and these challenges also affect simple design problems linked to complex social, mechanical, or technical systems. These issues are

1. a complex environment in which many projects or products cross the boundaries of several organizations, stakeholders, producers, and user groups;
2. projects or products that must meet the expectations of many organizations, stakeholders, producers, and users; and
3. demands at every level of production, distribution, reception, and control.

These ten challenges require a qualitatively different approach to professional design practice than was the case in earlier times. Past environments were simpler. They made simpler demands. Individual experience and personal development were sufficient for depth and substance in professional practice. While experience and development are still necessary, they are no longer sufficient. Most of today's design challenges require analytic and synthetic planning skills that cannot be developed through practice alone.

Professional design practice today involves advanced knowledge. This knowledge is not solely a higher level of professional practice. It is also a qualitatively different form of professional practice that emerges in response to the demands of the information society and the knowledge economy to which it gives rise.

In his essay "Why Design Education Must Change" (from *Core77*, November 26, 2010), Donald Norman challenges the premises and practices of the design profession. In the past, designers operated on the belief that talent and a willingness to jump into problems with both feet gives them an edge in solving problems. Norman writes:

> In the early days of industrial design, the work was primarily focused upon physical products. Today, however, designers work on organizational structure and social problems, on interaction, service, and experience design. Many problems involve complex social and political issues. As a result, designers have become applied behavioral scientists, but they are woefully undereducated for the task. Designers often fail to understand the complexity of the issues and the depth of knowledge already known. They claim that fresh eyes can produce novel solutions, but then they wonder why these solutions are seldom implemented, or if implemented, why they fail. Fresh eyes can indeed produce insightful results, but the eyes must also be educated and knowledgeable. Designers often lack the requisite understanding. Design schools do not train students about these complex issues, about the interlocking complexities of human and social behavior, about the behavioral sciences, technology, and business. There is little or no training in science, the scientific method, and experimental design.

This is not industrial design in the sense of designing products but industry-related design—design as thought and action for solving problems and imagining new futures. This MIT Press series of books emphasizes strategic design to create value through innovative products and services, and it emphasizes design as service through rigorous creativity, critical inquiry, and an ethics of respectful design. This rests on a sense of understanding, empathy, and appreciation for people, for nature, and for the world we shape through design. Our goal as editors is to develop a series of vital

Series Foreword

conversations that help designers and researchers to serve business, industry, and the public sector for positive social and economic outcomes.

We will present books that bring a new sense of inquiry to design, helping to shape a more reflective and stable design discipline able to support a stronger profession grounded in empirical research, generative concepts, and the solid theory that gives rise to what W. Edwards Deming described as profound knowledge (Deming 1993). For Deming, a physicist, engineer, and designer, profound knowledge comprised systems thinking and the understanding of processes embedded in systems, an understanding of variation and the tools we need to understand variation, a theory of knowledge, and a foundation in human psychology. This is the beginning of "deep design"—the union of deep practice with robust intellectual inquiry.

A series on design thinking and theory faces the same challenges that we face as a profession. On one level, design is a general human process that we use to understand and to shape our world. Nevertheless, we cannot address this process or the world in its general, abstract form. Rather, we meet the challenges of design in specific challenges, addressing problems or ideas in a situated context. The challenges we face as designers today are as diverse as the problems that clients bring us. We are involved in design for economic anchors, economic continuity, and economic growth. We design for urban needs and rural needs, for social development and creative communities. We are involved with environmental sustainability and economic policy, agriculture competitive crafts for export, competitive products and brands for microenterprises, developing new products for bottom-of-pyramid markets, and redeveloping old products for mature or wealthy markets. Within the framework of design, we are also challenged to design for extreme situations; for biotech, nanotech, and new materials; for social business; and for conceptual challenges for worlds that do not yet exist (such as the world beyond the Kurzweil singularity) and for new visions of the world that does exist.

The Design Thinking, Design Theory series from the MIT Press will explore these issues and more—meeting them, examining them, and helping designers to address them.

Join us in this journey.

Ken Friedman
Erik Stolterman

Editors, Design Thinking, Design Theory Series

Acknowledgments

I quickly learned that authoring a book is to become part of a large assemblage of writing technologies, manuscripts, books, thoughts, discussions, and of course people. Like an assemblage, the fullness of who and what contributes to authorship is hard to disentangle. And so, this can only be a partial (and human-centered!) acknowledgment of all who were a part of writing this book. One of the privileges of writing this book was the opportunity to engage in dialogue and discussion on the ideas I was trying to express with long-standing colleagues, new colleagues, designers, and students I met in writing the drafts and retelling the stories of the book in lectures, seminars, and informal discussions. These engagements were heartening, helpful, insightful, and added much more than I was able to commit to writing this time around.

I am most indebted to those who thoroughly read and reviewed the various drafts and full versions of the manuscript, including Gabriela Aceves Sepúlveda, Tamara Alvarez, Alissa Antle, Audrey Desjardins, Laura Devendorf, Jordan Eshpeter, Laura Forlano, Cindy Lin, William Odom, James Pierce, Robert Rosenberger, Oscar Tomico, Peter-Paul Verbeek, and the MIT Press anonymous reviewers. I wish I could detail all the ways they each improved the book and how their generosity of thought and critical reflections are the reason for many of the better passages. I also thank those who reviewed key chapters, including Kristina Andersen, Joep Frens, Lenneke Kuijer, Angella Mackey, Doenja Oogjes, and Pauline van Dongen.

During the two or more years of writing I was fortunate to be invited to give lectures and seminars on "the book" that allowed me to "road test" my thinking and arguments. These events were as invaluable as they were inspiring and played no small part in refining my ideas and expressions.

Special thanks to Sun Young Park of Stamps School of Art and Design and the Michigan Interactive and Social Computing Group (MISC) at the University of Michigan and her graduate students for hosting me for a graduate seminar on early drafts of the book, and Bruce Tharpe and Stuart Candy whose invitation to their amazing Design Salon in Detroit brought me to Michigan. Additionally, I thank Aynur Kadir for inviting me to give a lecture and to meet with the students and colleagues at the Games Institute at the University of Waterloo; Kristi Kuusk and Nithikul Nimkulrat for the invitation to give a keynote and engage those at the Design Research Society Experiential Knowledge Special Interest Group (EKSIG) 2019 at the Estonia Academy for the Arts in Tallinn; Janine Huizenga, Anna Arov, and Anja Hertenberger of the Royal Academy of Art, The Hague (KABK) for the opportunity to give a lecture, talk with students, and see their inspiring design projects; and Oscar Tomico and Tomas Dietz for the lectures at the Institute for Advanced Architecture of Catalonia (IAAC) and Elisava Barcelona School of Design and Engineering and for the pre- and post-COVID-19 seminars with the amazing graduate students of the Master in Design for Emergent Futures at IAAC/Elisava.

I am fortunate to have the support of two academic homes. There is my home away from home, the Industrial Design Faculty at Eindhoven University of Technology (TU/e) in the Netherlands and especially the Future Everyday Cluster. In Eindhoven there is an openness of mind and heart when it comes to design that fuels me when I'm there and keeps me thinking and making when I'm not. My academic home, the School of Interactive Arts and Technology at Simon Fraser University in Surrey, British Columbia, has supported me and my work for almost twenty years. I am especially grateful to those at the Everyday Design Studio (EDS), the design research studio of graduate students that nourishes me daily and beyond expression has sustained me intellectually, socially, and in making. I could not have dreamed of a better group of people to have to "design-with" on a daily basis. They include Will Odom, Armi Behzad, Jordan Espheter, Sabrina Hauser, Henry Lin, Doenja Oogjes, Xiaolan Wang, Tiffany Wun, Xiao Zhang, and Ce "Kimi" Zhong. Over the years, this writing has benefited from ongoing discussions and collaborations with those I've not yet mentioned, including Jeffrey Bardzell, Shaowen Bardzell, Eli Blevis, Lin-Lin Chen, Carl DiSalvo, Batya Friedman, Bill Gaver, Steve Harrison, Kate Hennessy, Tad Hirsch, Kia Höök, Caroline Hummels, Youn-kyung Lim, Troy Nachtigall, Carman Neuestaedter,

Acknowledgments

Daniela Rosner, Thecla Schiphorst, Sowmya Somanath, Erik Stolterman, Russell Taylor, and Stephan Wensveen.

I thank Doug Sery and all those with MIT Press who supported me throughout the process. I am grateful for receiving financial support to write this book from Simon Fraser University in the form of a sabbatical and for help with the publishing costs. I also received research grant support that contributed to parts of the book and related research projects from the Natural Sciences and Engineering Council of Canada, Social Sciences and Humanities Research Council of Canada, Netherlands Organisation for Scientific Research, and Horizon 2020—the Research and Innovation Framework Programme of the European Commission.

This book was written during the COVID-19 pandemic, a time when no one needed to be reminded of our interconnectedness with nonhumans and the potential change that results—good and bad. There is the sorrow of loss but also the possibility of progressive and radical change of a capitalist culture responsible for climactic disasters. This has unfolded alongside the much-needed calling out of racial injustices and calls for change from Black Lives Matter and Indigenous Lives Matter, which make it painfully obvious that to do and say nothing is complicity.

And so, during these moments it was a blessing to write quarantined with my sons Andre and Olin, who lead their lives in ways that make me hopeful and grateful. My deepest gratitude as well goes to Resja Campfens, who supports me in ways I don't even know and still made every effort to help me at each stage of writing, making clear that she is my partner in thought as in life.

Chapter 1: Introduction

This book is a posthumanist exploration of design. The arc in design of the last thirty to forty years has been to conceptualize, attend to, and prioritize human values. This arc, represented in a series of paradigms that includes human factors, ergonomics, human cognition, embodied interaction, cooperative work, human experience, human ethics, and labor, among others, has led to a greater social and behavioral understanding of what it is to be human. Humanist design or what is commonly referred to as human-centered design, has been overwhelmingly successful for some in shaping technologies to human needs and desires in matters of safety, health, well-being, pleasure, learning, and convenience. While this success has not been evenly distributed, the promise of success has. As a matter of capitalism, this promise arguably exploits through cheap labor and poor working conditions; as a matter of consumerism it manipulates others through ideas of consumption and productivity as the paths to well-being; or as a matter of idealism it fosters a naïveté in which the universality of good design will eventually be accessible to all through human progress.

Human progress is a tenet in design. Designers tend to believe that new solutions to user satisfaction, human pleasure and well-being, productivity, environmental sustainability, social injustices, neoliberalism, and systematic inequalities, to name just a few challenges, lie just around the corner, and a human-centered approach is the path to solving these issues. A question that propels this book is, What if human-centered thinking (and its underlying humanism) is not the answer to these problems but rather, in its dominant role, may be part of the problem?

In the name of human progress, almost all that is not human has been depleted or made extinct. In an ecological sense, design today contributes to the very reality of climate change and the ongoing extinctions of other species. In the most direct sense, design is exploitative in its relations to nonhuman species and materials that are mined for and reduced to human use. This leads to questioning the ideal of human progress or perfection of humanity as a goal. And for those concerned with design, the supporting role that design plays in this. One can believe in the enlightenment of humans, in an eventual ideal state, in which "humanity" will care for that which is not human—simply put, to see no "other" in what we call human, to end animal cruelty and extinctions, and to positively cohabit a thriving biosphere—or we can shift from future desires to rethinking design from a present understanding of differentiated humans entangled in an equal fate with all that is not human and material.

I describe this Pandora's box of humanist shortcomings as motivation to rethink design, and do so by investigating what posthumanist design might be. This is ambitious, maybe even foolish, and not without immense challenges. A critical challenge is that humanism is a long-standing project dating back to the eighteenth- and nineteenth-century Europe in which scholars reinterpreted the ideals of classical Antiquity and the Italian Renaissance. This has led to a pervasiveness of humanist thought that continues in the modernist era to infuse itself in the ways I think and act, and likely how you think and act. The posthumanist thinker Rosi Braidotti describes humanism as the dominant model for human civilization. It is a structuring force for cultural practices that makes it foundational to almost all matters of human life, from political ideals to legal principles to educational practices (Braidotti 2013). The design discipline is as much an outcome of humanism as any other discipline. However, in design, humanism is foregrounded and is an organizing principle. And so, to many readers, to consider a posthumanist design is counterintuitive at best, antithetical at worst, to the very idea of design. However, to limit design to its origins in humanist thought charts an unsustainable path forward that is not only a concern ethically but existentially.

And so, if we turn away from a humanist understanding of design and look toward a posthumanist understanding, what might that mean? It does not mean that all the concerns I outlined above will go away with posthumanist thinking, but arguably it reveals a clearer picture. One in which we are irrevocably entangled and bound together on shared terrain with nonhumans. Out of this reality, a position of greater humility is necessary.

One in which we accept that the human subject is emergent, fallible, and a matter of differences rather than a universalizing ideal that humanism offers. Posthumanism shifts the focus away from the power of self-reflexive human reasoning to situated, partial, and multiple ways of knowing. It points to an acceptance that human agency is not autonomous, perhaps even fragmentary, alongside an imperceivable number of other actors, nonhuman ones, with their own possible forms of agency. And from this humbled and shared position, which in itself might be a remarkable step forward, comes alternative approaches for how we better cohabit our world with species and matter that are not human. To restate in a more direct and positive fashion, the question that propels this book: What, then, does it mean to design for more than human-centered worlds?

However, this question raises another challenge. In exchange for a more than human perspective we lose the illusion of sovereign human power and the control of that power, only to gain the knowledge that in our entanglements we are more transformative than even we realized and in ways we certainly do not control. Nowhere is this conundrum more evident than in the current time of the Anthropocene. The presence of humans in our biosphere is of a geological scale that is as evident as it is impossible to grasp. Just as we get to know the power we truly wield, the awareness is of cold comfort: "We have also to absorb the disturbing fact that the drama has been completed and that the main revolutionary event is behind us" (Latour 2014, 1). The Anthropocene, which began anytime between the Renaissance and the Industrial Revolution, marks a point of change in our understanding—a change that is more existential than enlightening:

> But is there an inflection point of consequence that changes the name of the "game" of life on earth for everybody and everything? It's more than climate change; it's also extraordinary burdens of toxic chemistry, mining, nuclear pollution, depletion of lakes and rivers under and above ground, ecosystem simplification, vast genocides of people and other critters, et cetera, et cetera, in systematically linked patterns that threaten major system collapse. (Haraway 2016, 100)

Donna Haraway, quoted above, sees the Anthropocene as a transition point in which "our job is to make the Anthropocene as short/thin as possible" (Haraway 2016, 100). She argues this to resist the form of anthropos (human) implicit in the term Anthropocene, but also to present an opportunity to critically imagine "epochs to come that can replenish refuge," what she calls *Chthulucene* (Haraway 2016, 100). Chthulucene is a speculation on what could come after the Anthropocene that is a multiplicity of possibilities of kinship across humans and nonhumans.

And so, the challenge of the explorations of this book is that we simultaneously live within overlapping moments of humanism and the Anthropocene. In response, like Haraway and Chthulucene, this investigation of posthuman design, "conceived as such, is then both construction and reality" (Puig de la Bellacasa 2017, 33). It is a construction or speculation of what posthuman design might be as much as it is the grasping of the reality that to gather around notions of design is to gather with agencies more than human that are a perilous danger from within. While I marvel at the shared agency of things, their vitality and shaping of us and the world, and especially the possibilities this opens, I see the critical part of this challenge is to seek possibilities that are sustaining and accountable.

And so, what do I mean by posthumanism? What I do not mean are the various notions of what I'll call *afterhuman*, firstly reflected in ideas of transhumanism, which sees a technological becoming of humans in which new technologies become our *afterbodies* to extend past our intellectual and physiological limitations, with the aim of achieving greater perfection in what it is to be human (Bostrom 2005; Kurzweil 2000; Moravec 1999; Pilsch 2017). Transhumanism, as such, is an intensifying of humanism and so the opposite of what I mean here (Wolfe 2010). Katherine Hayles's idea of posthuman as expressed in *How We Became Posthuman* (Hayles 1999) critiqued transhumanism for extending humanist ideals into the realm of the posthuman, a humanist self within a technological afterbody that is largely disembodied and mutated into information and technological forms. Implicitly, humanist conventions of technology, humans, and embodiment remain intact while the corporeal human is transcended. What I mean by posthuman is therefore the opposite of afterhuman ideas of posthumanism. It begins by abandoning the autonomy of human subjectivity, central to humanism, for a relational subjectivity or what is often referred to as a *relational ontology* (see Barad 2007; Haraway 1985). For example, for Haraway, beings do not exist before relations (Haraway 2003). They are not independent entities but defined by the relations they form within the world. Maria Puig de la Bellacasa calls Haraway's relationality *thinking-with*, and in this spirit the question of posthumanism is not to think-after but to think-with (Puig de la Bellacasa 2012)—that is, to always think-with other humans, technologies, things, and animals. Braidotti refers to this as *critical posthumanism*, a way of thinking that is not about technology as a neutral or controlled extension of humans; rather, it is about becoming or being human, entangled thoroughly with the world in ways that can only be relational and expansive (Braidotti 2013). It is far less a technological question and far more a question of post-human subjectivity and its realities and possibilities.[1] In this sense, posthumanism is a refiguring of humanism. At its simplest, it is humans sharing center stage with nonhumans. A more accurate description, though, is that the nonhuman stage at the center that was solely occupied by humans, with all its other beingness, materiality, vitality, and technology, has moved from the background to the foreground alongside humans. So posthumanism for me is the sharing of the center between humans and nonhumans. To say that I am exploring a posthumanist design is to explore what it means to design-with; that is, to design with humans and nonhumans in ways that are fundamentally expansive and relational. Posthumanism allows for a rethinking of design in ways that displace the human at the center of thought and action with humans and nonhumans bound together materially, ethically, and existentially.

Critical and Creative Speculations

This book is a critical and creative speculation that interweaves design with posthumanist thinking as both a strategy and motivation to "unbuild" design. Design is reimagined as a plurality of trajectories that intersect and diverge in what I call *nomadic practices* (see chapter 2). This speculative act is a way to critically imagine alternatives like posthuman design. This desire for alternative formulations of design is an ongoing and diverse enterprise shared by many other design theorists. And, similar to this book, different philosophical ideas are often mobilized alongside design theories and practices to unpack and redress critical shortcomings of commonly held assumptions in design, like human-centeredness. Key among these is what is called *ontological design* (Escobar 2018; Willis 2006; Winograd and Flores 1987), the idea that design creates ways of being, which draws heavily on the philosophical ideas of *being* or existence, by the philosopher Martin Heidegger (1962). Advocates of ontological design aimed to redirect or radically reformulate human-centered design and its underlying humanist precepts, including rationalism (Winograd and Flores 1987), instrumentalism (Willis 2006), global capitalism (Fry 1999, 2012), and globalization (Escobar

2018). This work inspired and informed the project of this book as it shares certain assumptions and goals. Key among these is the claim that technologies and humans need to be viewed together as a meaningful whole rather than separately. And given that technologies are an outcome of designing, design is seen to be fundamental to being human (Winograd and Flores 1987). Anne Marie Willis calls this relationship a *double movement*, meaning that in humans designing the world, the world designs humans back, or more succinctly, *design designs* (Willis 2006). This pragmatist interpretation aims to redirect and critique the underlying instrumentalism and rationalism of human-centered design, arguing that the "horizon of possibilities" of being human in the world has been narrowed to concerns of functionalism or only imagined within the mind-body dualism of human cognition (Willis 2006; Winograd and Flores 1987). In the work of Tony Fry, this critique takes on the term *defuturing*, in which the unsustainability of neoliberal capitalism, through its sheer hegemony, is literally erasing and extinguishing other possible futures. Fry argues for a radical reformulation of design to transition from the humanist ideals infused in human-centered design to ideals of *sustainment* (Fry 1999, 2012). Sustainment is the redesigning of the world and humans to create new possibilities to be environmentally sustainable. Equally important contributions are made by Arturo Escobar, who argues for design to be a pluriverse, an array of Global North and Global South designs that are autonomous and communal, radically local assemblies of design, decolonizing acts of futuring that open new possibilities of being through design (Escobar 2018). From these important works I take the courage to have the ambition to rethink design, wholly and imaginatively.

Despite the commonalities in this project with ontological design, there are divergences as well. Philosophically, the posthumanist arguments infused throughout this book take as their beginning a critique of and then moving past Heidegger (Borgmann 1987; Ihde 1990; Latour 2004a; Verbeek 2005; Wolfe 2010). I will not rehearse the critique here but point readers to Peter-Paul Verbeek's analysis of Heidegger's ideas of technology as both a starting point and point of divergence for philosophies of technology (Verbeek 2005). The concern for philosophies of technology (and design) is that Heidegger's views of technology are ultimately transcendental and so less relevant to the material and technological world (Borgmann 1987; Verbeek 2005). Heidegger is concerned with the idea of *being* as it relates to humans but ultimately as a notion on its own. He reserves the status of *things*, such

Introduction 7

as Greek temples or water jugs, as the means to reveal *being*, in contrast to technologies or mundane objects that he sees as concealing *being* (Heidegger 1976). For Bruno Latour and other philosophers of technology, everything is a thing, not just the "celebrated *Thing* . . . the handmade jug," but things also include "the industrially made can of Coke" (Latour 2004a, 233). The implications for this book are that I also consider all things as things, and in practical terms, this orients my inquiry of design and technology on what is materially present alongside constructions of what might be possible. I am not focused on an ideal yet nonexistent future, as is *sustainment*, despite its necessity and theoretical importance. The aim of this book is to look at things to refigure design rather than prefigure a future of design.

As I said, I am inspired by the ambitions of ontological design to dramatically and necessarily reconceptualize design, an inspiration I find in other important works as well. Daniela Rosner's *Critical Fabulations: Reworking the Methods and Margins of Design* (Rosner 2018) adopts Saidiya Hartman's method of *critical fabulations* to investigate and make lively alternative histories of design as part intervention and part renewal (Hartman 2008). Rosner looks to uncover the "long-silenced narratives of practices" through feminist technoscience investigations informed by the works (and lives) of Donna Haraway and Lucy Suchman, and through the telling and retelling of these submerged narratives, including numerous case studies of her own design research. Rosner's work, though different from the approach here, is a near traveler for its ambitions and shared concerns. Similarly, though different yet again, is Lars Spuybroek's *Sympathy of Things* (Spuybroek 2012). Spuybroek's critical and creative speculation "time-travels" to reinterpret Gothic architecture through the nineteenth-century art critic John Ruskin. This is not a historical reconstruction but quite the opposite—a self-described *ill-disciplined history* that travels ahistorically with Ruskin to reveal a vitalist rendering of Gothic architecture en-route to a design theory or a philosophy called *gothic ontology* (Spuybroek 2012, 2017), an ontology that Spuybroek claims equally applies to digital matter and the digital production of architecture today. It is a flat ontology of *things* that overturns hierarchies like structure versus ornament or designer versus builder. Spuybroek emphasizes movement and change that drives the design of gothic buildings, illuminating the relations between guild sculptors, stone, and line as internal relations that compose and build together. These relations are a matter of sympathy among things, a reuse of a Ruskin term to signal a vital materialism and distributed agency that draw on philosophies of Henri Bergson and Alfred North Whitehead. A vital materialism that appears in this book, though drawing on works of Jane Bennett (2010), Diana Coole (2005, 2010), and Maria Puig de la Bellacasa (2017). And so Spuybroek's work is also a near traveler, with key intersections that include sidestepping modernist/humanist notions of design to refigure design anew and to anticipate the vital materialist argument of things, including the digital, that are expanded on in chapter 5.

Thomas Binder and colleagues draw even closer to concerns of this book. *Design Things* (Binder et al. 2011) is a collection of essays describing new investigations of participatory design (PD). I find particularly important their reconceptualization of PD and notion of things. Things in their reworking become *design things* that are a sociomaterial gathering that forms *publics*, or community gatherings that engage in shared concerns through design activities (Binder et al. 2015; Ehn 2008). The thinking is informed by Latour's posthumanist concept of *things* that is directly relevant to discussions in chapter 7, where I see their efforts as complementary to my explorations of the human and nonhuman collectives or constituencies required to responsibly foster designers of things. In *Changing Things*, Johan Redström and Heather Wiltse (2020) similarly bring philosophies of technology to bear on their conceptualization of things. Things for them mark a change in which physical and digital objects have become increasingly networked, fluid, and contextually determined. They describe things as *fluid assemblages*, after Gilles Deleuze and Felix Guattari (1987), as a way to identify and describe the changed nature of everyday technological devices. The work is important in its attempts to understand new digital technologies and unpack them theoretically. There are intersections with ideas I bring forward, though fundamental differences in their foregrounding of digital technologies and an acceptance of a degree of technological determinism that has them focus on a series of concerns different than mine.

In the communities of design and human-computer interaction (HCI) that I largely participate in, there is a marked increase in bringing posthumanist philosophies to questions of design in our various conferences and journals. Key among these is the work of Daniel Fallman (2010), which draws on Albert Borgmann's focal things and practice (Borgmann 1987) to ask the question, What do we mean by *good* in design if we are beyond questions of human use? Also important is Laura Forlano's sweeping introduction to design of the range of posthumanist thinking (Forlano 2017), which asks, in the context of posthumanism, who is the user, how are agency and power distributed, what new knowledges are required for design, and how are ethics reflected and embedded in such a design? These works and others signal the increasing and vibrant discussion between related philosophies and design.[2] And so, this book does not travel alone. Many other design speculators traverse this territory, unbuilding design into other possibilities and alternatives, and if not explicitly intersecting with this investigation, they are often nearby.

In my critical and creative speculation, I will deemphasize the role humans play to shed light on and to assert the role that things, as I see them, play and could play in design. For example, I draw on ideas that dislodge the anthropocentric hold on our thinking—ideas that inform a humanity that is understood within a broader spectrum of nonhuman species and nonhuman things alike. Animal studies scholar Cary Wolfe argues that this dislodging

> forces us to rethink our taken for granted modes of human experience, including the normal perceptual modes and affective states of homo sapiens itself, by recontextualizing them in terms of the entire sensorium of other living beings and their own autopoietic ways of "bringing forth a world"—ways that are, since we ourselves are human animals, part of the evolutionary history and behavioral and psychological repertoire of the human itself. But it also insists that we attend to the specificity of the human—its ways of being in the world, its ways of knowing, observing, and describing—by (paradoxically, for humanism) acknowledging that it is fundamentally a prosthetic creature that has coevolved with various forms of technicity and materiality, forms that are radically "not-human" and yet have nevertheless made the human what it is. (Wolfe 2010, xxv–xxvi)

Wolfe helps us in getting started by making clear the necessity to interweave what we understand to be human within the wider and more interconnected "sensorium" of nonhumans that we are in essence already a part of. This recontextualizes or reveals the potential to see our relations with things (nonhumans) in more multidimensional, interwoven, and intricate ways. He underscores this radically different understanding of humans as having "co-evolved" with things, that we are a "prosthetic creature," so tied to technology, matter, and nonhuman beings that they have become a part of us and shaped us. This clearly opens the door to rethinking not only the role that things play in design, but the role of design itself.

Things

And so, what do I mean by things? Here, I will explain and outline the key philosophical concepts that support my definition of a thing. I will briefly expand on this in the next section of this chapter and give the overview of the book, but alas, the reader will require patience to read the fullness of the definitions in the subsequent chapters.

Firstly, I offer a brief sketch or informal introduction to what I mean by things. Things are nonhumans made by both humans and nonhumans. These things are both concrete and conceptual in that the term describes in new ways what has already been designed while also pointing to what could be designed. I refer to things as concrete and specific entities that are embedded, situated, and experiential, although things can also be fluid, having no distinct boundaries, and are irrevocably relational. As matter or technologies, things are experienceable physically and virtually, although they can also be imperceptible, like chemical elements in a gaseous state, and remote, like microscale electronics and electronic processes. When referring to technologies, I typically mean digital technologies or material technologies like ceramics or textiles. However, I see these technologies on a continuum with other constructions like language, clothing, and shelter, and so sometimes in this book I refer to this broader understanding of technology.

That things are both concrete and conceptual resonates strongly with design. For example, a well-used concept across different ideas of design is that design is about the "ultimate particular" (Nelson and Stolterman 2012). This refers to the idea that a design outcome simultaneously manifests conceptually and materially. A chair holds the conceptual notions of a seated body, weight-bearing relief, comfort and rest, identity and power, wealth and social justice, art and culture, and so on. It equally refers to the particular avocado-green molded fiberglass Eames chair that I am sitting on that is paint splattered from the painting studio I found it in some thirty years ago when I was an art student. It is also political in that it can be contested as revealing design as a handmaiden to unsustainable industrial production, or a question of ownership, or that fiberglass as a material choice is unforgivable as it will never degrade. Nevertheless, I have kept the chair with me all these years, despite the fact that one leg is slightly askew, creating an uneven tilt and rock, depending on where I shift my weight.

Introduction

The term *thing* offers a pluralistic role of encapsulating various abstractions, politics, and embodied particulars. This power of things makes for a good vehicle to explore posthumanist design. To that end, I support this investigation of things with different philosophical concepts that unfold throughout the discussions in the book. I represent these relationships in the form of a stool (figure 1.1) with three supporting legs. I should make clear at the outset that at times it too will rock and tilt like my Eames chair.

There are three legs of the stool, and each comes into play in different chapters as I build the fuller argument for things we could design. The first leg is *mediating technologies*, which draws on ideas of technicity (Ihde 1990), natureculture (Haraway 2003), and technological mediation (Ihde 1990; Latour 1992; Verbeek 2005) that I will explain more fully in chapter 4. For now, it suffices to say that it describes how things, like technologies, are interconnected

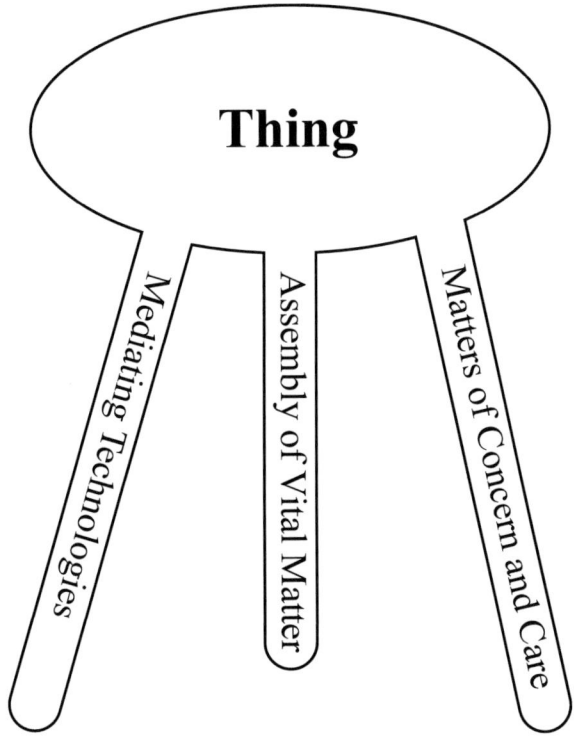

Figure 1.1
The philosophical concepts supporting the definition of *things*.

with who we are as humans, as *prosthetic creatures* (Wolfe 2010). Given this fundamental relationship with things, humans and things also co-shape each other; as such, the world is mediated through things and things through us. The second leg is *assembly of vital matter*, which draws on multistability (Rosenberger 2014), vital materialism (Bennett 2010), and agentic capacities (Coole 2005, 2013) that I will explain more fully in chapter 5. For now, this refers to how things are relational, seen as situated or belonging to assemblies and so not discrete. Things are also seen to have agentic qualities and intentionalities that contribute to their own making and the making of other things. The third leg is *matters of concern and care*, which draws on ideas of thingpolitics (Latour 2004b, 2005a) and more than human care (Puig de la Bellacasa 2017) that I will explain more fully in chapter 7. In short, this extends the idea of things into engagements with politics and ethics. In the etymological roots of the word *thing*, it is also a verb meaning to gather and a noun meaning a gathering. In this sense, things are political in that they gather issues or concerns, as with my Eames chair, while they also can mean to gather or assemble to engage these issues. From both these meanings of things, it's more than implied that things are also matters of affect and require ethical practices.

Outline of the Book

The book is structured in three parts that represent each of the three nouns in the title *Things We Could Design*: (1) design, (2) things, (3) designer.

Part I: Design (Chapters 2 and 3)
Earlier in this introduction, I discussed the shared ambitions of the critical and creative speculation of this book with others who also aimed to reconceptualize the discipline of design out of necessity (Escobar 2018; Fry 1999) or to make visible what has been obscured (Rosner 2018; Spuybroek 2012). I don't argue that design as a discipline is monolithic and undisputed, nor that it is without critical reflection and discourse that seeks to improve and adapt, part of the ongoing critique, reflection, and rebuilding of the discipline from within. However, there is also the option to radically speculate an alternative rather than to incrementally rebuild. This allows for establishing different rules and principles so as not to be weighed down by past decisions and long-held assumptions. This is the option I pursue here, as others have

done, in order to formulate an understanding of design with posthumanist commitments that reveals new possibilities for thinking-with design and out of necessity to break from humanist assumptions and epistemologies.

Nomadic practices is a theory that I develop in this part of the book to enable what is commonly called the discipline of design, to turn from humanism so as not to be singular in attention, hierarchical in knowing, or territorial in boundary setting. Design, as nomadic practices, is a multiplicity of intentionalities and situated knowledges, nomadic in their relations to other nomadic practices of design or other knowledges in general. Further, what makes a nomadic practice a matter of design is that it is an accountable claim for the design of *something*.

In order to unpack this further, I begin with the characteristic of design as a multiplicity of intentionalities. To start, let's consider answering the question of what it means *to design*. From a posthumanist perspective, specifically a postphenomenological perspective, the question of what it means to design is meaningless without knowing what is being designed. This is the underlying concept of *intentionality*, which reveals that humans do not exist independently of the world but are directed toward the world, or they are understood in relation to something. As Verbeek explains, humans cannot simply think, see, or feel; rather, humans "always think something . . . always see something . . . always feel something" (Verbeek 2008, 388). In posthumanist terms, to know what it means to design requires asking what it means to *design something*. For example, as I will later elaborate, to design a product to market globally versus to design an artifact to support your work routines are two different intentionalities. Herbert Simon famously offers an answer to the idealized question of what it means to design, to "[devise] courses of action aimed at changing existing situations into preferred ones" (Simon 1981, 129). The illusion of this definition is that it appears all encompassing, as if to apply to every instance of thinking to design, yet it offers no example of what it is that is designed. The definition is so abstract and idealized that as an answer to design it is simultaneously everywhere and nowhere. In plain terms, it is not of this world. To be of the world is to situate the question—that is, to specify the something to design. And so just as we can think, see, or feel many *somethings*, to design is a multiplicity of intentionalities—we can design *many* somethings.

A further modification is necessary to the revised statement of *to design something*, and that is to state who is doing the designing. Who is the designer or knower? And so, the fuller question becomes, What is the meaning of *a designer to design something*? It is important to make visible the designer/knower and to make them as embodied as the something to design. This is in contrast to the invisible and disembodied designer/knower of Simon's definition of design. This way of knowing design arises from Haraway's *situated knowledge* (Haraway 1988), an embodied objectivity that makes clear that to know is to be embodied, as I discussed above with respect to intentionality. And as a result, knowers are embodily situated, relative to what is known and to other knowers. This materialist understanding affirms that knowledge is perspectival or positioned in relation to who is doing the knowing. This situated perspective is also reflected in the knowledge created and in *how* that knowledge is created. This explains the other characteristic that a particular design of nomadic practices is situated in its knowing. In other words, the designer/knower is different when it comes to designing a product to bring to market or designing an artifact to improve one's work. Haraway argues that to account for the knower and its embodiment is more objective than an all-seeing disembodied knower. As a result, nomadic practices offer differently situated knowledges of design that are intersecting and divergent.

The last characteristic of nomadic practices is that it is nomadic. Drawing on Deleuze and Guattari's "nomadism" (Deleuze and Guattari 1987), design is refigured from a single territorial discipline to multiple, concurrent, allied, non-allied, collaborative, competitive, and contradictory knowings of design. Deleuze and Guattari often speak of territorializing and deterritorializing that can be seen as a spectrum between sedentary and nomadic (Deleuze and Guattari 1987). Along this spectrum, design as a discipline can be seen as sedentary, typically establishing settlements built on foundational knowledge and forming border walls to establish and protect its territory. The settlement itself is often organized and divided hierarchically. By contrast, design as a multitude of nomadic practices can traverse the landscape, territorializing and deterritorializing, following the somethings nomadic practices design wherever that may lead, often crossing paths to contest or form allegiances with other nomadic practices. In a word, nomadism offers a structure for design as nomadic practices, supporting the different intentionalities and situated ways of knowing in a way that is nonhierarchical, relational, and expansive.

A nomadic practice is accountable by the quantity and quality of the gatherings around its particular notion of design. That is the ability of the nomadic practice to attract and create a shared intentionality. It is also accountable by who makes the claim that a particular nomadic practice is a form of design, and a nomadic practice is accountable for the way in which it traverses the landscape and what it leaves behind. Lastly, the power of nomadic practices is that collective knowing across all the nomadic practices is deeper and more diverse than any singular knowing of design.

In chapters 2 and 3, I more fully argue and develop nomadic practices. I begin with prior strategies for critiquing disciplines that also serve as guiding paths toward the development of nomadic practices. These strategies include paradigms (Kuhn 1962), programs (Redström 2017), and generative metaphors (Agre 1997). And by way of demonstrating the utility of nomadic practices as an alternative to disciplinary structures, I use the conceptualization to describe three different nomadic practices: *designing artifacts* to contribute to human progress by supporting complex human use and practices; *designing objects* that aspire to higher principles of morality and goodness; and *designing products* for economic gain and well-being as a matter of financial transactions. However, the main goal in developing nomadic practices is to find a structure with posthuman commitments over humanist ones in order to create the speculative room to investigate a nomadic practice of *designing things*.

In chapter 2, I gather a range of artifacts or things to be part of the discussion. These include a collection of what are known as *slow technology* artifacts such as *Photobox*, an antique oak chest that randomly prints four or five photos a month from an owner's Flickr archive (Odom et al. 2014); the *Long-Living Chair*, a Charles and Ray Eames rocking chair that can record and display its usage over a period of ninety-six years (Pschetz and Banks 2013); and *Olly*, a wood and aluminum music player that processes Last. FM listening history metadata to occasionally select a song from its owners' past but offers no control over what is selected or when (Odom et al. 2019). In chapter 3, I gather an array of objects, artifacts, and products, including Braun Pocket Receivers, portable radios small enough to fit in one's pocket designed in the late 1950s and early 1960s; the *Kar-a-Sutra*, a concept car that was designed in 1972 by Mario Bellini of the Italian Radical Design Movement; and the *Fairphone*, a modular mobile phone and campaign to address the use of conflict metals from the Democratic Republic of Congo in mobile phones.

Part II: Things (Chapters 4 and 5)
Chapters 4 and 5 detail what I mean by things, expanding on the first two legs of the supporting philosophical concepts *mediating technologies* and *assemblies of vital matter* to describe features of things as interconnected, transformative, relational, and vital. It is an attempt to account for things, to understand them, to allow them to newly illuminate design while also beginning to construct ideas of how to design things.

Things and humans are interconnected in that we cannot consider what it is to be human without things. Chapter 4 expands on the philosophical concepts of *mediating technologies*, which is the first supporting leg of the idea of things (see figure 1.1). This feature draws on ideas of technicity (Ihde 1990) and natureculture (Haraway 2003). For example, Donna Haraway argued for a concept of the *cyborg* as a figure that represents the rejection of the boundaries between human, animal, and machine. She writes that "the cyborg would not recognize the Garden of Eden" (Haraway 1985). This is echoed in Don Ihde's description of humans living within a *technologically textured ecosystem* (Ihde 1990, 3). Ihde makes clear that this goes beyond our current industrialized realities to be a varying but effective constant in being human. He claims that humans have always lived with things. In referring to a mountain climber, he states that even as we disclose new understandings of the world, such as mountain peaks that have not been summited or rarely seen vistas, these are disclosed in concert with things. These things are highly specialized climbing equipment, synthetic clothing, lightweight camping gear, electronics, and specially processed food that enable humans to venture to remote mountaintops. Even when things do not have a direct role in our perceptions and actions, things like airplanes, helicopters, cars, wagons, roads, bridges, stairs, stone paths, compasses, GPS, maps, and photographs make remote landscapes and mountains accessible and perceivable.

This argument claims we are inseparable from things. It gives a great deal of power to design since it makes clear that to design things is fundamental to any consideration of what it is to be human.

Things are transformative, which arises from the first characteristic that we are not separate from technology. It extends the implications to see the inseparable relationship between us and things as transformative. When a climber wrapped in climbing gear looks at a mountain, the mountain is transformed into a landscape to be climbed. The mountain invites ascents, revealing itself to be a series of paths to the summit. The climber perceives through the ropes, cams, and carabiners that have become a part of her that her ability to climb has been dramatically extended. For the climber to not attempt to climb, or by her very situation to not be in the act of climbing, is almost implausible. In the philosophy of postphenomenology, this connectedness or the relations of humans and technology co-shapes our subjectivity and objectivity (Verbeek 2005). This also refers to the supporting philosophical concepts of *mediating technologies* (see figure 1.1). In addition to technicity and natureculture, that things are transformative refers to the idea of *technological mediation* (Ihde 1990; Verbeek 2005). This means that through our interconnectedness with technologies we act and perceive the world with and through things in which things are non-neutral. Things shape human perceptions and actions in ways that are inherent to things. This offers a break from seeing technologies as exclusively shaped by humans, to be socially constructed (cf. Bijker, Hughes, and Pinch 1987) or exclusively shaped by the technology, to be technologically determined (cf. Kurzweil 2000). The alternative role for technology offered by postphenomenology is exactly both: Our world is shaped by humans and things together. In philosophical terms, humans and things are co-constituted. Technological mediations decenter humans as the privileged shaper of things and world. It also reveals a dimensionality of things in which human-technology relations can take on different relations, from being embodied like eyeglasses to being simultaneously present and absent, like the background technologies of a refrigerator (Ihde 1990) and cyborgian fusions like cochlear implants (Verbeek 2008).

The transformative relations of humans and things building on their interconnectedness can be more complex if we extend the connections into what is called an *assemblage*, an assembly of heterogeneous elements that function together (Deleuze and Parnet 2002). In returning to the climbing example, we can view our climber as an assemblage that includes her fellow climbers, carabiners, cams, ropes, and an inordinate number of other climbing things I partly detailed earlier, that ascend the mountain together. In addition, climbers of high-elevation expeditions, like summiting K2 or Mount Everest, routinely summit with supplemental oxygen systems made up of an oxygen canister, a connected mask, an oxygen reservoir, and a regulator. This substitutes the rare and extraordinary human aerobic capacity of some climbers with readily available nonhuman supplemental oxygen systems for all.[3] Latour calls this a *delegation*, another form of technological mediation in which breathing oxygen from the air is delegated to a nonhuman device (Latour 1992). This reassembles the assemblage of climbers underscoring the transformative and dynamic interconnectedness of things. Further, what has been seen in the past as mere equipment, a supplemental oxygen system, is clearly here an agential actor that contributes to the climbing of the whole assembly.

This argument describes how things change us through our interconnectedness. This relationship also shows that things share the foreground with us in that they too act and interpret our world. Additionally, the relations of things and humans are expansive, creating complex interactions and entanglements that do not idly share the center together but act dynamically and interchangeably and are open to reassembly. And so, while to design things is powerful in its transformations of the human and the world, this claim reveals that the human role in design is shared, partial, and interchangeable.

In chapter 4, where these arguments take place, I also gather things to be part of the discussion. These include Pauline van Dongen's *Phototrope* (2019), an illuminated running garment that makes runners more visible at night; *+Lichtlijn*, a traffic light for mobile phone users by HIG Systems (Scully 2017); the *Prayer Companion* by the Interaction Research Studio (Gaver, Blythe, et al. 2010), a device designed to support the prayer life of cloistered nuns; and what is known as the Great Pacific Garbage Patch, the largest collection of plastics and trash floating in the northern Pacific Ocean.

Things are relational means that we can only understand humans, things, and the world in relation to each other. In other words, the very example of our mountain climber that has woven her way through this opening chapter is in relation to the mountain that we have discussed climbing—with or without oxygen canisters. Those canisters mutually shape the relation of the climber and the mountain, as do the ropes and carabiners. To purists in the mountaineering community, the idea of using supplemental oxygen to summit mountains is tantamount to "doping" or cheating, whereas for most climbers, an oxygen canister is simply one of an array of synthetic clothing and equipment that adds to the performance of climbing. Ihde refers to these different interpretations of things as *multistability* (Ihde 1990, 144). He sees in any technological artifact or thing more than one stability or variation dependent on the particular embodied contexts. Things do not exist in a vacuum; rather, they are embedded in different relations, configurations, or networks that determine how they are interpreted. One community of climbers sees a supplemental oxygen system as simply another part of the assembly, while another sees it as the "steroids" of climbing. Ihde draws on phenomenology to focus on the variances between different and particular embodied interactions in the world or, as he states, things are *variantly embedded* (Ihde 1990). This leads Ihde to see technologies, in our case things, as essentially ambiguous, structured in multiple perceptions and meanings that are relational rather than essential.

In the form of assemblages, things belong to a collective agency or "the ensemble nature of action and the interconnections between persons and things" (Bennett 2010, 37). Citing the massive power failure in the Northeastern United States and Canada in 2003, Jane Bennett explains that it is impossible to find individuals responsible for the collapse of the electrical grid. The grid is an assemblage, a "volatile mix of coal, sweat, electromagnetic fields, computer programs, electron streams, profit motives, heat, lifestyles, nuclear, fuel, plastic, fantasies of mastery, static, legislation, water, economic theory, wire, and wood" (Bennett 2010, 25). This same distribution of humans and nonhumans and their interconnectedness is what makes the electrical power grid function and what makes it fail—a failure in which things are as equally culpable (or not) as humans. For Bennett, assemblages move us past "the belief that humans are *special* . . . outside the order of material nature" (Bennett 2010, 36–37). With this in mind, it would be an "injustice" to see any human as having sufficient autonomy to be responsible or blamed for what occurred. However, if responsibilities are shared by things, then things share in the politics and are open to contestation alongside humans.

This argument establishes that things are not fixed but hold different stabilities of meanings determined by the relations and embodiments they form. For design, ambiguity and multiplicity become the rules for things, and it is the variances between the different possible stabilities that are important and, in some ways, more defining. The relationality of things makes it necessary and only possible to see things and humans as interconnected or in assemblages that further opens the door to a sharing of agencies, responsibilities, and politics between humans and things.

Things are vital in that they enact or manifest a force inherent to them and their materiality. The concept of intentionality, which I discussed earlier in relation to nomadic practices, reappears here. As described, humans cannot be understood in isolation but rather in relation to the world. However, things or technologies are also directed at the world in ways embodied and unique to them. Verbeek considers different types of intentionalities in relation to technology, such as how an omnidirectional microphone records background sounds that humans typically filter, revealing different sounds within a room. In this sense, he sees a *composite intentionality* between technological and human intentionalities. For example, radio telescopes create visualizations of distant stars by "seeing radiation that we cannot see" and, as a result, composite intentionality makes accessible "ways in which technology 'experience' the world" (Verbeek 2008).

The argument that things are vital also draws on the second supporting philosophical concept of things, *assembly of vital matter* (see figure 1.1), which utilizes ideas and vocabulary of what is known as *vital materialism* (Barad 2007; Bennett 2010; Braidotti 2013). Similar to agency and intentionality, vitalism is seen as a human characteristic, typically atop a chain of organic life and not extended to nonliving or nonhuman things. Returning to the 2003 power failure, Bennett describes the electrical grid as vital: "very active and powerful nonhumans: electrons, trees, wind, fire, electromagnetic fields" (Bennett 2010, 25). She describes one factor in the power failure as the massive and inexplicable patterns of movement of electricity. As Bennett states, "electricity sometimes goes where we send it, and sometimes it chooses its path on the spot, in response to the other bodies it encounters and the surprising opportunities for actions and interactions that they afford" (Bennett 2010, 28). The vital materialism of electricity is an inherent force of action that while without purpose (in the human sense) is not without effect.

In keeping with mountaineering, we can see another example of the vital forces of materiality. Over two days in 1996, eight climbers died on climbing expeditions on Mount Everest. Jon Krakauer, who described the events in the best seller *Into Thin Air* (Krakauer et al. 1999), came out against the use of supplemental oxygen systems by climbers unless in emergencies. In his view, the supplemental oxygen systems cultivated summit attempts and too much risk taking by unskilled climbers. However, for alpine climbers and designers of oxygen systems, it is known that these systems are far from foolproof, and in the case of these climbers, systems failed or were depleted of oxygen. The systems are subject to extreme cold and winds that freeze regulators and valves, harden the plastics of the face masks, and can become increasingly unwieldy to operate by tired and possibly oxygen-deprived or frostbitten climbers. The vibrant forces of temperature, oxygen, snow, and wind are as much a part of the supplemental oxygen systems as the climber and the clothing these systems are strapped on. We can add to our human and nonhuman climbing assemblage weather, temperature, air pressure, humidity, and oxygen. With this in mind, vital forces play out in ways and at scales we cannot expect. To add to the tragedy and challenges that conspired against the climbing assemblage on those two days, researchers from the University of Toronto found that on May 10, 1996, massive currents of air or jet streams pushed the stratosphere to just above 8,000 meters, where the climbers experienced an even further reduction of the already perilously low oxygen content of the "death zone" (Moore and Semple 2004).

These examples, the Northeast power failure and the Everest climb, are tragic (some attribute as many as a hundred deaths to the 2003 outage) and reveal vital materialism in dramatically negative ways, as matters of danger and human catastrophe. However, electrons flow unpredictably through our power grids at every instance, and the effects of temperature and air pressure variances are a constant matter of weather; it is simply that at the limits of human experience, especially at magnitudes and scales that are beyond human, the nonhuman vitalism or force is most apparent. This vitalism of matter, whether dramatic or mundane, reveals what Diana Coole refers to as the *agentic capacities* (Coole 2005), a form of agency of things that can *create* through effects and combinations across an assembly. Agentic capacities can also appear lively and directional, though without clear purpose, as in combining organic matter to produce a particular black dye (Erichsen 2019) or the data collection and processing of digital network services. Agentic capacities can also be seen as untraceably causal, a diffracted sharing of agency or intentionality that leads to unforeseen outcomes. Discussing agency from the perspective of things reverses the orientation to see humans as having "affinities" with nonhumans rather than nonhumans adopting human characteristics. Bennett underscores this point succinctly, writing that "one moral of the story is that we are also nonhuman and that things, too, are vital players in the world" (Bennett 2010, 4).

This argument describes how we share agency and vitality with things. It asserts that agency and intentionality, traditionally viewed as uniquely human traits, are shared with things through technological intentionality and agentic capacities. A type of vitalism, inherent forces are part of the materialism of humans and nonhumans alike that have an array of creative and agential effects. The challenge is to understand the value of seeing any of this as design and the roles that shared agencies play in design. Further, any new realization of what it means to be a designer or to design would need to acknowledge that humans are already nonhumans and that things are also vital agents in designing things.

In chapter 5, where I discuss the relationality and vitality of things, I again gather design examples to be part of the discussion. These include Laura Devendorf and Kimiko Ryokai's *Being the Machine* (2015), a digital fabrication system that guides makers in building three-dimensional forms out of everyday materials; design investigations of technologies for the home known as *Tilting Bowl* (Wakkary et al. 2018), a ceramic bowl that tilts; and *Morse Things* (Wakkary et al. 2017), ceramic bowls and cups that communicate to each other through Morse code. James Pierce and Eric Paulos's *Obscura 1C Digital Camera* (2015) is a *counterfunctional artifact* that requires destroying the camera to retrieve the digital photographs. Chapter 5 also describes a textiles research and creative partnership known as the *Burgundian Black Collaboratory* led by Claudy Jongstra and Jenny Boulboullè (Erichsen 2019), and the *Mineral Accretion Factory* by the School of Art of La Réunion (Énon 2019) that fabricate tables underwater through an artificial reef production process.

Part III: Designer (Chapters 6 and 7)

Chapters 6 and 7 are about the designer or the "we" in the title of the book. Given the posthuman commitments that have refigured design and configured things up to this point, there is no room for the idea that a designer is exclusively human. This part describes how designers are assemblies of humans and nonhumans that share agencies that together design. The chapters articulate the importance of keeping these assemblies together with the lifeworlds they help create in what I call a *biography*, and the necessity to pay equal attention to what makes designers as much as what makes things through what I call a *constituency*. The aim of part III is to expand on the philosophical concept of things as *matters of concern and care* that lead to seeing the designer in ethico-political terms.

Designer as biography sees the designer as an assembly of nonhumans and humans that together inscribe themselves into the same lifeworld they cohabit. The term biography is intended post-anthropocentrically to reflect that a designer is a combination of humans and nonhumans, but its real purpose is to define a way to make the designer of things accountable for what it designs into the world and what it leaves behind. In other words, the value of the designer of things cannot be separated from the lifeworld it contributed to through designing things—that is, a lifeworld understood in the fullness of its entanglements and politics. Biographies tie together the interdependencies of the assembly and lifeworld of a designer into one entity that may live on well beyond the human lives of the designer of things. I argue this is critical to getting beyond the willful exclusion of matters of concern and care that attach to the things that are designed. This occurs today in design by restricting design concerns to the *design problem*, which excuses the designer from engaging or encountering the politics of things, rendering these as unintended consequences for others (nondesigners) to address. Yet, given the distribution of agencies and the vitality of things, unintended consequences are inherent and so need to become fundamental to any considerations of design.

In understanding the designer of things as both human and nonhuman, I draw out the shared agentic capacities as a matter of designer as force that now situates the agentic capacities of things in relation to a designer rather than a thing. In this context, the agentic capacities are seen as contributors to the creation and designing of things. The designing of things by things occurs through effects or combinations across an assemblage, the lively or purposeless trajectories and diffracted and untraceable causality that are described in chapter 5. In the designer of things, the unique human contribution is language, and so to speak on behalf of nonhumans is what I call a *speaking subject* of the designer. As the speaking subject, humans give a rationale or purpose for the designer and what is being designed. In this way, the speaking subject is often at the origins or beginning of designing a thing and may reappear again in the life of a thing when it is iterated upon or redirected toward a new purpose. The speaking subject also speaks on behalf of its nonhuman collaborators, explaining their agentic capacities, meaning, value, and overall participation as the designers.

In chapter 6, I gather the following things: *Living in a Prototype* (Desjardins 2016; Desjardins and Wakkary 2016) engages the complexities and relationalities of making, transforming, and adapting the space one lives in as reflection on the Internet of Things (IoT). *Greenscreen Dress* is an exploration of wearing garments with digital display capabilities, or what is known as dynamic fabric, on a daily basis for close to a year (Mackey et al., "Blending

Clothing and Digital Expression," 2017). Superstudio's *Supersurface* (Branzi 1984) is an installation of a six-foot cubic room of mirrored tiles that repeats itself endlessly. And Aleph Zero/Marcelo Rosenbaum's *Children Village* is a dormitory for over 500 students of the Canuanã school in remote northern Brazil (Wainwright 2018).

The constituency of a designer is a political structure that convenes humans and nonhumans together to "discuss" design before there is a commitment to assemble a designer and to design things. The constituency assembles to discuss, debate, contest, and enact design to form and inform the designer of things in ways that are expansive and political. The human role in a constituency is as the convener that means to assemble and maintain the collective. It is also an extension of the speaking subject role to speak on behalf of and ensure the participation of nonhumans. A constituency is the radical kin to the idea of a design studio in other nomadic practices, although it emphasizes the gathering of a collective or any formal gathering to consider designing things. Constituencies aim to build on these assemblies with the new aim of designing-with.

The third philosophical assumption supporting the idea of things, *matters of concern and care*, is important in relation to constituencies (see figure 1.1). It draws from Latour's *matters of concern*—the bringing together of the many associations and attachments related to things that are open to discussion and contestations. In essence, they are contestable, negotiable, and represent a plurality of voices. To let things speak is to hear or make visible matters of concern that can also be called *thingpolitics* (Latour 2005a). That is a world of contestations, mediations, and affinities, which is the same messy world that designers and things cohabit through their biographies. *Matters of care* are drawn from Maria Puig de la Bellacasa and extend Latour's matters of concern to more precisely draw out the "affective and ethical connotations" of concerns (Puig de la Bellacasa 2017, 42). Bellacasa offers a notion of care and ethics grounded in nonhuman agencies that sees ethics and care as situated—that is, they arise from relations with nonhumans, matter, and things rather than a priori or as fixed values. I build on these concepts to not only consider how constituencies gather and make visible the nonhumanness of the designer of things but how ethics and care emerge through the formation of constituencies.

In chapter 7, I gather for discussion several counterexamples of biographies that I call *anti-biographies*. These include the patent for the ubiquitous plastic shopping bag by the Swedish package designer Sten Gustaf Thulin, known as the *bag with handle of weldable plastic material* (Gustaf Thulin 1965); the M-16/AR-15 rifle designed in the late 1950s by the designer Eugene Stoner and the weapons company Armalite; the Weather Channel Weather App for mobile phones and tablets that provides location-aware data on the weather; and the Camden Bench, designed in 2010 by Factory Furniture, a design firm that specializes in street furniture. I also include for the discussion on constituencies *Lifepatch*, a do-it-yourself biology (DIYbio) collective based in Yogyakarta, Indonesia.

Balancing Language and Things

The attention given to things in posthuman philosophical thought inspires, fuels, and informs the arguments in this book. However, it is important to make clear that I write this book as a designer and someone who is trained in creative practices and design research but not philosophy. And so, my concern here is with design. Having said that, I have argued that there is both the potential and need for greater interaction between philosophy and design research (Wakkary et al. 2017, 2018). Given my focus on design in writing this book, I set out to balance language and things. And as a practical way of doing this, each chapter has its own prologue that precedes it, where I describe design artifacts, objects, products, and things that are relevant to the chapter that will follow. This balancing act arises from recognizing the limits of using philosophy, theory, or written language, for that matter, to describe, articulate, and reveal the nature and importance of things. I struggle with the idea that language itself is a technology in the broad sense that mediates our actions, perceptions, feelings, and thoughts and tends to obscure if not dematerialize things. I share the desire and goal of Bennett, who argues that "a vital materialist theory of democracy seeks to transform the divide between speaking subjects and mute objects into a set of differential tendencies and variable capacities" (Bennett 2010, 108). I take this to heart and explore this idea further in chapter 7, but at this point it is sufficient to say that our ability to transform the imbalance between "speaking subjects" and "mute objects" is more theoretical than actual. Despite this, and in large part to advance my arguments, I have made every effort to make things present in this book in all their particularities and embodied knowledge. I assume that things anticipate much of what I will say and can challenge whatever I articulate through language. So, take the things presented here as part "witnesses," part resistance, and a caution on the limitations of writing about things.

In thinking of myself as a speaking subject among mute nonhumans that witness, resist, and make humble any claims I will make in this book, I recall a strange moment years ago, one of many that led to my writing this book. One evening when returning to my home in Vancouver from Simon Fraser University where I am a professor, I encountered in our living room the *table-non-table*, our family's companion cat *Rusty*, and an early version of what I called the *hook* (see figure 1.2). The *table-non-table* was part of my design research that would come to be called a *counterfactual artifact*, as it was designed to be non-normative with respect to the conventions of designing technologies as a way to investigate the normative nature of designed technologies. The *table-non-table* is a stack of paper on an aluminum chassis that suggests it is a table, but it unpredictably and periodically moves. It was a way to destabilize or defamiliarize technologies and everyday experiences in order to study them (Wakkary, Desjardins, and Hauser 2016; Wakkary et al. 2015; Hauser, Wakkary, et al. 2018). The *hook* is similar, though it aims to emphasize its nonutility to allow us to see how designed things become part of ensembles of everyday life that we relate to and interact with in unselfconscious and unknowing ways. *Rusty* is our family cat, one of four in our household that was conceived in our neighborhood and continues to live with his mother, though rarely harmoniously. The *table-non-table* and *hook* were designed by me and the graduate students in my research studio known as the *Everyday Design Studio*. These things were in my home because a part of our design process is to live with the things as we make them, to experience their nuanced effects and how they shape our daily life. As the speaking subject in this encounter that I had the wherewithal to photograph (see figure 1.2), I was strangely rendered mute. I was very uncertain about whether what I was *witnessing* was alien to me or very much a part of me. There was the strangeness of the conflation of home and work and finding myself experiencing the oddness of the things I made. It was as if there was a reversal from being the researcher to being research participant in one of my own studies! My routine arrival home from work had become defamiliarized. But the stronger sense I had was that I was an intruder on this nonhuman affair. *Rusty*, the *hook*, and *table-non-table* appeared self-contained in their own microsphere or bubble, as

Introduction

Figure 1.2
Rusty, our companion cat, with the *hook* and the *table-non-table* (the design research projects) in my home.

the philosopher Peter Sloterdijk would describe it. A bubble formed out of an "optical encounter, an infectious face-to-face" that signals a conjoining of entities out of "intimate mutual recognition" that Sloterdijk regards as *inter-faciality* (Sloterdijk 2011, 139, 147). Admittedly, he was talking about humans coming in eye contact rather than nonhumans "gazing" at each other. No doubt, one interpretation is that Rusty was sniffing the hook in a feline friend, foe, or food interaction, yet that was not what occurred to me at the time. I experienced being a mute witness to and excluded stranger from this inter-facial loop of nonhumans that I mistakenly felt I had a sovereign or potential all-knowing relationship with. It was appalling for me to simultaneously recognize and disabuse myself of this fallacy. Further, I wanted badly to be the interlocutor, to be in discussion with *Rusty*, the *hook*, and *table-non-table* if for no other reason than to ask, What is going on? And so, this encounter and the questions of what is going on with nonhumans in the things we design and why don't I know, as the human designer of these things, are if you like, the origin story for this book.

This story leads me to one other point that I want to make to conclude this introductory chapter. That is, the variants of the role I play in this book—as the mute witness of nonhumans who impossibly wants to be the interlocutor, or the speaking subject among mute things, or the balancer of language and things—are not without limits and privileges that are not shared by everyone. As a matter of privilege, I write as a senior, straight, married male academic who in large part can afford intellectual risk taking; moreover, I can be challenged for not making more of my position to take more risks on behalf of others. Many of my biases are products of colonization. In my case, I am a child of Indonesian immigrants to Eastern Canada; my mother is from Solo and Jakarta in Java and father from Manado in Sulawesi. They came to Canada to study to become a chemist and endocrinologist. Growing up in a racialized immigrant family sensitized me to the multiple realities of how the world appears, some of which were accessible to me and those like me, and others not. However, the world I experienced throughout my life was largely white middle class, which would lead me to identify as middle class if not fully white. I tell you this, as an addition to the story, to locate me as the human narrator in this story of things.

Part I: Design

Chapter 2 Prologue: Photobox, Long-Living Chair, and Olly

Chapter 2 "unbuilds" design as a discipline to create a new starting point from which to discuss design. In this prologue, I highlight design exemplars that emerge from what is known as *slow technology*, a radical shifting away from the emphasis on speed in the design of technology. I see in slow technology aspects of the type of "unbuilding" that I seek as a way to open design to nonhumanist perspectives. Slow technology can be seen as a critical research program aimed at destabilizing and shifting foundational ideas of designing technology (Hallnäs and Redström 2001). The privileging of speed in today's design aligns with other values like immediacy, utility, and functionality. I also see in slow technology a proto-example of the idea of nomadic practices that I develop in chapter 2. In nomadic practices there is no discipline of design to critique or become a part of. Rather slow technology is a variant design in its own right that is independent of other ways to design. The design of slow technology is to design through temporality in a way that values reflection, aging, and materiality.

Photobox

The *Photobox* is an antique oak chest that encases a printer connected to the Internet (Odom et al. 2014). It was designed as part of design research into *slow technology* by William Odom, Mark Selby, and their colleagues. It randomly prints four or five photos a month from an owner's Flickr archive (see figure 2.1). The random nature of the "functionality" makes it difficult to anticipate how the *Photobox* will behave. Further, the printed photos are within the box and so hidden from view. The only direct interaction with *Photobox* is to open its lid to see if any photos have been printed or not.

Figure 2.1
Photobox.
Source: Courtesy of William Odom.

The infrequency, inaction, and unpredictability make the experience of the technology one of anticipation, reflection, and surprise. Odom and his colleagues conducted fourteen-month-long field studies of *Photobox* to see how this slow engagement with a person's typically large digital photo collection might affect attitudes about digital materials and domestic technologies (Odom et al. 2014). They found people's attitudes changed and that people took a more reflective interest in the photos taken. From this Odom and his colleagues see opportunities to design for anticipation and for reflection on one's past, both key dimensions to temporality in technologies.

Long-Living Chair

The *Long-Living Chair* is a Charles and Ray Eames rocking chair that was redesigned by Larissa Pschetz to record and display its usage over a period of ninety-six years (Pschetz and Banks 2013). Motion sensors, a simple processor, and a display are embedded in one of the chair's rockers to record and visualize periods of rocking and periods of rest (see figure 2.2). The display

Figure 2.2
Long-Living Chair and details of the digital component and display representing use over ninety-six years.
Source: Courtesy of Larissa Pschetz.

creates a vertical bar for each year and the brightness of the pixels reflects the intensity of use and periods of inaction. In addition, the embedded component is stamped with the date the rocking chair was produced. The display is intended to attract attention only rarely. This is achieved by the slow change of the display in which a single pixel represents over 140 hours or may take six days to appear. Further, the display itself is in an inconvenient location that is not visible while sitting or rocking in the chair. The digital display in this way re-creates the incremental dynamic of wear and usage over a long period of time. Further, the mere presence of the display frames the age and life of the chair in ways that elicit reflection rather than interaction.

Olly

Olly is a music player designed by Jeroen Hol, Bram Naus, and Pepijn Verburg that processes Last.FM listening history metadata to occasionally select a song from its owner's past but without giving the person any control over what is selected or when (Odom et al. 2019). *Olly* was originally a student project in a master's class taught by William Odom and me in the Industrial Design Department at the Eindhoven University of Technology and later became a design research project within the Everyday Design Studio also led by Odom and myself. The class was an exploration of the idea of *unawareness* in domestic technologies (Odom and Wakkary 2015). *Photobox* can be described as "unaware" because while it was designed to be lived

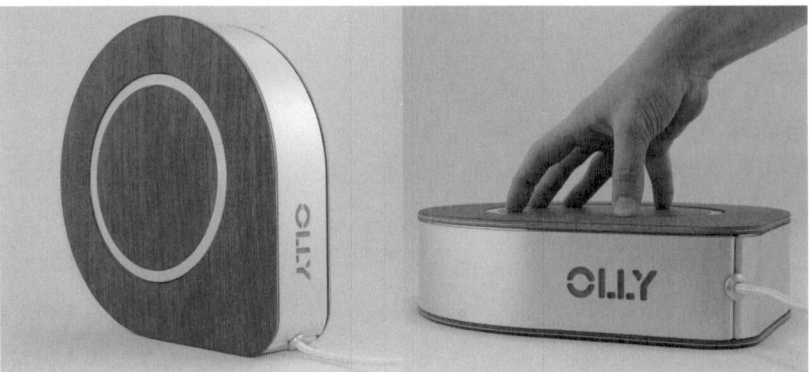

Figure 2.3
Olly music player.
Source: Jeroen Hol, Bram Naus, and Pepijn Verburg.

with, it acted on its own accord with minimal to no human input or interaction. *Olly* emphasizes this quality in *slow technology*. Its central feature is its internal wooden disc encircled in aluminum (see figure 2.3). When a song is surfaced from the past, it is not immediately played. First, the disc begins rotating to subtly indicate a song has been selected and is available to be played. The speed of the disc's rotation is relative to how deep into the past the song was listened to by *Olly*'s owner (e.g., the deeper into the past, the slower the rotational speed). To play the song, the owner must physically spin the rotating disc further. If the song is not played within a relatively brief time window, *Olly* will abandon it and stop spinning until another song is eventually surfaced; the process continues indefinitely. Similar to *Photobox*, we deployed *Olly* in three homes for fifteen months to explore how its slow pace might support reflections on the past (Odom et al. 2019).

Chapter 2: Nomadic Practices

In this chapter I develop the idea of nomadic practices as an alternative to conceiving of design as a discipline. Nomadic practices is a theory for structuring design that is guided by posthumanist commitments (DeLanda 2016; Deleuze and Guattari 1987; Haraway 1988; Verbeek 2008). The aims of the theory are to create openings to investigate posthumanist design within an epistemological structure that avoids humanist ideals and assumptions and, by removing these hurdles, to see design as more expansive and open to all kinds of different and concurrent explorations.

Nomadic practices can be described as an epistemological theory. Epistemology concerns itself with how knowledge occurs and what form it takes. To date, conceptions of design draw on humanist understandings of a discipline as an autonomous body of knowledge that has clear boundaries with other disciplines. A characteristic of humanist disciplines is that knowledge is produced through objectivist positions that are neutral and encompassing and that the knowledge produced is unified in its concepts to be seen as foundational or universal. By contrast, nomadic practices draw on posthumanist epistemologies in which knowledge production is situated, embodied, and partial—that is, knowledge is structured without foundations or universality but rather is nomadic in that it is situated and pluralistic.

In relation to material practices, posthumanism is grounded in a materialist understanding and also offers new epistemological concepts for embodied knowing that together are useful in rethinking design further. The posthumanists cited in this book embrace minoritarian positions of belonging to minor sciences or "studies" over disciplines (Braidotti 2012; DeLanda 2016; Deleuze and Guattari 1987), whether science studies, feminist studies, technology studies, or animal studies. The positions of these thinkers avoid labels of subdisciplinary, multidisciplinary, interdisciplinary, or even transdisciplinary as a further disavowal of humanist precepts and ideals of knowing that can equally apply to design.

By way of a brief introductory summary, nomadic practices view design as a multiplicity. This means that at any moment, a multitude of nomadic practices can call themselves design, or more accurately, a multitude of gatherings assemble around unique notions of design. These multiple gatherings do not compete over a single claim of the meaning of design. Rather, each is on its own path, pursuing a particular *something* of design, though open to intersections, divergences, contestations, or alliances. I describe this characteristic as a *multiplicity of intentionalities*. Additionally, nomadic practices are not structured on a universal or foundational knowledge like a discipline or subdiscipline. Knowledge of a particular nomadic practice is situated within that nomadic practice. This means there is no independent knowledge of design outside of any given nomadic practice, although each practice can overlap with others and collectively share what is known. I describe this characteristic as *situated knowing*. Lastly, nomadic practices are *nomadic*, as the name implies. This means that they are not about claiming domains or setting boundaries. Nomadic practices follow the somethings they design wherever they lead and, in this way, they traverse in parallel, almost always on the move. What makes a nomadic practice accountable is the quantity and quality of the gatherings around a particular something to design or the ability to attract and create a shared intentionality. It is also accountable by who makes the claim that a particular nomadic practice is some kind of design, and not so much by the credentials of who makes the claim but that someone stands up to account for making the claim. Lastly, a nomadic practice is accountable for how it traverses the landscape and what it leaves behind.

Design as a discipline is not monolithic or undisputed. If anything, the discipline has been subject to ongoing critique, constant critical reflections, and a never-ending series of radical rebuilding. It is a short history full of upheavals and disruptions. I will describe some of these upheavals in detail in the next section as they played out in human-computer interaction (HCI) as paradigmatic change of the second wave to third wave HCI or generative metaphors of embodiment over mental cognition. I could have easily chosen other examples as such changes have occurred over and over, such as the shift to reflective practice from technical rationality (Schon

1984), or the move to a design cognition of designerly ways of knowing from design as science (Cross 2006), or the semantic turn toward human-centered design from technology-centered design (Krippendorff 2006). More recently, adherents have argued for an ontological design (Escobar 2018; Fry 1999) or feminist correctives of the ongoing reformulations of the foundation of design (Rosner 2018). Shared among these is a territorial battle, the challenge of one body of knowledge by another in which the two are mutually exclusive. Also shared is that the bodies of knowledge are relatively unified concepts or coherent theories described in different ways as foundations, discourses, metaphors, or practices that have some form of universalizing power or hold sway as the dominant or majoritarian position. I take aim, so to speak, at the idea of foundational knowledge and universality as the way to know design by offering an alternative.

This move away from design as a discipline aims to liberate thinking about design by embracing multiplicity; it sees design as concurrent, conflicting, and overlapping alternatives rather than a singular body of thought. I begin developing the idea of nomadic practices by drawing on past attempts to reconsider disciplines that have been applied to design (Bødker 2006; Harrison, Tatar, and Sengers 2007; Redström 2017), including paradigms (Kuhn 1962), programs (Redström 2017), and generative metaphors (Agre 1997). I then turn to reshaping key elements toward a posthumanist framing by drawing on philosophical ideas of intentionality (Verbeek 2005), situated knowledge (Haraway 1988), and nomadism (Deleuze and Guattari 1987). Lastly, I detail the structural features of a nomadic practice that I outlined above. The idea of nomadic practices developed in this chapter is used in chapter 3 to describe current design practices as nomadic practices rather than a discipline. In chapters 4 and 5, nomadic practice is used as a theoretical vehicle to articulate and explore the nomadic practice of designing things.

Paradigms, Programs, and Generative Metaphors

The development of nomadic practices begins with drawing on prior ways of reconceptualizing science, technical practices, and design. These include paradigms (Kuhn 1962), programs (Redström 2017), and generative metaphors (Agre 1997). There are many characteristics and elements to be taken from these approaches that I will expand on and some shortcomings that, for my aims, will need to be addressed.

Paradigms

Paradigms or paradigm shifts argued by Thomas Kuhn (1962) are a radical rethinking of science and progress. Kuhn recasts the development of science from being a progressive trajectory of increasing approximations of scientific truths to a series of disruptive breaks between different scientific paradigms. A paradigm, according to Kuhn, is an exemplar in science, such as Ptolemy's calculations of planetary movements, Newton's laws of motion and gravity, or Maxwell's theory of the electromagnetic field. These paradigms, in a given period, provide the theoretical beliefs, values, instruments, and techniques to solve scientific problems. The capacity for a paradigm to contribute to scientific problem-solving is what Kuhn refers to as a period of "normal" science (Kuhn 1962, 92). Here, for a given time, the goals, theories, and experimental approaches to science adhere to the paradigmatic theory in a cumulative and productive fashion that we tend to think of as scientific progress.

Kuhn's radical departure is to make the case that stable periods of "normal" science come to an abrupt end in a "revolution" phase—a crisis in which scientific "anomalies" of a time, unassailable by the paradigm of the day, come to seriously undermine the existing paradigm. For example, James Clerk Maxwell's mathematical discovery of electromagnetic waves and continuous fields changed interpretations of reality based on the physics of material particles in mechanical movement. The shift from one paradigm to another is disruptive rather than cumulative (Kuhn 1962, 92). The subsequent paradigm, in the example above, swept aside Newtonian theories. The observable and empirical approaches of Newtonian physics gave way to a new order of mathematics and postulations of the directly unobservable, like radio waves and the speed of light. The importance of this formulation is that paradigms are, in Kuhn's view, incommensurable—meaning that there is little in common when it comes to measuring and assessing theories from different paradigms. Herein lies the rejection of scientific development as the cumulative building on earlier theories, with each progressive theory a closer approximation to scientific truth. In contrast with Karl Popper's ideas of falsifiability (Popper 1959), in which a good theory is one that can be refuted, Kuhn argued that the revolutionary phase is not a rational process. Rather, the revolutionary phase is wildly open to competition among different and incompatible ideas.

In design and HCI, the concept of paradigms was put to good use in Susanne Bødker's *When Second Wave HCI Meets Third Wave Challenges*.

Bødker characterizes the development of the field of HCI as a succession of waves. In particular, she addresses the rise of a "third generation or wave, that one might identify as a break with the second wave, theoretically and technologically" (Bødker 2006, 1). She characterizes the second wave as HCI and design's focus on designing technologies in work settings for communities of practice. This wave opened design and HCI to sociological perspectives. She identifies anomalies or unsolvable puzzles, to use Kuhn's terminology, in second wave HCI as challenges of a burgeoning third wave. These challenges are, broadly, the wider use contexts, applications, and settings for technology that moved beyond the workplace to homes and everyday settings. This shifted the concern of the field to cultural, emotional, and experiential aspects of technology and use. And in many respects, the challenges invert second wave concerns into matters of "non-work, non-purposeful, non-rational, etc." (Bødker 2006, 1–2).

This is a good example of the constructive nature of paradigms. Characterizing the field of HCI as successive waves describes new values and shifting foci without having to argue against progress or ideal truths. The incommensurability of paradigms is seen as a series of successive waves within the discipline, in which the latter wave replaces the previous wave. The incommensurability of paradigms holds the benefit of challenging humanist ideas of progress as ways of understanding disciplines. However, the successive winning out of a new dominant paradigm does little to shake free the disciplinary model of a foundational and territorial organization of thought and action. For a step in this direction, I turn to the idea of programs as developed by Johan Redström (2017).

Programs

In *Making Design Theory*, Redström (2017) addresses a central shortcoming of a disciplinary approach—foundational knowledge. He does this by arguing that the disciplinary foundation for design should be dynamic and transitional rather than stable. The key concept in this ongoing reflexive change in design is a "program." In some respects, he normalizes the "revolution" phase of paradigms by adding the idea of programs as a purposeful and experimental mechanism for critical reflection on the foundations of a discipline. Programs are a set of beliefs and design ideals that encapsulate and foreground a particular worldview of designing. In this way, they can guide the design actions and thinking of designers within a program.

The real potential of programs is when there are multiple concurrent and competing programs operating within the practice of design. This affords the possibility of looking at programs from the "outside," as a matter of difference, in order to reflect on what else designing could be. It allows a form of meta-reflection that enables progressive change. A good example of a design research program is Redström's work with Lars Hallnäs on *slow technology* (Hallnäs and Redström 2001) that I introduced in this chapter's prologue. The worldview experimented with a what-if agenda that designed technologies to create moments of reflection and mental rest rather than increasing performance and efficiency. I discussed more recent work in slow technology in the prologue to this chapter: *Photobox* (Odom et al. 2014), *Long-Living Chair* (Pschetz and Banks 2013), and *Olly* (Odom et al. 2019). Here a program offers a vehicle for a purposeful and critical examination of foundational concepts for design—namely, usability and productivity—through designing alternative "slow" technologies.

Redström adapts Imre Lakatos's idea of *programme* (and changes the spelling to program, which is used throughout), which was in part a response to Kuhn's paradigms (Lakatos 1976). Lakatos's program is meant to reconcile Popper's theory of falsifiability, discussed earlier, with Kuhn's less rational and more evolutionary idea of how competing theories lead to a new paradigm. In Lakatos's view, science is supported by collections of theories that individually may be proved false but, as a collection, are in practice irrefutable until the whole collection is proved otherwise. This collection of theories forms a program that is implied to be an evolving foundation for a new paradigm (Lakatos 1976).

In Redström's hands, programs go through a degree of radical change. He situates his adapted version of programs within the discipline of design as a mechanism to destabilize the discipline. This is in contrast to Lakatos, who saw change as a step approach toward a unified foundation for science. Redström sees this stability as highly problematic for design and needing to be actively defended against. Stable theories are problematic because design is concerned with producing contingent and provisional knowledge in the form of "products, concepts, and structures" rather than laws and absolute measures. Redström argues that fluid and shifting foundations are better for exploring possible realities through design (Redström 2017, 135). With Redström, programs are assigned the role of experimenting with and generating alternatives that productively challenge and destabilize the discipline of design, as is the case with slow technology.

There is much that is valuable here for nomadic practices. Redström makes the difficult maneuver of adapting the epistemological language of natural sciences to design, which is a very necessary move for nomadic practices. Equally important is the concurrency of programs that creates a field of alternatives which may align or contradict in different ways. Redström applies this as a way to reflexively maintain a transitional theoretical foundation for a discipline. As I will explain later, an important feature of nomadic practices is the establishment of interweaving trajectories of design or distinct perspectives on what is being designed that extends Kuhn's incommensurability into parallel rather than sequential movements.

Programs are a step away from the disciplinary stasis of paradigms. The idea of transitional theoretical foundations unsettles the ground of design as a discipline, but does it go far enough? Redström keeps the notion of design as a discipline and a singular theoretical foundation however kept unstable. In considering further distancing from disciplinary structures to conceive of design, I look to Philip Agre's concept of *generative metaphors* (Agre 1997) that eschews the paradigmatic idea of disciplinary foundations.

Generative Metaphors

Philip Agre extended the idea of generative metaphors to make the case for what he referred to as a "critical technical practice" based on the original concept by Donald Schon (1993). He argued that such a critical technical practice was necessary to shift from the underlying Cartesian rationalism in computer modeling and artificial intelligence (AI). Agre's idea of a critical technical practice implicitly draws on Kuhn's rejection of progress and ideal truths but explicitly rejects Kuhn's disciplinary framing of paradigms and foundational knowledge:

> A critical technical practice would not model itself on what Kuhn (1962) called "normal science," much less on conventional engineering. Instead of seeking foundations it would embrace the impossibility of foundations, guiding itself by a continually unfolding awareness of its own workings as a historically specific practice. It would make further inquiry into the practice of AI an integral part of the practice itself. It would accept that this reflexive inquiry places all of its concepts and methods at risk. And it would regard this risk positively, not as a threat to rationality but as the promise of a better way of doing things. (Agre 1997, 9–10)

In rejecting Kuhn's disciplinary thinking, Agre focuses on the idea of *technical practice*. A technical practice is understood as historically specific, rather than autonomous, as one might see a discipline. A technical practice is also concerned with "building" as a distinct activity, in the sense of making and constructing entities like software (Agre 1997, 10). This turn to technical practice is directly comparable to design. The framing of concepts and methods, as practice, moves the discussion further from under the shadow of disciplinary science as the ultimate reference point for ways of knowing. The radical nature of critical technical practice is, as Agre states, to commit to a reflexive inquiry around a practice. And further, this reflexivity is willing to scrutinize and jeopardize the very concepts and methods that make up the practice. In thinking about how to guide a reflexive inquiry of one's own practice, Agre uses and adapts the idea of *generative metaphors*.

Agre draws on Schon's idea of utilizing metaphors, the "stories" of a field that drive inquiries in research, as a way to understand the "social reality" of a given practice (Agre 1997, 34). For example, using the idea of a network of connections and nodes as a metaphor for society would be a generative metaphor. Agre describes a generative metaphor as "an open-ended mapping from one discursive domain to another (economics and physics, reproductive physiology and cultural gender roles, evolutionary biology and social structures), and a metaphor is 'generative' in the sense that a research community can extend its own discourse by carrying one element after another through the mapping" (Agre 1997, 34). Generative metaphors cross the boundaries of "discursive domains," like social sciences and computer science in the example above. They are orthogonal in that a metaphor can "carry" thoughts and actions across the various disciplines to extend a given discourse—for example, network topologies as an analysis for social bonds.

Another idea that draws on Schon is that a generative metaphor mutually shapes what deserves attention within a practice and how that attention should be structured theoretically and methodologically. For example, Agre saw in cognitive science the generative metaphor of "mentalism," in which the human mind acts like an internal information processor, computing stimuli and perceptive data to reason on external responses and behavioral actions in the world. The then-current theoretical and methodological formulations of cognitive science were clearly structured by the metaphor of an interior computing mind. The greater concern for Agre was what future trajectory lay in store given the hold of this metaphor. In the mode of reflexive inquiry, he counters with a generative metaphor of "interactionism"—that is, mutual involvement, participation, and reciprocal shaping between humans and their environment (Agre 1997, 53).

The mutual naming and framing of concerns by generative metaphors reveals how the selection of a metaphor for attention shapes the actions of those in the practice (Schon 1993). The worldview of the generative metaphor is put into practice, so to speak, by determining what that practice is and what it will become, similar to Redström's programs. And as Agre articulates, as a consequence, any given generative metaphor places other concerns at the margins of the practice. In a cognitive science practice based on the "mentalist" metaphor, embodied and contextual concerns are set at the margins. Agre's real concern is that without a critical awareness of how generative metaphors work, what is at the margins remain invisible to the field, and hence no alternatives arise to shift a practice away from a problematic direction or eventual stasis and repeating of itself. Hence the need for a critical technical practice that is able to diagnose and deconstruct the underlying generative metaphor that "will have an utterly pervasive influence on the techniques, methods, and priorities of a field" (Agre 1997, 47). The *modus operandi* of a critical technical practice is to provide alternative generative metaphors by starting with what is relegated to the margins and then doing the hard work of developing new techniques, methods, and priorities that can enable a shift of concerns from margin to center.

The applicability of generative metaphors to design practice is evident in the work of Steve Harrison, Deborah Tatar, and Phoebe Sengers. In *The Three Paradigms of HCI* (2007), these authors use Agre's approach to address many of the same issues in HCI that Bødker (2006) discussed in her paradigms of second and third waves. Notwithstanding the use of the word paradigm, Harrison and colleagues use generative metaphors as a way to articulate the state of HCI at the time and its possible future trajectory. They deconstruct the practices of HCI into different generative metaphors of interaction, allowing them to further analyze the field as different "centers" and "margins" of concerns. Based on this analysis, they argue for an intervention through a third generative metaphor of "situated perspectives," in which situated and embodied interactions, which were formerly marginalized by metaphors of mind and information processing, take center stage. In this case, it is evident that the critical work of deconstructing dominant metaphors and the seeking of alternatives can begin with paying attention to what is marginalized within any generative metaphor of the practice. Further, Harrison and colleagues make clear that multiple generative metaphors may coexist, signaling a potential plurality of practices.

The contributions of generative metaphors to the development of nomadic practices are substantial. Generative metaphors separate practices from foundational knowledge. Its own emergence is historical, and, in this sense, it inherits disciplinary practices without the structures. It argues that knowledge and methods are self-contained in practices that, while at risk, also are open to sweeping change. Lastly, generative metaphors can coexist and operate in ways that cross disciplinary boundaries and, in the process, extend the discourse of a given practice and can be seen as nomadic.

Toward a Posthumanist Epistemology for Design

Across paradigms, programs, and generative metaphors there are many characteristics and elements to build on in developing nomadic practices, especially by augmenting and refining these aspects with posthumanist commitments. Key among these elements to build on are what I see as the *making of practices, practices without foundations*, and *practices as transversals*.

Making of practices. Agre is indebted to Schon's definition of practice (Schon 1984) as a form of knowledge production in its own right rather than an application of disciplinary knowledge external to the practice. Schon famously argued that professions like engineering are reflective practices with their own epistemological and methodological grounding, rather than technical extensions of the disciplines of physics and math. The distinct grounding of practices arises from their situated and embodied natures that privilege experiences and contexts over laws and principles. This relation to experience makes explicit the practitioner of the practices. In Agre, this arose as the "naming and framing," which Schon sees as the mutual shaping of the practice and practitioner, whereby what is attended to by a practitioner shapes the practice and in turn the practitioner.

Practices without foundations. Agre (1997) and Redström (2017) do the valuable and difficult work of adapting reconceptualizations of science to technical practices. In so doing, their formulations of practice take on a critical relation to the idea of foundations, the theoretical concepts and assumptions of a given practice. Redström's program aims to destabilize the foundations of design, to keep theories and assumptions of a discipline in a transitional state. This, in Redström's view, is a better fit with the contingent nature in which knowledge is produced in design. Agre eschews foundations and disciplines altogether to focus on practice. Practices in Agre are a social construction that can be continually deconstructed like a literary text. Like any text, a practice has a coherent story or a dominant narrative that can be undone by parts of the narrative that are excluded and put to the margins.

Practices as transversals. Redström and Agre take advantage of the incommensurability of Kuhn's paradigm to emphasize pluralism and movement of competing notions of design. Redström describes programs as mechanisms to productively destabilize disciplines, keeping them from stasis. This destabilization is most effective when multiple programs coexist in a critical relation to each other and the original foundations of design. Generative metaphors are freed from any relations to a foundation and so can also coexist. In place of foundations, they are structured as a dynamic of center and margins, in which the exclusionary force of the main metaphor creates alternatives at the margins of a practice. And through critical intervention, what lies at the margins can eventually take center stage.

These aspects of making practices—practices without foundations and practices as transversals—are elements to build on. However, there are shortcomings that will also need to be addressed. The mechanics of generative metaphors is center to margins, which creates a dualism that is not sufficiently expansive. Another shortcoming to address is that the multiplicity of programs and generative metaphors are a fixed and hierarchical relationship between critiques to foundation or margins to center. This type of fixed relationality is not in a sense relational enough. Lastly, implicit in paradigms, programs, and generative metaphors is an anthropocentric hold or privileging of human agency. Posthumanism, in contrast, assumes epistemologically the agentic contributions of nonhumans, which adds to the expansiveness.

Intentionality, Situated Knowledge, and Nomadism in Nomadic Practices

In the next section, I will introduce posthumanist concepts that will help shape these elements further and set the theoretical scaffolding in place for nomadic practices. In particular, I will discuss the postphenomenological ideas of intentionality to support ideas of embodied variations (Verbeek 2008). To draw out and make good, for my purposes, on the idea of a practice without foundations, Donna Haraway's feminist perspective on objectivity as a matter of situated knowledge will be invaluable (Haraway 1988). And to set the terms for a concept outside of a disciplinary structure, the element of practices of transversal opens the door toward multiplicity and movement that can be further refined when considering Gilles Deleuze and Felix Guattari's ideas of nomadism (Deleuze and Guattari 1987).

Intentionality of Nomadic Practices
In the introductory chapter, I discussed how in phenomenological terms, humans, as a notion, cannot be seen in isolation but rather in relation to the world. This is a matter of intentionality, or we can say that intentionality makes visible the inextricable bond between us and world (Verbeek 2008). Intentionality, in the phenomenological tradition of Edmond Husserl and Maurice Merleau-Ponty, is the central concept by which to understand the relationship between humans and their world. The importance here is that the way in which we are directed toward reality constitutes ourselves and the world together:

> Humans are always directed toward reality. They cannot simply "think," but they always think something; they cannot simply "see," but they always see something; they cannot simply "feel" but always feel something. As experiencing beings, humans cannot but be directed at the entities which constitute the world. Conversely it does not make much sense to speak of "the world in itself" either. Just like human beings can only be understood from their relation with reality, so can reality only be understood from the relation human beings have with it. The "world in itself" is inaccessible by definition, since every attempt to grasp it makes it a "world for us," as disclosed in terms of specific ways of understanding and encountering it. (Verbeek 2008, 388–389)

Phenomenological intentionality is distinct from the more general meaning of intentionality, which is to form intentions or set goals. Rather, phenomenological intentionality illuminates the way experience is structured through our embodiment, situatedness, and contingencies. This creates a relationality that shapes what we make of the world and, in turn, this experience shapes us. This shows intentionality to be bidirectional: The designer shapes the *something* designed as it in turn shapes the designer. Intentionality also reveals that the subject-object is not only mutually constituted but variant. In this way, designers are formed by what they design in ways that can vary; as such, however we constitute the designer, it is not only relational but composed of differences and differently structured experiences of the world.

Additionally, Verbeek, drawing on Don Ihde (1990), describes intentionality on the part of technologies; that is, experiences are not entirely human but structured by and through technologies, be they glasses, a thermometer, or a radio spectrometer (Verbeek 2008). Relatedly, Diana Coole draws on phenomenological intentionality to articulate "agentic capacities" across a spectrum of "prepersonal, corporeal processes and at the other [end], a transpersonal, intersubjective interworld" (Coole 2010, 124). This opens intentionality of nomadic practices to combinations of humans and nonhumans.

The importance for nomadic practices is that we can begin to see practices like design as formed by different intentionalities that constitute different types of designers designing differently. In other words, we cannot see "designers" as simply "designing" but rather as designing *something*. Equally, we cannot see "design in itself" but rather only in relation to "designers designing something." And that *something* is structured in different ways that are embodied, situated, and contingent—meaning that designers, as a matter of co-constitution, are also relational and multiple. Nomadic practices begin with the principle that designers and what is designed are multiply fashioned in numerous variations that are both coherent within and through intentionality.

Situated Knowledge of Nomadic Practices

In my discussion of paradigms, programs, and generative metaphors, I hope to have mapped an alternate route around disciplinary structures toward a concept without foundations, hierarchies, and the claiming of territory for describing the variant knowings and actions of a given design. Disciplines operate within an illusion of a total and autonomous body of knowledge. Such a body is attended to by disciplinarians who occupy a seemingly objective and therefore a truly uninhabitable perch to police, govern, and monitor the foundations and perimeters of the discipline (Krippendorff 2016).

Haraway famously and simply called this a "god trick." That is the "promising vision from everywhere and nowhere equally and fully" (Haraway 1988, 584). Haraway argues against the transcendent or objective models of knowing by offering a localized understanding of knowing referred to as "situated knowledge" (Haraway 1988). This is described as an embodied objectivity that is accountable by virtue of making clear that knowers are situated, in a particular and local position, relative to what is known and to other knowers. And this localized embodiment, the perspective of the knower, is reflected in the knowledge created and in *how* that knowledge is created. Situated knowledge makes unavoidable the limitations of knowing, given the knowing subject in every case is a result of differences, contingencies, embodiments, and incompleteness, while at the same time, these situated knowledges collectively form a "radical multiplicity" of knowledge (Haraway 1988, 579).

Yet, not wanting to give in to relativism or give up on reality or the spirit of objectivity, Haraway positions an embodied and visible knower in place of an all-seeing invisible knower as a measure of credible knowledge. This turns objectivity into a matter of accountability. This accountability arises from the visible knower being made present in the process of knowing. Further, as a result of the perspectivism of the situated knower, an additional and necessary accountability comes into play, taking the responsibility that any interpretations of reality are partial and incomplete and gaining trust by acknowledging this limitation. In situated knowledge, objectivity is not derived from neutrality in knowing. For Haraway and feminist thinking, there is no desire for a "theory of innocent powers to represent the world," a desire that marks humanist and masculine ideals of objectivity (Haraway 1988, 580). Feminist objectivity, in this way, embraces knowing in its multiplicity:

> Subjectivity is multidimensional; so, therefore, is vision. The knowing self is partial in all its guises, never finished, whole, simply there and original; it is always constructed and stitched together imperfectly, and therefore able to join with another, to see together without claiming to be another. Here is the promise of objectivity: a scientific knower seeks the subject position, not of identity, but of objectivity, that is, partial connection. There is no way to "be" simultaneously in all, or wholly in any, of the privileged (i.e., subjugated) positions structured by gender, race, nation, and class. (Haraway 1988, 586)

Situated knowledge dismantles the assumption that through the rigors of technique and method, or conversely through the politics of identity, the all-seeing position is achieved and only from this vantage point can claims be made on what is true and needs to be known. The assumption of who can claim to know is dismantled. In situated knowledge, the claim to know is not a privileged position but is privileged as the way to know:

Nomadic Practices 49

"So, with many other feminists, I want to argue for a doctrine and practice of objectivity that privileges contestation, deconstruction, passionate construction, webbed connections, and hope for transformation of systems of knowledge and ways of seeing" (Haraway 1988, 584). And within this multiplicity of limited and contradictory claims, there is the ability to "join with another"—or, as Haraway puts it, a "positioned rationality"—which is "the joining of partial views and halting voices into a collective subjective position" (Haraway 1988, 590). Positioned rationality is not about resolution or "claiming to be another" but about making collective claims of knowing.

The importance of this discussion is that understanding design from the perspective of situated knowledge also opens design to being understood in multiplicity. The issue is not which claims are truer toward an ideal notion of design but rather that all claims about design that hold an embodied objectivity are accountable claims for what in a collective fashion—with all the contradictions and partial knowing intact—is a collective design. The value of the claims can be seen in the visions and productive interpretations of how we know and see design.

Nomadism in Nomadic Practices

Nomadism is central to the idea of nomadic practices by supporting and pushing further the notion of practices as transversals. Up to this point, I've discussed the principle of intentionality as the binding of subject-object or designer-designed together in ways that not only structure what each means but are open to a multiplicity of variations. Situated knowledge makes explicit the perspectivism behind ways of knowing. It also shows that this plurality of perspectives does not atomize the meaning of design into unrecognizable bits of relativism. Rather through "positioned rationality," a collective subjective view of design emerges that accounts for the embodied knower or knowers of design. Yet in a design without foundations or fixed definitions, how do we understand what form these alternatives take and what features they hold?

To answer these questions, I draw on "nomadism" as described by Deleuze and Guattari (1987). They often speak of opposing poles on a spectrum including, for example, the territorialized and deterritorialized. Eva Aldea concisely illustrates nomadism as a spectrum of orders between sedentary and nomadic:

> Under the sedentary order, exemplified by the image of agricultural land, distinct parcels of land are distributed to determined groups of people. Areas of land are divided and demarcated, in order that the ownership of the land is clear. Any movement across sedentary land is defined by borders and boundaries: as you move from one distinct place to another, from field A to field B, roads and walls determine the route you have to take.
>
> In contrast, under the nomadic order, exemplified by the image of the desert, a number of people are scattered across an expanse of land, without clear borders or exclusive ownership. The route from point A to point B is not determined in the same way as under the sedentary order. Rather, stopping places are subordinated to the journey itself: meeting places, encampments, watering holes instead of fields, cities, castles. (Aldea 2014)

Deleuze and Guattari use this language of territories and movement to describe an array of organizations from political systems to the military to the sciences. In *Thousand Plateaus*, they offer an illustrative example by comparing the games of chess and Go (Deleuze and Guattari 1987, 352–353). Both are strategy games. Social structures of differentiated power are represented in the chess board and pieces (see figure 2.4), including kings, queens, knights, and lowly serfs or pawns. The object of chess is to "kill" or remove your opponent's pieces from the board. Go is abstract, without representations or structures, and so the pieces are typically either white or black (see figure 2.5). The aim of Go is to surround and occupy more territory than the other player.

The sedentary order in Deleuze and Guattari is typically associated with "the State" or organizational authority. Chess is a game of the State, not only historically but structurally as well. Chess pieces are, to use Deleuze and Guattari's term, "coded," meaning they have intrinsic properties or an internal nature that defines them in terms of movements, actions, and capacities. These codes are unchangeable. For example, a knight piece is intrinsically different from a queen because the knight can move on the board in the shape of an "L" whereas a queen can move in any straight line across the length of the board. A player is understood as the totality of all her pieces on the board. These pieces are part of a hierarchical organization, from pawns to king, and have power relative to their place in the hierarchy. This echoes the idea of agricultural land as sedentary, members of which are clearly divisible and accorded individual capacities. Even the board of chess is a matter of borders and boundaries divided between opponents down the center of the board. Go, a completely different strategy

Nomadic Practices 51

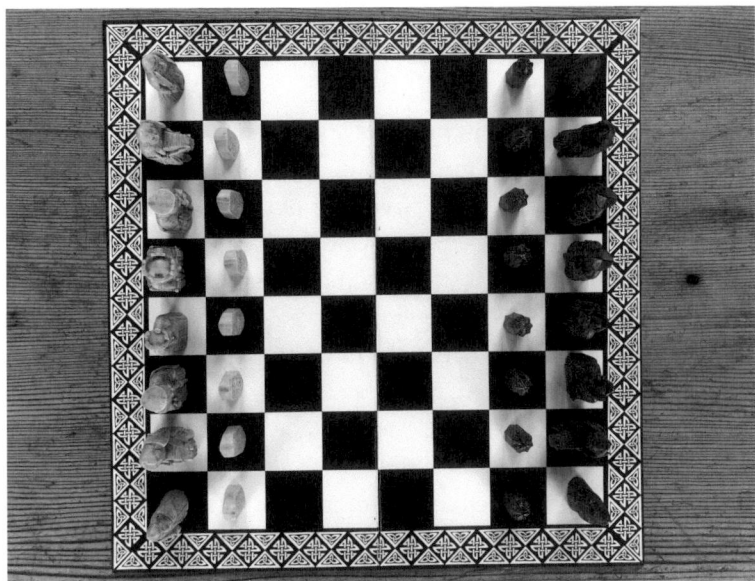

Figure 2.4
Chess board and pieces.

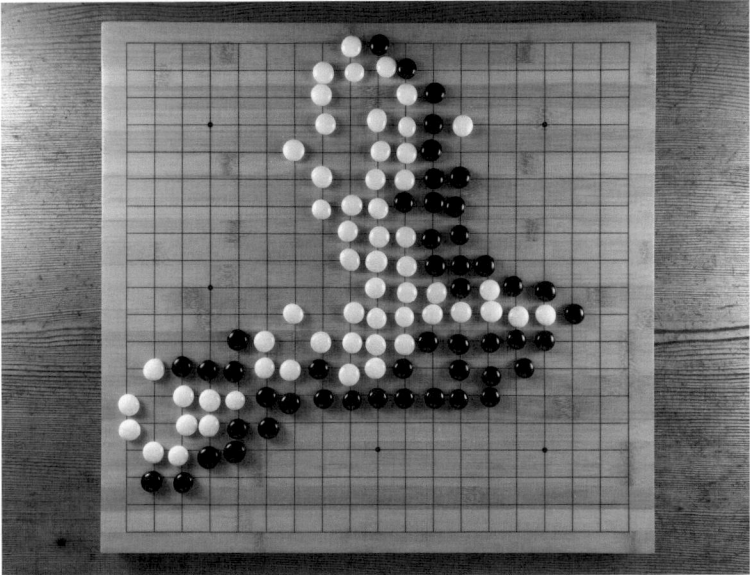

Figure 2.5
Go board and pieces.

game, is what Deleuze and Guattari see as nomadic in its order. The pieces are "anonymous, collective, or third-person" (Deleuze and Guattari 1987, 352), featureless and nonreferential. Typically, the pieces are either black or white stones or pellets, but in principle any two contrasting forms will do. Go pieces have no coded or intrinsic properties, only situational properties acquired externally through the placement of other Go pieces. This establishes a clear difference in gameplay: Chess pieces are "structural," posing threats to opponents in concert with other chess pieces and the positions of the opponents' pieces. Go pieces are more nebulous, becoming parts of patterns and constellations. In the right circumstances, one Go piece can change the entire arrangement of the board and the game in a single move. Ultimately, as a war game, Deleuze and Guattari see chess as "institutionalized, regulated, coded war with a front, a rear, battles," whereas Go "is a war without battle lines, with neither confrontation nor retreat, without battles even" (Deleuze and Guattari 1987, 353).

Deleuze and Guattari describe war machines (the military apparatuses of structures and strategies) and not just strategy games of war as assemblages along the spectrum of sedentary and nomadic. More closely related to my aims of a nondisciplinary framing for design, Deleuze and Guattari describe sciences as sedentary and nomadic. Major science, what I have described as disciplinary, is sedentary. Minor science, what I have described as practices, is nomadic. Again, it is important to caution that this is a distinction on a spectrum rather than an explicit opposition; what Manuel DeLanda (2016) refers to as "parameters" is a matter of emphasis, in one direction or another. Major science is axiomatic, producing laws and principles by which to question or investigate phenomena. Minor science follows phenomena, allowing the phenomena to pose problems. DeLanda details this distinction further:

> Deleuze and Guattari include other characteristics of minor and major fields in addition to the contrast between the problematic and axiomatic approaches, and between the practice of following phenomena rather than interrogating them using predefined categories or laws. The authors [Deleuze and Guattari] argue that while minor science concerns itself with flows, major science treats fluids as a special case of a theory of solids; while minor science deals with becoming, major science concerns itself with what is stable, eternal, identical, and constant. (DeLanda 2016, 96)

DeLanda expands on Deleuze and Guattari's analysis of major and minor sciences in a case study of chemistry, which like most scientific fields aspires to the status of a major science all the while demonstrating the nomadic characteristics of a minor science (DeLanda 2016). Here, I've expanded on this idea to make the point that nomadic practices will treat design as a minor science, emphasizing the nomadic parameter of pursuing phenomena to generate problems in ways that constantly move across territories, settling and unsettling (territorializing and deterritorializing in the language of Deleuze and Guattari), all the while avoiding laws, principles, foundations, territorial claims, and hierarchical structures.

Nomadism contributes centrally to the idea of nomadic practices, revealing an enabling approach to traverse across territories, avoiding disciplinary structures. Equally important, it moves to the fore the ongoing emergence of the phenomena of which a given design "follows" or "gathers" around. Lastly, it makes understanding a particular nomadic practice of design a matter of describing the relational features it holds.

Nomadic Practices

At the risk of making the "destination" of the chapter seemingly abrupt in relation to the journey of getting here (though in keeping with the nomadic approach), I will end with a succinct description of the features of nomadic practices. Nomadic practices can be described as having three features:

- *Multiplicity of intentionalities* is the plurality with which designers and the something designed are mutually constituted across different nomadic practices. Nomadic practices are shared intentionalities in which designers gather around different ways to structure possibilities of designing.
- *Situated knowing* is how knowledge of the particular *something* to design of nomadic practices is created. The knower or designer is embodied, situated, and made visible with respect to any claims of what is known about design. As a result, nomadic practices offer multiple ways to know design, resulting in knowledge that is diverse and collective.
- The *nomadism* of nomadic practices refigures design from a single territorial discipline to a multiplicity of concurrent, allied, non-allied, collaborative, competitive, contradictory, or aligned practices of design marked by who gathers around a particular something to design. There is a plurality of gatherings that traverse across a landscape, territorializing and deterritorializing as they go, following the somethings they design for wherever that may lead, often crossing paths to contest or form allegiances with other nomadic practices.

The accountability or credibility of nomadic practices is established in various ways. One is through the embodied objectivity of making visible the knower of the nomadic practice and the ways of knowing. Second, the nomadism structures nomadic practices as gatherings of knowers/designers around a particular notion of design and its accompanying *something*. As a gathering, a nomadic practice is accountable based on who and what it gathers both in quantity and kind. Further, nomadic practices are much more fluid and dynamic than disciplines since they can grow or fade depending on the attraction to gather (or not) within a given shared intentionality.

To give up on a claim to universalism as nomadic practices does is to also abandon ideas of generalizable knowledge. In many respects, epistemological theories of design like conceptual constructs (Stolterman and Wiberg 2010) or intermediate knowledge and strong concepts (Höök and Löwgren 2012) have already argued against universal principles in exchange for propositional and materialist understandings of how design knowing is generated and shared. Nomadic practices take this a step further, and in doing so it emphasizes a collective approach to knowledge and its creation. First, generative metaphors make clear that regardless of how we may now reconceptualize design practices, we will have inherited a history of knowing that can be appropriated and above all else shared. However, this asserts the need to investigate historical narratives beyond the hegemonic, as with the critical work of undoing long-silenced narratives of design (Rosner 2018) or exposing the past racial encodings of technology (Benjamin 2019). Moving forward, nomadic practices are dynamic and on the move such that their trajectories are defined by intersections, divergences, contestations, and temporary alliances with other nomadic practices in which knowing and know-how cross-pollinates and is shared. Thinking of knowledge collectively and as shared across nomadic practices rather than as an abstract and generalizable theoretical foundation for all practices points to what Haraway refers to as a "radical multiplicity" of knowledge that is far richer and more diverse than a singular discipline (Haraway 1988, 579).

So, what can be done with nomadic practices? Informed by posthumanist approaches, nomadic practices can be said to open design to alternative formulations that are not solely bound to humanist assumptions. In chapter 3, I will put nomadic practices to work and use the theory to interpret current approaches to design to see what a nondisciplinary view of today's design might look like. Then in part II of the book (chapters 4 and 5), I will look past current formulations of design and use nomadic practices to speculate on the idea of a posthumanist variant of design—designing things.

In conclusion, the theory of nomadic practices has a particular and pragmatic role to play in this book. I use it as an intellectual argument to pry open space in discussing a shared intentionality of design that was not afforded in humanist notions of discipline. However, I am aware that I hold a privileged position from which to make this argument—a privilege received in large part through the rise of design as a discipline during my academic career—and so I have benefited professionally and scholarly as a result. Ironically, in this way, I can afford to make this claim. Having said that, while there is some power in not being weighed down by former affinities, there is clearly power in offering the collective benefit of an expansive and generous way of knowing design(s).

Chapter 3 Prologue: Fairphone, Pocket Receivers, and Kar-a-Sutra

In chapter 3, I apply nomadic practices to current design to show that it is an effective alternative to viewing design in a disciplinary fashion. In this prologue, I present a range of design works that later help me in chapter 3 to elaborate on the different *somethings* of design and the different nomadic practices that are constituted through what I discuss as *artifacts, objects,* and *products*.

The Fairphone

The *Fairphone* began as a campaign in 2009, led by Peter van der Mark and Bas van Abel, to raise awareness in the Netherlands about the use of conflict metals from the Democratic Republic of Congo in mobile phones. The campaign was a coalition of Dutch telecommunication providers, nonprofits, and the Waag Society, a Dutch foundation for the creative industries (Van der Welden 2014). Van der Mark was a public relations specialist and van Abel an industrial designer. As part of the campaign, they invited the Dutch public to work with them to design a "conflict free" smartphone: "They had neither the intention nor the expertise to make a commercial product. They hoped that any resulting prototype would be a non-functional concept device destined for exhibition at a local museum" (Akemu, Whiteman, and Kennedy 2016). However, years later, in 2012, after successful media reception, receipt of a public grant, international partner interests, and an angel investment, *Fairphone* incorporated and became a social enterprise. Van Abel became the CEO, stating that company would "produce a cool phone that puts human values first" (Akemu, Whiteman, and Kennedy 2016). Yet the newly formed company did not have a prototype, sufficient industry or technical knowledge, and the funding to go into production. Nevertheless, *Fairphone* in 2013 initiated a crowdfunding campaign and, remarkably, by the end of the year, presold 25,000 nonexistent smartphones for 325 euros each. More remarkably, with funds in hand, new technical staff, support from partner mobile operator networks like Alpha-Mobile and Beta-Mobile, and an outsourcing arrangement with a Chinese manufacturer, the Fairphone company filled all the orders by February 2014 (see figure 3.1).

Central to the concept of *Fairphone* is self-evidently the value of fairness. What began with the aspirations of fairness as a matter of ethical sourcing of minerals soon expanded to include "a people-first approach, fair and conflict free resources, the use of recycled materials, e-waste solutions across the supply chain, fair technical and design specifications, and transparent pricing" (Van der Welden 2014, 6). This translated into design specifications for the actual *Fairphone*. While its form factor and user interface were in no way unique, the "fairness features" of the phone include housing made of recycled polycarbonate, nonconflict materials; dual SIM cards to reduce one owner's need for multiple phones; open source operating system (Android OS) with root access for the owner; fully accessible and repairable parts; and modularity for additional changes. Fairphone released a third version named *Fairphone 3* in September 2019.

The *Fairphone* can be seen as a concept of progressive human values from production to product. Its development and conceptualization of an artifact of "good" makes it an illustrative (if partly a boundary) case of what I will describe as the nomadic practice of *designing artifacts*.

Braun Pocket Receivers T3, T4, and T41

The *Braun Pocket Receivers* are portable radios small enough to fit in one's pocket (see figure 3.2). Braun, as a product company and maker of radios and record players, had considered portable radios since the 1930s. However, it was not until the transistor technologies of the 1950s that electronics could be produced that were small enough, robust enough, and sufficiently low power to be truly considered portable. An earlier version, the T1, was the first radio project by the designer Dieter Rams (Lovell, Kemp, and Ive 2011). Rams, perhaps the most influential of industrial designers, became synonymous with Braun, helping to transform it into one of the first "design companies" that made "good design" central to its business and marketing strategies.

Fairphone, Pocket Receivers, and Kar-a-Sutra

Figure 3.1
Fairphone, first edition.
Source: "Unboxing Fairphone" by Rainer Stropek, licensed under CC BY 2.0.

Figure 3.2
Braun Pocket Receivers T41 (left), T4 (middle), and T3 attached to record player (right).
Source: "Untitled" by Martin Wichary, licensed under CC BY 2.0.

His functionalist style of design, often associated with the aphorism "less but better" (Rams 1995), came to represent a trajectory of modernist design from Bauhaus through to the Ulm School of Design to Braun.

In the late 1970s, Rams consolidated his thoughts on design in what has become known as the "ten principles for good design" (Rams 1995). Before then, at the time of the *Braun Pocket Receivers*, it was clear that Braun's design team already operated from a set of principles by which to design. Rams affirmed Richard Moss's characterization of industrial design at Braun as being "defined by three rules: the rule of order, the rule of harmony, the rule of economy" (Rams 1995, 30). Rams, for example, saw that, within a harmony of design, aesthetics has a functional purpose to "facilitate a positive emotional response between a device and its user" (Rams 1995, 30). Notably, Braun can be credited with bringing technology into the home in a way that was celebrated and made visible, rather than hidden or disguised as furniture. Rams added an additional "rule" to Moss's characterization: one of longevity. Longevity is achieved through the focus on necessity and conciseness that would "exist beyond all fashion and point towards the essential." And Rams continues, "It is therefore no coincidence that numerous Braun appliances could be produced and sold for decades with little change to their overall design" (Rams 1995, 31). In large part, during his time at Braun, this was true. Rational principles external to the fashions and happenings of the time governed the form and design. This was also evident across product and functional domains. One glance at Braun products—from kitchen mixers, blenders, and juicers to shavers and slide projectors—reveals a strikingly similar sparseness: the radii and slope of lines; dark contrasting horizontal and vertical slits; similar mix of white to gray thermoplastics, metals, and glass; and similarly economical and precisely shaped switches and buttons.

The design of the Braun Pocket Receiver T3, designed in 1958 by Rams (see figure 3.2), translated horizontal slits used in his previous radio project, the TI, into a square array of perforated holes that act as a speaker grille. The T3 and later radios (T4 and T41) are housed in an off-white thermoplastic shell, a relatively new material at the time developed by Braun, that forms the rectangular shape of the radios. In each case, the power and volume buttons are recessed into the form. The station dial of the T3 is a rotary dial that is flush with the surface of the radio. The circles, rectangles, perforations, and slits repeated themselves in many variations throughout Braun design, becoming emblematic of Braun and Rams. This was clearly the case with the subsequent T4 (1959) and T41 (1962) radios. In these later versions, the speaker grille is changed into a circular pattern of perforated holes. In the T4 (figure 3.2), the station dial is placed in the housing, rotated from a recess in the side and viewable through a narrow rectangular window. In T41 (figure 3.2), the play of circles and rectangles harks back to both the T3 and T4 in that the station dial is now a larger window revealing a pie-shaped view of the internal dial that is at the same radius of the original touch rotary dial of the T3. The Pocket Receivers were also part of a system design in which each receiver could be connected to a portable phonograph (turntable) to play vinyl records. The P1 record player, as it was known, was of the same width as the receivers and so could be joined together by the metal handle and leather strap of the P1 to be carried more easily. This became a part of a modular approach to Braun's devices, in which dimensions were standardized so separate parts of systems could be combined and the overall system extended.

The *Braun Pocket Receivers* are clearly commercial products, but they are products of an era in which the design of an object could hold value in surplus of the economic exchange it also represents. Here the values are transcendental, external principles of what makes good design—specifically, what makes a good design *object*. In chapter 3, I will discuss how the *Braun Pocket Receivers* are illustrative of the nomadic practice of *designing objects* in which idealized human values are made manifest in the detail form, function, and symbolism of the something, the object, designed.

Kar-a-Sutra

The *Kar-a-Sutra* is a concept object that was designed in 1972 by Mario Bellini (figure 3.3) for an exhibition at the Museum of Modern Art in New York titled *Italy: The New Domestic Landscape*. The exhibition, curated by Emilio Ambasz, investigated the "limitations and critical problems" of design that had uniquely emerged in then-contemporary Italian design. The investigations of these designers included "a wide range of conflicting theories about the present state of design activity [in the late 1960s and early 1970s], its relation to the building industry and to urban development, as well as a growing distrust of objects of consumption" (Shaw 1972).

Kar-a-Sutra, a pure concept design, was not intended as a product and so did not function. Bellini saw the design object as a "vehicle for conversation and change" (Niera 2017). This makes it among the first critical design objects. The "car" is essentially a box on wheels with a forty-five-degree slope at the front and of similar length and width of a large sedan of the time. The body of the car is like a greenhouse, with glass sides and a glass roof. The plates of glass can be removed and, through pneumatics, the roof can be raised an additional two feet. The emphasis of the design, though, is on the interior. It has a large loading capacity of almost twenty square feet of floor space. The interior is completely fitted with cushions that are ten inches high by two feet square. The cushions can be arranged in any combination to form seats, armrests, beds, sofas, and so on. This flexibility encourages the inhabitants to arrange the interior as it suits them, allowing those inside to stand, sit, kneel, or lie facing in any direction. Additionally, the foam of the cushions is a type of "memory foam" that keeps its last molded shape. Given this flexibility and indeterminacy of the space, Bellini referred to the interior as a "plastic field" (Bellini 1972).

Fairphone, Pocket Receivers, and Kar-a-Sutra 63

Figure 3.3
The *Kar-a-Sutra*.
Source: Mario Bellini Studio and Museum of Modern Art, New York.

The *Kar-a-Sutra* is a design object for speculation and critique. Its expressed aims are to speculate on the idea of mobility in a new way. Bellini calls it the making of "MOBILE HUMAN SPACE," as opposed to the "AUTOMOBILE-MAN system" (all caps is in the original) of the traditional consumerist car (Bellini 1972, 202). As the provocative name of the design suggests, Bellini aims to deeply humanize the modern automobile, to wrap its design around the needs and desires of people in transport and, in so doing, provide "human space in motion." The emphasis is to make cars more livable and, by implication (similar to Rams's longevity), to create a longer-lasting connection with people and therefore avoid "some critical limit in the extent of its [the car's] indeterminate multiplication" (Bellini 1972, 203). Herein lies the consumerist critique of the instrumentalized and commoditized mode of transportation that cars had become:

> In present-day automobiles, however, we have no option other than to enter, sit either alone or, less comfortably, in motionless groups of five or six; smoke, think, read a bit, talk to the passenger next to us or behind us, switch on the radios [and] watch the landscape from the corner of our eye, and finally get out. More important, we can speed along, accelerate, roar down the road like real sports heroes, loving the automobile itself and hating the people in cars we overtake; we can permit others to admire our virility and economic power, of which our car is a symbol; we can implicate the car in obscene attempts at lovemaking; we can ruin ourselves for the car, kill others with it, or die in it ourselves. (Bellini 1972, 202)

The *Kar-a-Sutra* is a design object that urges and critiques its way to a new set of values. In chapter 3, I will discuss how the *Kar-a-Sutra* is also part of the nomadic practice of *designing objects*. Similar to the *Braun Pocket Receivers*, its details, form, function, and symbolism advocate for change through a prescriptive set of human values.

Chapter 3: Designing Artifacts, Objects, and Products

In this chapter, I show how nomadic practices can conceptualize design as different variants. In particular, I describe the nomadic practice of *designing artifacts*. And for comparison's sake, I briefly discuss *designing objects* and *designing products*. The value of emphasizing the differences is that each nomadic practice reveals its own autonomy and "logic" of a particular form of design that does not need to be resolved into a single discipline. And as a collection of variants, nomadic practices form a greater diversity and potential for design. Ultimately, I want to use this idea of nomadic practices to develop a posthumanist understanding of *designing things* that I take up in part II of this book.

The Nomadic Practice of Designing Artifacts

The nomadic practice of designing artifacts is motivated by human progress—that is, to design artifacts that improve human lives politically, technologically, or socially. This thinking is most evident in the interdisciplinary work of human-computer interaction (HCI) researchers and practitioners. HCI is a diverse field of study and practice with concerns ranging from participatory design to human cognition and behavior and ethnography. As a traditional description, HCI is the research and practice into the design and use by humans of interactive technologies. In HCI, humans take on the universalizing concept of the user. The idea of the user remains a dominant concern, though its definition has evolved over time.

Participatory design (PD) contributed to this evolution by considering users as co-designers and stakeholders situated in particular work or community contexts. PD emerged in Scandinavia from systems design with a commitment to users shaping their own technologies. This began through collaborations of unions and academic researchers in a form of action research and design and later more broadly in community contexts in which skills and knowledge are exchanged to arrive at a process of designing together. Computer-supported cooperative work (CSCW as it is commonly known) also contributed to the evolution of the ideas of use and user in this story of artifacts. Similar to PD, CSCW focuses on technologies as system design issues, in particular, considering users as social groups interacting with networked systems, system software, and organizational systems. Adhering to the concerns of the design of such systems, CSCW brings together HCI researchers with organizational theorists, social psychologists, anthropologists, cultural theorists, and sociologists. In many respects, CSCW looks beyond the technical and design matters of systems to investigate social structures and organizations in the workplace, the home, and more broadly. As an ongoing concern, CSCW opens HCI to nontechnical issues within the context of human use of technologies.

Much of the development of the idea of artifacts in design occurred in the late 1980s and early 1990s. The strength of these arguments is that they are largely still in effect some thirty years later. Admittedly, I've simplified internally diverse and complex perspectives that many might wish to view separately. Yet, in taking a step back, looking for transversals, intersections of common interests and shared articulations, it is useful not to see HCI, PD, and CSCW as separate endeavors but rather as interrelated approaches with shared interests in the role that design of technologies plays in improving human lives.

Artifacts as Somethings

In the story of this nomadic practice, the *something* that is designed is an *artifact*. In this case, an artifact is constituted or can only be understood as *something* for *human use*—more specifically, use that is enduring in the form of practices that are embedded contextually and typically seen in terms of human behavior, cognition, or social routines. In addition to being embedded in complex use and practices, artifacts refer to incredibly diverse forms and concepts, showing artifacts to be very flexible in what they signify. And in related ways, artifacts are seen to embody conceptual and theoretical claims.

Artifacts Are Embedded in Complex Use and Practices

The development of the concept of artifacts moved attention away from low-level types of uses, such as discrete tasks in operating a computer, to more complex and situated uses. Nowhere is this more evident than in PD. In PD, use is "engaged"; it is embedded in practice that is a matter of professional training, skill, and knowledge learned and embodied over years (Ehn 1988). It is in this relationship between use, artifacts, and practice that the larger concerns of democracy and participation in PD were crystallized.

The embedding or situating of use extends beyond specific practices to encompass all use. Wanda Orlikowski (2000) makes a clear distinction between artifact-in-itself versus artifact-in-use, what she refers to as "technology-in-practice." Orlikowski describes use as contextualized and situated, drawing on Lucy Suchman's idea of "situated action," in which actions, dependent on material and social circumstances, occur on a moment-by-moment basis in ways that are highly situated (Suchman 1987).

In its broadest sense, the dynamic of artifact and use is such that artifacts are shaped by past practices, reasoned on contextually, and function within the sociomaterial circumstances of a given situation.

Artifacts Are Highly Flexible

Artifacts take on different forms and even temporal states. This is one of the most salient features of artifacts. This wide range, or flexibility, means there is a great diversity in what is referred to as an artifact. For example, an artifact can represent a large number of different types including "hardware, software, applications, interfaces" (Carroll and Rosson 1992); "scenarios, prototypes, mock-ups" (Bødker et al. 1988); "video scenarios" (Binder 1999); "medical records" (Berg and Bowker 1997); or "routines or models" (Ackerman et al. 2007). On a more concrete level, artifacts can refer to a diverse range of particulars including a "training interface for a word processor" (Carroll and Carrithers 1984), "computer-based newspaper production" system (Ehn 1988), "order slip at an espresso bar" (Ackerman et al. 2007), or "rush cheat sheet" (Halverson and Ackerman 2008). What these types and particulars have in common is that they all support human goals through use.

The flexibility of artifacts extends temporally as well. Artifacts operate across time from the present to the future, meaning that a present artifact is typically viewed together with its possible future iteration. In PD, understanding the use of a present artifact is the analytical grounding for an imagined future use of a related or similar artifact: "The future use situation is the origin of design, and we design with this situation in mind. To design with the future use activity in mind also means to start out from the present practice of the future users" (Bødker et al. 1988, 382). PD incorporates this temporal continuum of artifacts into the design process as well. Design process outcomes like "scenarios, prototypes, mock-ups" (Bødker et al. 1988) are seen as "design artifacts" or representations of the design process (Bødker et al. 1988; Binder 1999). These artifacts are typically not wholly or partially usable, yet they represent future possibilities of use stretching forward in time as a way "of anticipating new or changed computer artifacts and use situations" (Bødker et al. 1988, 384).

From a cognitive psychologist viewpoint, John Carroll and Wendy Kellogg also see artifacts as analytical and generative iterations across time: "We envision a reciprocal relation between the articulation and re-articulation of a set of psychological claims and the iterations of design" (Carroll and Kellogg 1989, 7). Here the "reciprocal" relationship is between analytical claims in psychology alongside the generative function of design in which claims can be made concrete and experimented upon. Similarly, Andrew Crabtree and his colleagues see a reciprocal role of ethnography and design in HCI, in which ethnography can be said to be the analytical present and design is considered the generative future in which ethnographic findings guide or hold implications for future design requirements (Crabtree et al. 2009).[1]

This flexibility of artifacts cannot be overstated. It gives artifacts the conceptual capacity to represent and change human practices and behavior. It is also remarkably unique that artifacts are perceived simultaneously in their present and future states.

Artifacts Embody Conceptual Claims about Humans

The embedded and highly flexible nature of artifacts shows them to be deeply entangled with human matters in ways that give insights into human practices and behaviors. It is then no surprise, particularly in the academic and research contexts of HCI, that artifacts are seen to embody theoretical and conceptual claims about humans. "HCI artifacts themselves are perhaps the most effective medium for theory development in HCI" (Carroll and Kellogg 1989, 7), and more specifically "HCI artifacts embody psychological claims in contexts of use: aspects of the interface engender psychological consequences and in this sense make claims about the user's behavior and experience" (Carroll and Kellogg 1989, 8). Carroll and Kellogg describe artifacts as a convergence or "nexus" of theoretical claims that operate in a number of ways. Artifacts give "coherence" to the theoretical claims, since these claims are made tangible in artifacts and situated within "real use" (Carroll and Kellogg 1989, 9). Relatedly, artifacts manifest use at a level of complexity that would be impossible to capture in a lab setting. And above all else, artifacts turn HCI theory into empirical claims, readily observable and testable.

The theoretical capacity of artifacts in complex use settings gives an advantage to HCI in terms of theory making and research. Viewing artifacts as "the bundle of material and textual properties packaged in some recognizable form, e.g., hardware, software, techniques" (Orlikowski 2000, 262) creates an opportunity to extend theories of human interaction in novel and empirical ways. For example, Edwin Hutchins's theory of distributed cognition defines "cognitive artifacts" as artifacts that participate in, extend, and improve human cognition. Artifacts and humans together form a distributed version of cognition that enables performing complex tasks like navigating a large Navy vessel in a busy harbor (Hutchins 1996). Further, past human skills, reason, and experiences are embodied in cognitive artifacts in such skills as math, memorization, navigation, and others. This allows humans to use these skills without relearning them, freeing up cognition for further complex actions (Becvar, Hollan, and Hutchins 2008). "In this sense the artifact becomes the partially saved solution of a problem that has been solved many times before. . . . The tools themselves are the residua of the cognitive processes of an expert" (Halverson and Ackerman 2008, 11).

The embodying of concepts and theories in artifacts creates a twofold complexity that serves the aims and intentionality of the nomadic practice to both understand and improve the lives of humans. As a result of being situated in use contexts, artifacts represent the complexities of use and human behavior. And the same situated nature of artifacts can positively change human use and behavior. Given the capacity to embody theoretical claims, artifacts create an invaluable empirical perch from which to study and influence human behavior in ways that are seen to be testable and verifiable.

Given the way in which artifacts have been defined and developed, it is hard not to overstate their power. Artifacts configure a design that is broadly connected to the substantive goings-on of humans, from practices to social routines to behaviors. An artifact is widely diverse in terms of what it constitutes both tangibly and temporally. As I said earlier, nomadic practices work across differences, drawing out affinities and transversals. There are clear epistemological differences across the various researchers I've drawn upon, from sociomaterial readings in works like Orlikowski (2000); ethnomethodological commitments to objectivity in Crabtree et al. (2009); empirical commitments in cognitive psychology orientations of Carroll and Kellogg (1989); and the commitments to hermeneutics and embodiment among PD researchers. Yet, despite these differences, there is an ability to gather around artifacts as *something* to design that centers on human use and practices.

The Intentionality of Designing Artifacts

A central characteristic of a nomadic practice as discussed in chapter 2 is *intentionality toward something*, which in the case of nomadic practice of designing artifacts is self-evidently artifacts. Artifacts as I've been describing them in practice are a set of structured possibilities for human progress through design. We can see this structure in slightly different ways throughout the practice, yet constant is the privileging of progress. Another characteristic of intentionality of nomadic practices is the mutual constitution of the designer and what is designed. This plays out very clearly in designing artifacts.

The something that is designed in this nomadic practice is artifacts that contribute to human progress. For example, in PD, artifacts are seen to enable labor and community stakeholders to shape and improve their own future practices through co-designing artifacts. The roots of these ambitions lie in the ideal of emancipatory politics in industrial democracies. As Pelle Ehn states, the goal for PD is to bring "democracy inside the factory gates and office doors" (Ehn 1988, 247):

> I have earlier identified work-oriented design of computational artifacts not only with technical and practical research guiding interests of instrumental control and intersubjective communication, but also with the research guiding interest in emancipation. This interest focuses on knowledge and understanding for emancipation from hypostatized forces of history and society and is directed towards creating conditions for independent individuals in a society of free cooperation and communication. This comes close to the democratic ideal, but there is a supplementary emphasis on the **process of democratization**. (Ehn 1988, 247)

Designing Artifacts, Objects, and Products 71

Ehn threads together the significance of democracy in the workplace through design with the move toward the democratic ideal of open cooperation and free information sharing. He ends with the charge to design to take at its core the *process* of this democratizing effort. He goes on to specifically ask of design and research: "What are the practical constraints and possibilities for democratic design and use of computer artifacts at work? How can research contribute in this direction?" (Ehn 1988, 247–248). The something to design in PD is clearly to contribute toward a democratic ideal through a democratic process for designing artifacts.

In ethnographic-related HCI work, the matter of explicit human progress is rarely stated. Rather, ethnographic efforts aim to reveal or uncover present realities that can be said to be impediments to progress or a thickening of reality to better understand what would be considered human progress with a particular group of people in their own social contexts. In ethnomethodologist approaches to artifacts, the concern is the revealing of "social facts" in a "theoretically unmediated fashion" to lay bare the goings-on in a social setting (Crabtree et al. 2009). This interpretive certainty is a bit of a battleground of commitments in the way social realities are revealed such that there is a range from the "unmediated" reporting of some to "analytical orientations" of others who critically reveal through theoretical lenses like postcolonialism (Irani et al. 2010) or decolonization (Halbert and Nathan 2015), as examples. Nevertheless, the actualities of the social relations awaiting description or the critical digging to reveal power relations point to creating an accurate account of contexts from which the use of artifacts may seek improvements.

Progress can also be seen as scientific that reveals more clearly the path toward technological improvements and their use. In HCI, artifacts are seen to contribute to scientific progress in understanding human use and behaviors. Carroll and Kellogg see HCI as a complex science: "Interpretations of the claims embodied by HCI artifacts evince the hallmarks of scientific progress, at least insofar as we can determine this now. The claims embodied in artifacts are absolutely specific; they are always already instantiated in the world. It is incumbent on the analyst to faithfully extract a system of testable empirical claims" (Carroll and Kellogg 1989, 13). In Carroll and Kellogg's account, theoretical claims converge to be materially instantiated in artifacts, as I discussed earlier. Manifest in artifacts, theoretical knowledge becomes coherent and empirically accessible within a rich context that suggests ecological validity. On a higher level, this idea of artifacts as empirical claims for HCI theory squarely puts HCI forward as a complex science capable of substantial and credible contributions to the progress of HCI and other fields.

These assumptions of the progressive nature of designing artifacts are embodied in commitments of how artifacts are designed and understood. The commitment is to empiricism. For artifacts, the way to know if new knowledge is created and if progress is made is to collect, analyze, and assess empirically. The roles of artifacts are the means to produce validated theory and directly impact use and practices. These embodiments consolidate quite a range of design and research methods from PD games of simulated use, ethnography, and contextual inquiries; a range of empirico-analytical approaches including hermeneutics, ethnomethodologies, critical analysis, reflexivity, usability analysis, and user testing; and user-based methods including stakeholder engagements, co-design, and user-centered design.

Given these orientations toward the world, it is no surprise that the "classical" designer fades to the background. Artifacts are seen to be produced cooperatively, socially, or scientifically. The intentionality of artifacts is one in which reality is produced through use and so "designed-in-use." That artifacts are not exclusively created through the design process and designers is a defining quality of this nomadic practice. The designer of artifacts is co-constituted as multiple stakeholders that contribute to the design of artifacts. Relatedly, Gerhard Fischer developed the concept of *meta-design*, in which designers enable and support users in the process of designing complex artifacts through processes and tools (Fischer and Scharff 2000). PD developed a design process based on *language-games* to support the competences of users as active agents in the design process (Bødker et al. 1988).

In these cases, the goal is to bring users and their knowledge of use directly into the design process of creating artifacts. CSCW takes these aims a step further by declaring that the meaning and particular ends of artifacts are invariably determined through use. For example, Paul Dourish states:

> Critically, how technology is used in practice is not the same as the designer's conception, in two ways. Firstly, at a gross level, people often find ways of using technology that are unexpected or unanticipated. . . . Secondly, at a more particular level, even when the general patterns of technology use do conform to expectations, the meaning of the technology for those who use it depends on how generic features are particularized, how conventions emerge, and so on. (Dourish 2001, 26)

Designing Artifacts, Objects, and Products

Dourish sees that artifacts are shaped in direct ways by users by being *appropriated*, used for purposes other than the original intentions of the designers, and that artifacts are understood through the sociohistorical or social contexts of use. Artifacts are not seen as "stable, static, and closed software systems" but as malleable material, functionally and conceptually, adapted to the practices they become embedded in (Dourish 2001, 28). In this sense, artifacts and designers are co-constituted as largely social processes that can be empirically studied.

The Fairphone Is an Artifact

I will illustrate the nomadic practice of designing artifacts by applying it to the *Fairphone*. I chose the *Fairphone* as an example of an artifact since it holds all the critical qualities yet shows the reach or extensibility of the idea of artifacts. The Fairphone is not an academic or research pursuit, and neither is it a commercial product. As discussed in the prologue to this chapter, the Fairphone began as a conceptual matter, specifically a campaign to create awareness around ethical issues of the use of conflict minerals in mobile phones.

The *Fairphone* is a concept of human progress with ethical values that lends it qualities of what I also describe as an object. However, I view it as an artifact since its main goal is to improve human lives through the functionalities of mobility and communication. As an artifact it holds the incredible conceptual power to embody an abstract claim like ethical sourcing that transcends any particular material instantiation or can in effect operate without such an instantiation. It contributes to the central notion of human use by claiming to offer *ethical use*. The *Fairphone* is a highly flexible concept. It primarily existed as a theoretical vision of ethical good without a specific or tangible form until very late in its development. In many respects, it embodies a future good of design and technology. The *Fairphone* is designed by selecting and combining *existing* ethical options. As a result, and true to a nomadic practice of designing artifacts, the designer is a consensus-making body of diverse stakeholders that unsurprisingly takes the form of a social enterprise that combines commerce with democratizing strategies for design. In this sense, the Fairphone can be said to have been designed cooperatively and socially and so is emblematic of an artifact.

By Comparison: The Nomadic Practices of Designing Objects and Designing Products

The virtue of nomadic practices is that they crystallize and give description to variants of design, each with their own structure and logic. This is the nomadism of the theory. To highlight this, I move to a brief but purposeful discussion of two other nomadic practices: *designing objects* and *designing products*. I do this for comparison's sake, to underscore the productive differences that are highlighted through a relational and nomadic viewpoint. I begin with the nomadic practice of designing objects. In the foreword to *Dieter Rams: As Little Design as Possible*, Jonathan Ive, the former chief design officer of Apple, writes a telling description of what makes a design object that is well worth citing at length:

> When I was a young boy growing up in London, my parents bought a wonderful juicer. It was a Braun MPZ 2 Citromatic. I knew nothing about Dieter Rams or his ten principles of good design. But to a little boy uninterested in juicing, I remember the Citromatic he and his team designed for Braun with shocking clarity. It was white. It felt cold and heavy. The surfaces were without apology, bold, pure, perfectly-proportioned, coherent and effortless. There was an honest connection between its blemish-free surfaces and the materials from which they were made. It was clearly made from the best materials, not the cheapest. No part appeared to be either hidden or celebrated, just perfectly considered and completely appropriate in the hierarchy of the product's details and features. At a glance, you knew exactly what it was and exactly how to use it. It was the essence of juicing made material: a static object that perfectly described the process by which it worked. It felt complete and it felt right. While my memories are, of course, in the past tense, the product remains all these things. I was completely enchanted with it then, and I now find, with surprise, that this object resonated so deeply with me that nearly forty years on I remember my sense of it with startling clarity. . . . [Rams's] genius lies in understanding and giving form to the very essence of an object's being—almost describing its reason for existence, as so perfectly illustrated by the Citronic juicer of my childhood. (Lovell, Kemp, and Ive 2011, 13)

In this nomadic practice, the *something* is an *object*. Ive's account of his childhood memory of the *Braun MPZ 2 Citromatic* is emblematic of how to describe an object (figure 3.4). Unlike an artifact, the meaning of an object does not emerge from use. Ive is clear that his younger self was "enchanted" by the *Citromatic* despite being "uninterested in juicing." That "at a glance," the juicer revealed its essence and how it functions. An object is understood as an object-in-itself, unlike an artifact. It is only in this sense that a young

Designing Artifacts, Objects, and Products

Figure 3.4
Braun MPZ 2 Citromatic by Dieter Rams and Jurgen Greubel 1972.
Source: das programm.

boy can distill the value and importance of an object without explicit recourse to its use, its social setting or the social relations it produces, or the economic values it is enmeshed in. The importance of the juicer is viewed without context. This spirit of seeing an object-in-itself echoes the nineteenth-century art critic John Ruskin, who saw the modernist observer and painter as one who views the "inner nature" of the world without convention or "consciousness" of any external meanings (Ruskin 1885). He referred to this as the "innocent eye," an eschewing of the pictorial conventions or social constructions of what something might be. As Ive observes, Rams is able to give the form its own "essence" of being that is self-reliant. Objects are self-referential, directed at themselves as a matter of design qualities of proportions, form, materials, and relations among parts that come together in a coherent and meaningful way. What Ive referred to as "shocking clarity."

Ruskin's claim of a modernist vision of an unencumbered "innocent eye" was in defense of the English painter Joseph Turner, whose near-abstract landscapes were assailed for their lack of realism. Ruskin's defense of Turner was that the realism of the day was no more than pictorial conventions and social constructions that overlooked the deeper and essential aspects of nature. This ethos of pureness of perception is the very trajectory of much modernist art from Cezanne through to the abstract expressionists of the twentieth century. However, art historian Jonathan Crary is quick to point out that the term "innocence" is misleading:

> Rather it is a question of a vision achieved at great cost that claimed for the eye a vantage point uncluttered by the weight of historical codes and conventions of seeing, a position from which vision can function without the imperative of composing its contents into a reified "real" world. It was a question of an eye that sought to avoid the repetitiveness of the formulaic and conventional, even as the effort time and again to see afresh and anew entailed its own pattern of repetition and conventions. (Crary 1992, 96)

Crary argues that the object-in-itself, independent of existing codes and conventions comes at a cost. That cost is the belief that objects or paintings hold their own truths and that it is the job of the artist or designer to reveal the essence of the object-in-itself.

At this juncture in the nomadic practice of designing objects, we are a far cry from artifacts. Objects claim or pursue a transcendental knowing that reflects back on itself, manifest and self-evident in the design of the object. The transcendental principles—the higher order of meaning and pursuit, beyond the material and particular—is articulated in Rams's "ten principles for good design" (Rams 1995), among others (e.g., Hara 2018). Though this is a representation of the principles, they are manifest and self-evident in a well-designed object, as Ive determined with the *Citromatic*. Many of the principles were clear and evident in the juicer to Ive's young mind when encountering the object without him explicitly knowing the principles. In the prologue to this chapter, I discussed the *Braun Pocket Receivers T3, T4, and T41*, all designed by Rams and his team. I discussed how before Rams set out the fuller set of ten design principles, the team operated from four principles of order, harmony, economy, and longevity that were universally applied to Braun products from kitchen appliances to shavers to the portable radios. These principles governed the design of the *Braun Pocket Receivers T3, T4, and T41* (see figure 3.2). Crary's point is that the transcendental

Designing Artifacts, Objects, and Products   77

vision required to design good objects, the dismissal of the formulaic and conventional, results in new repetitions and conventions. We see this indeed in the pocket receivers, as the patterns of circles, rectangles, perforations, materials, and switches achieve a new order that in its details are interchangeable from radio to radio. This newer order of design creates a new set of conventions representative of the higher order of transcendental goals for design rather than changing sociohistorical codes and conventions. In the case of Braun, these are the principles that Rams established for all of his design. In this sense, the different pocket receivers should be seen less as *iterations* and more as *instantiations* of the ideal portable radio object being pursued. Like artifacts, objects occupy a unique temporal state—one that is the complete opposite to artifacts. Unlike artifacts, objects remain stable and untouched over time. An ideal object is timeless. Artifacts exist in iterations over a temporal continuum from the present to the future and are expected to be understood in both their present and future iterations. Objects extend the present ideal state unchangeably into the future over time. This is what Rams referred to as the principle of longevity. And as stated in the prologue, the aim of Rams's Braun appliances is to be "produced and sold for decades with little change to their overall design" (Rams 1995, 31). The timelessness of objects is such that Ive recalls that the object, the *Citromatic*, "resonated" deeply with him for nearly forty years (Lovell, Kemp, and Ive 2011, 13).

Designing objects has a normative function to create objects that are "good" in ways that are enduring, essential, and universal. As a result, the designer is co-constituted as a moralist. A designer of objects is a masterful technician who can see how objects can make moral arguments for what should be, in ways that are aspirational and corrective. The mastery is in the alignment between knowing what is good and putting that into practice through techniques that bring together proportions, form, materials, and relations among parts, to uniquely reveal the good of the object-in-itself. This pursuit is ongoing as the designer is expected to be self-reflexive, continually questioning and cultivating the ideal of design objects. In the case of Rams, this is mainly a matter of aesthetics but one that is implicitly corrective. For example, in the prologue to the chapter, I discussed how the *Braun Pocket Receivers* are commercial products, however produced in an era when a goal for the design of an object could be more than and different from the value of the economic exchange. Additionally, the idealism of Rams's design challenges products to aspire to more than commercial success. Ive ascribes a virtuous role to designers like Rams, who "created objects that were neither vehicles of self-expression nor purely means to make money" (Lovell, Kemp, and Ive 2011, 14). Ironically though not surprisingly, Rams has criticized Apple and Ives for designing products that promoted endless consumerism for purely commercial gains (Hustwit 2018).

The explicit aesthetics and implicit corrective measures of Rams's approach can be described as *affirmative* with respect to designing objects. Relatedly, what is known as "critical design" can be seen as a *critical* approach to designing objects in which the corrective measures are made explicit and aesthetics plays an implicit role (Malpass 2017). Similar to the affirmative approach, vision is privileged such that objects can be understood through sight alone. Critical design takes full advantage of the way objects can be fully meaningful symbolically without experiencing their use or function. Critical design can be traced to the anti-design movements of United Kingdom and Italy of the late 1960s, like the work of Superstudio, an architecture collective founded in Florence in 1966 that disavowed the building of structures as a form of anti-architecture, offering dystopic concepts like *Supersurface* (1972), a global grid system over the surface of the earth that proposed a life free of objects and architecture (see chapter 6 and chapter 6 prologue). Anti-design emerged again in the late 1990s as critical or speculative design in the work of Anthony Dunne and Fiona Raby (Dunne 2008). Critical design persists through to today in industrial design and design-oriented HCI practices (Malpass 2017).

Superstudio, together with Archizoom Associati in 1966, wrote what became known as the manifesto for the *Radical Design* movement, a collection of iconoclastic architecture and industrial design studios like UFO, Gruppo Strum, 9999, Archizoom, Studio 65, and Superstudio (Didero et al. 2017). This movement was the impetus for the Museum of Modern Art exhibition *Italy: The New Domestic Landscape* (Ambasz 1972). The *Kar-a-Sutra* (1972) by Mario Bellini signals clearly the shared nature of affirmative and critical approaches to designing objects. *Kar-a-Sutra* makes the moral argument to humanize mobility in the age of automobiles through the prescription of livable mobility. The concept is aimed at creating a "lasting connection" with people, minimizing the impact of the endless production of automobiles. The humanized *Kar-a-Sutra* is intended to overturn the instrumentalized commute of moving human bodies through space in favor of a means of transport that is richly and socially connected to our daily lives. More importantly, *Kar-a-Sutra* internalizes the joy of mobility into the pleasures of cohabitation rather than the externalized expressions of violence and power that the car had become (Bellini 1972). The power of the critique of the object arises from its capacity to communicate symbolically through vision alone and the "narrative of use" rather than actual use.

The *Kar-a-Sutra* is not a functioning car, though it was built to scale. The object was presented in a way that would become classic critical design storytelling, a photographic essay of *defamiliarization*, in which seemingly commonplace settings and activities are made unfamiliar, triggering reflection and rethinking. Bellini photographed the *Kar-a-Sutra* in a rural setting far from roads or any urbanization. And rather than showing the car being driven, the series of photographs were of mimes inside and outside the car (see figure 3.3). The website *Car Design News*, in an article commemorating the *Kar-a-Sutra* as the first-known concept car, described the Bellini's presentation as follows: "Even the official Kar-A-Sutra photoshoot challenged conventions. Instead of a few leggy fashion models attending the car in an exotic location, the Sutra was pictured in the spiky remains of a freshly harvested cornfield, with a troupe of creepy-looking mimes showing the Sutra's various interior arrangements. The resulting photos cemented the car's outré reputation. It was a perfect anti-presentation for the ultimate anti-car" (Smith 2016).

By negation, the idea of the nomadic practice of designing products is presented alongside the object. The "anti-car" of the *car as object* is in fact the moral argument against the *car as product*. The *something* of the nomadic practice of *designing products* is conjured up in *designing objects* in its most negative manifestation. The car as product in *Kar-a-Sutra* is a utility machine masked by the seduction of virility and violence that Bellini bemoans as "loving the automobile itself and hating the people in cars we overtake; we can permit others to admire our virility and economic power, of which our car is a symbol" (Bellini 1972). The *something* is a product characterized by economic efficiencies wrapped within narratives of personal satisfaction as a means to create a fair exchange between profit and consumer goals. The *intentionality* of products is largely an economic matter. Harold van Doren, an industrial designer of the 1930s and 1940s and one of the cofounders and president of the Society of Industrial Designers, defined industrial design as "the practice of analyzing, creating, and developing products for mass-manufacture. Its goal is to achieve forms which are assured of acceptance before extensive capital investment has been made, and which can be manufactured at a price permitting wide distribution and reasonable profits" (Van Doren 1954). In a more concrete and recent example, the sportswear company Columbia employs what it calls "tariff engineering," which specifies the design decisions of the percentage use of materials like rubber soles, zippers, and waterproof nylon in order to lower import taxes when importing American-designed but Chinese-manufactured products into the United States. Adding a wafer-thin sheath of fabric over the sole of a boot or shoe that wears off within days of use avoids the 37.5 percent tariff on rubber soles. Adding as little as 10 percent of a jacket's weight with down reduces the tariff to only 4 percent. As the company spokesman says, "It's part of the thought process, part of the creative thinking, part of the D.N.A." (Tankersley 2018). In the nomadic practice of *designing products*, the technologies, forms of production, manufacturing, distribution, and financing continuously innovate to meet the unchanging intentionality of products.

From the critical perspective of *designing objects*, Rams's idealism is an affirmative argument for change of the very desires of *designing products*, whereas Archizoom and Superstudio's 1966 manifesto for the exhibition *Superarchitettura* ironically and absurdly negates the argument for products. The manifesto states that "the superarchitecture is the architecture of superproduction, of superconsumption, of superinduction to superconsumption, of the supermarket, of superman and super-petrol" (1966) (figure 3.5). At the heart of the criticism is a mocking of the commitments of *designing products* to mass consumption and style. Though different in approaches, Rams and critical design share the imperative of objects as a moral argument, one as affirmation and the other as negation.

The designer as moralist is unique to designing objects co-constituted in intentionality toward designing moral objects. And in direct contrast to artifacts, the designers of designing objects are the historically configured designer-creator that is named and celebrated. Every aspect of a given object is traceable or has provenance that leads back to the named designer. Here, the social, economic, and scientific conditions of objects take a back seat, reversing the order of artifacts, by downplaying the use and context and celebrating the designer as master.

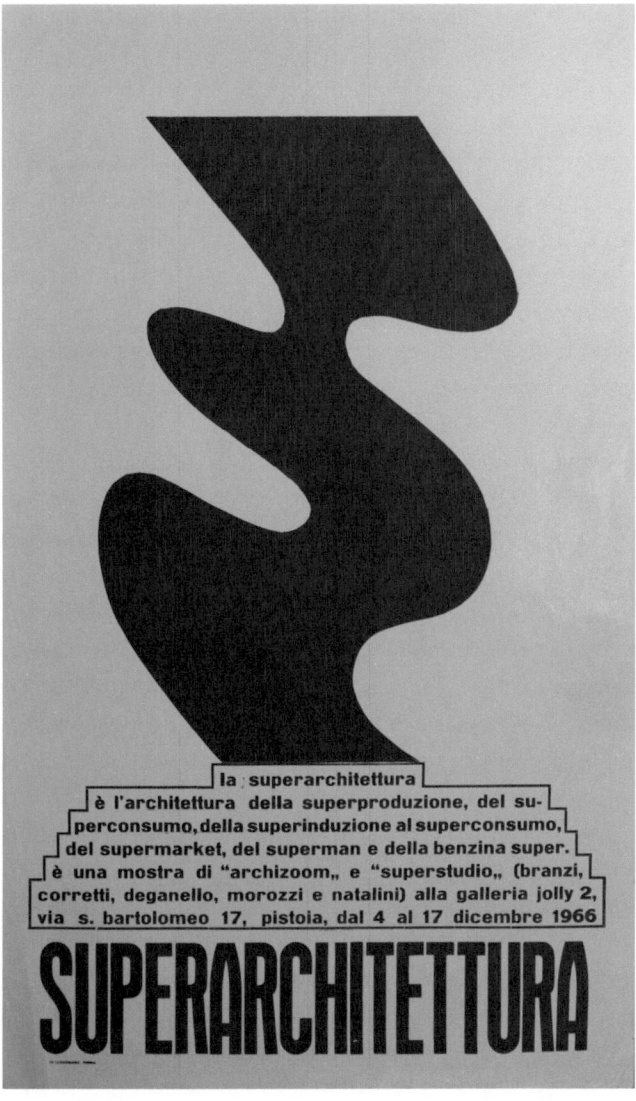

Figure 3.5
The poster and manifesto for the 1966 *Superarchitettura* exhibition.

Situated Knowledges and Nomadism of Artifacts, Objects, and Products

Each of the nomadic practices of artifacts, objects, and products are autonomous in the sense that the knowledge each produces is embodied within the intentionalities of the particular designers and *somethings* designed. That is, the knowledge of design is situated and particular to that practice. For example, the knowledge making of artifacts generates a large number of design methods, which is not surprising, given that artifacts are socially created, aim to progress human needs, and are empirically validated. Methods allow for knowledge sharing of design among multiple actors as designers, and methods allow for repetition and iterative improvements of design making that are externalized and can be assessed. Knowing in designing objects is a matter of aesthetic principles, techniques, and critical awareness, whereas products focus on manufacturing, marketing, or distribution. This autonomy is independent of common knowledge external to the practices, which is not to say that sharing and overlaps in what is design do not occur; rather, they take place through nomadic intersections, contestations, and alliances. The nomadism of the practices is evident in that even in these examples they overlap and intersect. *Braun Pocket Receivers* intersect with products and the *Kar-a-Sutra* takes aim at and contests nomadic practice of designing products as an object. In many ways, products rely on the innovations of user-oriented artifacts or aesthetic objects as resources to commercially optimize for markets. Though the differences among these are clear, the nomadic practices also are porous with various relationships and overlaps between them.

In summary, artifacts pursue human progress in ways that make the artifact matters of complex use and practices tangibly and temporally flexible and vehicles of theoretical arguments and claims. Objects, by comparison, are cultural aspirations governed by transcendental principles of a higher order of morality and goodness that make good objects timeless and of a standard more enduring than social conventions or economic gain. Products produce commercial value through innovations in manufacturing, marketing, and overall economic development. In this context, products aim to serve the human economic goals of fair transactions between profit and consumer satisfaction.

The aim of this chapter is to demonstrate how nomadic practices can be used to understand design outside of the disciplinary structures of a singular design. Rather than pursue a common foundation from which differences are either excised or ordered through hierarchies and prescribed importance, I've attempted to draw affinities together into design variants, beginning with the current design practices that we know, such as artifacts, objects, and products. There is no limit to the potential number of variants of nomadic practices of design. In chapter 4, and the beginning of part II of this book, I will describe one such possible nomadic practice of design that extends into the intermingling of human and nonhuman aspects of what we can call design. I will begin to argue for a posthumanist design as the nomadic practice of *designing things*.

Part II: Things

Chapter 4 Prologue: Phototrope, +Lichtlijn, New Faces, New Identities, Prayer Companion, and the Great Pacific Garbage Patch

In this prologue, I describe design works, discussed further in chapter 4, to help me elaborate on what I mean by things that are interconnected and transformative. Among the works discussed are Pauline van Dongen's *Phototrope* (Van Dongen 2019) and Saúl Baeza's *New Faces, New Identities* (Baeza Argüello et al. 2021), which are emblematic of the embodied and mediating quality of things. *+Lichtlijn* by HIG Systems (Scully 2017) is part of a traffic light system at a traffic intersection in the Netherlands that helps to describe the interconnectedness and assemblages of humans and things. *Prayer Companion* by the Interaction Research Studio (Gaver et al. 2010) is a device to assist cloistered nuns in prayer that reveals the interweaving of technicity with spiritual life. Lastly, I discuss what is known as the *Great Pacific Garbage Patch*, not as a work or thing of design but rather to make clear the ongoing assembly and reassembly of things to show their long-lasting interconnectedness and transformative capacities.

Phototrope

Phototrope is an illuminated running shirt that allows runners to be seen at night and to coordinate running exercises and tempos with other runners (figures 4.1 and 4.2). *Phototrope* is designed by Pauline van Dongen and her studio, along with Marina Toeters of by-wire.net. It is made of dark blue synthetic fabric that is typical of a running garment. However, it also includes other novel design elements and materials:

> Sewn into the fabric are streamlined shapes made of semi transparent, silver-colored prismatic foil. The foil is thin and flexible and is perforated with small holes. Textile based LED ribbons, emitting white colored light, are trapped inside tunnels behind the foil. The prismatic structure of the foil causes the light of the

Figure 4.1
Phototrope as seen from the front.
Source: Courtesy of Pauline van Dongen.

>LEDs to be refracted in a playful and subtle multi-colored way. The upper back is covered by a larger piece of prismatic foil that connects two pleats on either side of the shoulders. The two pleats create a distance between the body and the foil, thereby creating a space for the light to diffuse. The LED ribbons and prismatic foil are placed in such a way that the light is visible from all sides of the body. A hidden zip on the lower back of the garment reveals a pocket containing a 3D printed casing with electronics. The electronics allow for connectivity and interaction. (Van Dongen 2019, 167–173)

The illuminated shirt increases the visibility of runners at night but also adds a unique look and use of materials when worn during the day. *Phototrope* and other fashion work by van Dongen critically and creatively explore the relations between technologies and fashion. Her work aims to treat new technologies like those that are digital and solar as materials to design with similar to designing with textiles and fabrics as materials. Van Dongen critiques the separation of technologies from garments in wearables or fashiontech, choosing to manipulate, interweave, and shape all the materials concerned into garments that shape us through embodiment and materiality (Van Dongen 2019; Toussaint 2018). In chapter 4, *Phototrope* elaborates on how the

Figure 4.2
Phototrope as seen from the back.
Source: Courtesy of Pauline van Dongen.

embodiment of things underscores the interconnectedness between humans and things and the resulting co-constitutive effects of this relationship.

New Faces, New Identities

Artist and designer Saúl Baeza has been creatively exploring facial prosthetics as wearables that allow for the creation of multiple "identities" through facial recognition software (Baeza Argüello et al. 2021). To date, he and his collaborators have designed several facial prosthetics that represent a form of fashion-critical wearables that explores drag, queer, and trans identities (see figure 4.3). Baeza experiments with different approaches to design and fits differently shaped prosthetics that can be worn by different people. When "read" through the biometric sensing of facial recognition systems, the prosthetically adorned face is seen as a new and unique individual. For his experimentations he uses Apple's FaceID system to refine and test the wearable prosthetics. In the following chapter, *New Faces, New Identities* more explicitly reveals how humans together with things can be transformative to the point of creating new human identities from a technological perspective.

Figure 4.3
Two examples of *New Faces, New Identities* wearables by Saúl Baeza (2020).
Source: Courtesy of Saúl Baeza.

+Lichtlijn

In 2017, in the town of Bodegraven in the Netherlands, the city council voted to install the *+Lichtlijn* by HIG Traffic Systems (Ricker 2017) at the intersection of Goudseweg and Vrije Nesse. The system embeds LED strips in the sidewalk that are synchronized with the existing traffic light system (figure 4.4). *+Lichtlijn* is at the right angle for mobile phone users who, while looking down at their phones, will still see the traffic signal within their line of sight. As discussed in chapter 4, *+Lichtlijn* concretely elaborates on the transformative capacity of things in the form of assemblages.

Prayer Companion

The *Prayer Companion*, by Bill Gaver and his colleagues at the Interaction Research Studio at Goldsmiths University of London, is a bespoke device

Figure 4.4
+*Lichtlijn* by HIG Traffic Systems in Bodegraven, Netherlands.
Source: HIG Traffic Systems.

designed to support the prayer life of the Poor Clare sisters, cloistered nuns living in a convent in northern England (Gaver et al. 2010). A display on the top of *Prayer Companion* shows headlines from various online news feeds and text from different online sources. The display is updated frequently, making itself constantly available as a provider of contemporary news and other concerns that could be a relevant source for the nuns' prayers. The information is scrolled as text across a liquid crystal display (figure 4.5). The physical form understatedly evokes a tau cross and stands approximately thirty-five-centimeters tall (figure 4.6).

Gaver and his colleagues had several aims with *Prayer Companion*. One motivation for the project was to explore how, through their design work, they could support spiritual experiences through computation. Relatedly, the work focuses on the nuns' commitments to spiritual life as the way to understand affinities of the people for whom technology is designed. This point is made in opposition or as a critique of design that targets people in broad categories, such as the "aging or elderly," rather than through shared activities and interests. The Interaction Research Studio has a long history of advocating for design-oriented human-computer interaction (HCI) that opens designing with computation to materiality, aesthetics, ambiguity, and interpretations of use (Gaver et al. 2010). The *Prayer Companion* is a good example of this designerly approach to HCI and, as discussed in chapter 4, it is helpful in navigating the dynamics of the spiritual as a matter of technicity or interconnectedness of things.

Figure 4.5
The *Prayer Companion* as viewed from above.
Source: Courtesy of and © Interaction Research Studio.

Figure 4.6
The *Prayer Companion* in the monastery.
Source: Courtesy of and © Interaction Research Studio.

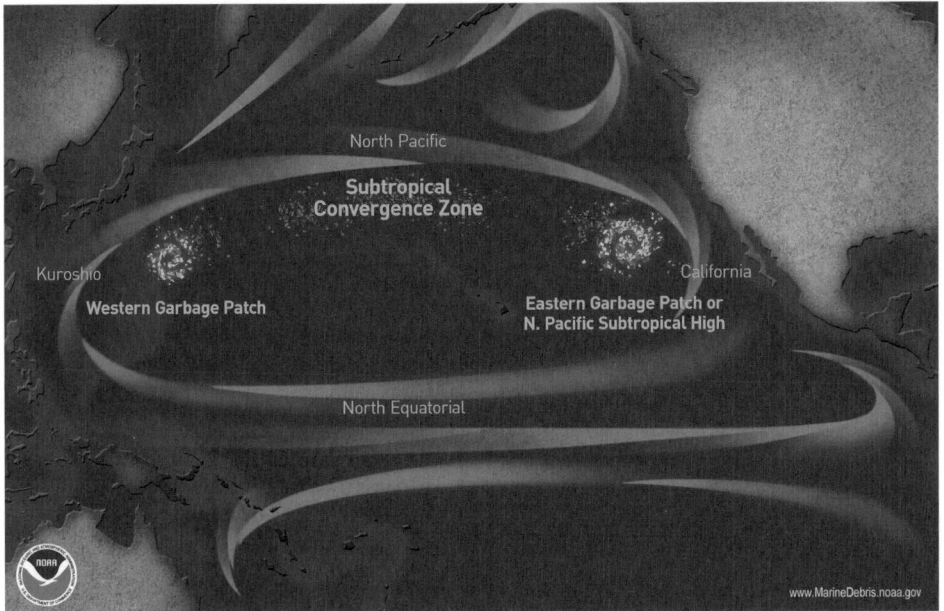

Figure 4.7
The *Great Pacific Garbage Patch* formed by three or more constantly moving gyres.
Source: Courtesy of the National Oceanic and Atmospheric Administration, US Department of Commerce.

The Great Pacific Garbage Patch

The *Great Pacific Garbage Patch* or Pacific Trash Vortex is perhaps the largest collection of plastics and trash floating in the Northern Pacific Ocean. The plastics are caught within the North Pacific Gyre, a confluence of four prevailing ocean currents that creates a large clockwise movement of the ocean waters. The Ocean Cleanup, a nongovernmental engineering environmental organization, estimates the area of floating trash is approximately 1.6 million square kilometers in size with upwards of 100 kilograms of plastics per square kilometers or about 80,000 metric tons of waste[1] (see figure 4.7). In chapter 4, I discuss the *Great Pacific Garbage Patch* not as a thing itself, but rather to show the persistence of things even as waste and their continual enrollment in one assemblage after another.

Chapter 4: Things Are Interconnected and Transformative

In the first part of the book, comprising chapters 2 and 3, I engaged in an "unbuilding" of design into a series of nomadic practices. This allowed for reconceptualizing design in order to move it away from the underpinnings of disciplinary structures and to embrace a multiplicity of "designs" that are concurrent, conflicting, and overlapping alternatives. It is from this necessary reconceptualizing of design, shedding its structural origins in humanism, that I am more able to engage in a posthumanist exploration. And so, this chapter and the previous prologue mark the beginning of the second part of the book, comprising chapters 4 and 5. This is the core of the book that tackles the idea of *things*. In this chapter, I delve more deeply into the two features I discussed earlier: *things and humans are interconnected*, and *things are transformative*. This chapter charts these unique features by signposting the key commitments of the practice of designing things. In chapter 5, I expand on the latter two features: that *things are relational* and *things are vital*.

Here, I begin with a focus on the first of the three philosophical concepts that support the idea of things, *mediating technologies* (see figure 4.8). This concept draws on ideas of technicity (Ihde 1990), natureculture (Haraway 2003), and technological mediation (Ihde 1990; Verbeek 2005) that I will explain more fully below. Additionally, in the next few pages, I will refer to *technologies* rather than *things*, especially as this is the term used in postphenomenology that I heavily draw upon. Later in this chapter, I explain how these ideas of technologies are used to develop my idea of *things*.

Technicity: Technologies and Humans Are Interconnected

In the first chapter, I discussed how Don Ihde illustrates the fundamental relationship between humans and technologies through a thought

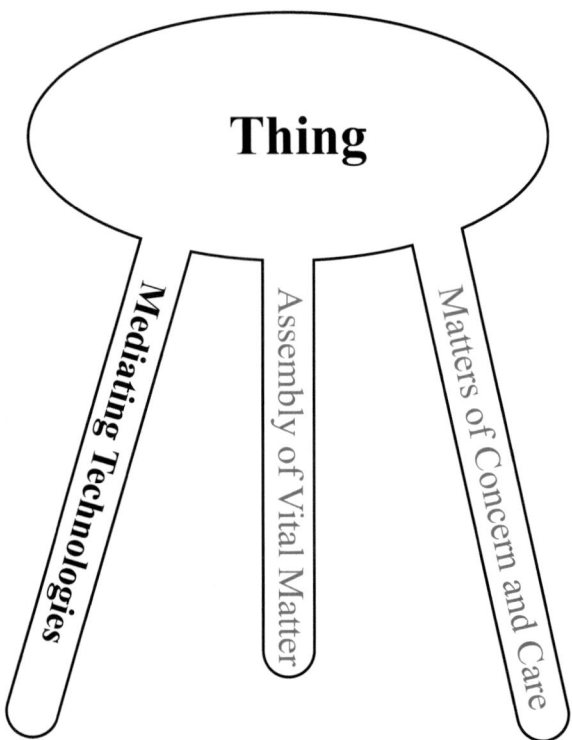

Figure 4.8
The philosophical concept of *mediating technologies* that support this part of the discussion of things.

experiment. He reimagines the mythical trope of the "Garden of Eden" by considering humans within an idyllic and nontechnological environment: "Imagine a *New Eden*, a new tale of beginnings, in which a New Adam and a New Eve, like the old, appear first, naked and placed in the nontechnological Garden" (Ihde 1990, 12). Ihde engages his thought experiment knowing it will fail but in the process reveal that humans can only be seen as technological beings or "prosthetic creatures" as Wolfe (2010) describes humans. In such a garden, nontechnological humans would have severely limited communication (body gestures), limited food with no food storage (fruit and grubs), no shelter or clothing, no protection from the elements or predators, and would be limited to live within a narrowly hospitable temperate zone. "What this initial imaginative exercise reveals is that it might be possible for humans to live non-technologically as a kind of abstract possibility—but only on the condition that the environment be that of a garden, isolated, protected, and stable. The price for such a nontechnological existence is to be enclosed. Here would be the '*milieu of nature in purer form*'" (Ihde 1990, 12). Ihde argues that the only way we can imagine a world of humans without technologies is to conjure up an image of nature that is perfectly suited to the naked and nontechnological human.[1] Only in such a humanly centered environment would technology have no place. As Ihde states, "By taking up technologies, humans left the nontechnological Garden to inherit the Earth. The price for that inheritance is to have taken up a technology" (Ihde 1990, 14).

Ihde goes on to question the opposition between nature and technology as a way to argue against the false dichotomy of natural human versus technological human that pervades many arguments about technology. For example, he cites well-known instances and discoveries of animals and tool use—or what he refers to as "proto-technologies" (Ihde 1990, 15). The dichotomy of nature-technology is dismantled through a reassessment of the divide between human animals and nonhuman animals and their shared *technicity*. The extent of technological use shows a porous divide between humans and nonhuman animals. Haraway (2003) refers to this porosity or dissolution of boundaries as *natureculture* and to animals as companion species. Ihde cites Jane Goodall's research with primates, in which she observed chimpanzees constructing and using tools like grass or twigs to find food. In a similar example, New Caledonian crows have been observed to use "hooked stick tools" for foraging for food (Troscianko and Rutz 2015). A more recent study on New Caledonian crows by Sarah Jelbert and her colleagues found that these crows not only used "found tools" or "proto-technologies," but they also created or replicated technologies (Jelbert et al. 2018). In this study, crows were "trained" to use different-size cards as tokens; if a card is inserted in something like a vending machine that the researchers created, a treat would be dispensed. The birds were first trained that large tokens would work and small ones would not work. Later, premade tokens were replaced with whole sheets of paper of similar color to the tokens (figure 4.9). The birds, seemingly unfazed, created tokens from the paper by tearing it with their beaks and talons into the proper size and shape (figure 4.10). The researchers then changed the vending machine to only being operated by small tokens instead of the large tokens. The crows adapted by changing their designs accordingly. The point is that the use of and creativity with technologies by nonhuman

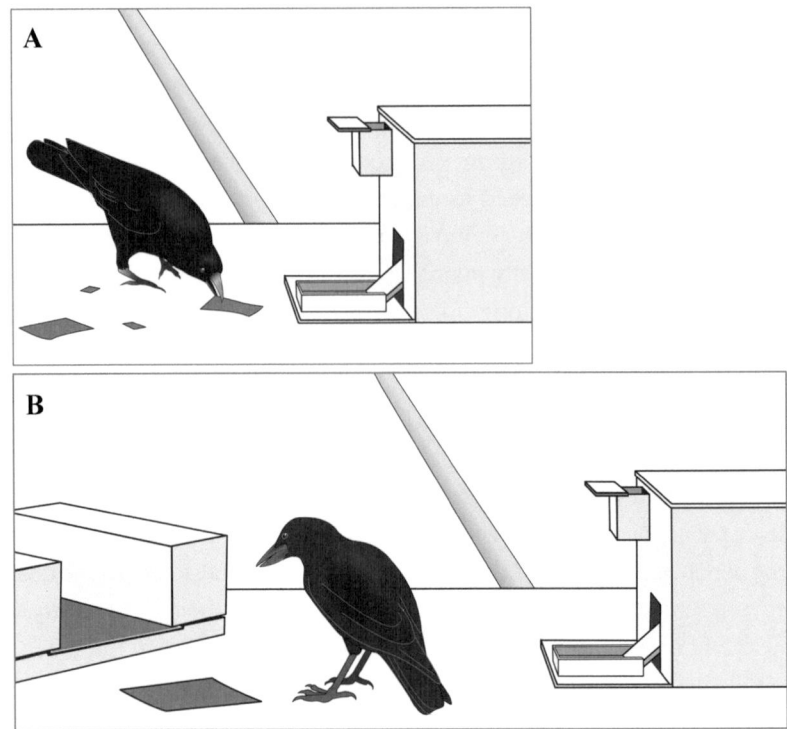

Figure 4.9
The experimental conditions for the study with New Caledonian crows: (a) premade tokens for the crows to use; (b) provision of large sheets of paper for crows to create their own tokens.
Source: Jelbert et al. (2018), licensed by CC BY 4.0, illustration by Vivian Ward.

animals is greater than recognized, thus blurring the boundaries between humans, nature as nonhumans, and technology. Not only is tool use not distinct to humans, but as Jelbert and her colleagues show, nonhuman animals like the New Caledonian crows demonstrate a form of "cultural cumulative evolution"—that is, the accumulation of improvements over time through learning, language, or imitation. Typically, this trait is thought to be unique to humans; however, in the case of the vending machine tokens, the crows' technology use and creativity appear to evolve through cognitive processes or self-learning (Jelbert et al. 2018). Further, this cumulative evolution happens through technologies that place the technicity of nonhuman animals on a continuum with the technicity of human animals. By technicity, I mean the

Figure 4.10
A New Caledonian crow inserting a crow-made token into a "vending machine."
Source: With permission of Dr. Sarah Jelbert.

lifeworld of technologies or the irreducible entanglements of human animals (and nonhuman animals) and technologies (Barad 2007; Feenberg 2017; Haraway 1985; Heidegger 1962; Ihde 1990; Latour 2005a; Stiegler 1998; Verbeek 2005).

Seeing humans and nonhuman animals on the same continuum of technology use and creation opens the doors to new research in design, such as the emergence of animal-computer interaction or ACI (Mancini 2011). ACI challenges the human-centered orientation in design by arguing for a "non-speciesist" (Dunayer 2004) approach to research and design of technologies (Mancini 2011; Mancini and Lehtonen 2018). As Wolfe (2010) points out, humans are animals, and what makes animal forms distinguishable are their unique embodiments or perceptual apparatuses along with their varying forms of technicity. This breakdown of the separation of humans and nature makes the terms human and nonhuman fluid with respect to animals, raising issues of ethics and, for Wolfe (2012), challenging the biopolitical hierarchy between humans and nonhuman animals. Braidotti (2013), in turn, argues for an *egalitarianism* between human and nonhuman animals, while Haraway (2003) sees in the continuum a remaking of the human subject that in hybrid and cyborgian terms is inclusive of nonhuman animals and technologies.

At this juncture, what is important is that the ontological divides that bolster humanist concepts of nature, animals, technologies, and humans in actuality give way to interconnectedness and fluidity that make separations and assumed hierarchies problematic. The interconnectedness is so pervasive as to decenter humans, such that humans, nonhuman animals, and technologies (or things) share the foreground—opening to a postanthropocentric view. And for the discussion at hand, the nomadic practice of things, the interconnectedness of humans and technologies is a fundamental feature.

Technologies Are Transformative

This interconnectedness with things and transformative capacity is rooted in the *intentionality* between humans and world. In chapter 2, I discussed the philosophical concept of intentionality that informs postphenomenology. I used this concept to describe a key characteristic of nomadic practices (see chapter 2, Intentionality of Nomadic Practices). In addition to contributing to the idea of nomadic practices, intentionality is also important in understanding technologies and, as a consequence, understanding things.

As a reminder, intentionality in the phenomenological tradition of Husserl and Merleau-Ponty argues that humans, as experiencing beings, are always directed toward the world or reality—meaning that we think, feel, or act toward something rather than simply "feel" or "think." This unavoidable directing or experiencing of the world structures that world for us. As humans are understood in relation to reality, reality in turn is only understood in relation to humans. This means that an objective world or "world-in-itself" is not accessible to us since every attempt by us to grasp the world makes it a "world for us," revealed by the particular ways we understand and experience it (Verbeek 2005). Verbeek sees intentionality as a central concept in understanding the relations between humans and the world (Verbeek 2008). As such, intentionality as a concept is also central to any understanding of technologies. In the case of technology, Verbeek sees a *cyborg intentionality* at play. Building on Ihde's postphenomenological concept of mediation, Verbeek argues for different forms of intentionality in the interaction between humans and technologies—namely, *mediated intentionality, hybrid intentionality,* and *composite intentionality* (Verbeek 2008). All three types of intentionality are important to discussions in this book, so I will expand on each as we encounter them. In this chapter and as a way of explaining the transformative nature of technologies, I focus on *mediated intentionality*.

The transformative aspect of things can be elaborated on through mediated intentionality that has its roots in Ihde's concept of *technological mediation* (Ihde 1990; Verbeek 2008). In mediated intentionality, "human intentionality is *mediated* by a technological device. Humans do not experience the world *directly* here, but always *via* a mediating artifact which helps to shape specific relations between humans and world" (Verbeek 2008, 389). As Ihde sees it, technologies inherently shape perceptions and actions (Ihde 1990). Verbeek elaborates on this point by asking us to consider how a word processor allows an author to not only write text but also compose with it by copying and moving whole passages, inserting references and footnotes, creating outlines and so on, in comparison to writing by hand with pen and paper: "These writing technologies are therefore not neutral means, but rather play an active role in the relation between author and text" (Verbeek 2005, 115). In chapter 1, I illustrated mediation at work in mountaineering gear that transforms a mountain into a landscape to climb. Technologies co-shape how humans are present in the world and perceive the world. In addition, technological mediation as a form of intentionality is co-constitutive, meaning that the human entanglement with technology is a mutual becoming, in which humans and technologies influence what each other becomes. Verbeek elaborates by stating that mediation is not a phenomenon occurring between a "pre-given world of objects and pre-given human subjects. Rather, human beings and their world are constituted in the 'act' of mediation" (Verbeek 2016, 194). To paraphrase Rosenberger and Verbeek, technologies help to form the "subjectivity" of humans and the "objectivity" of their world: climbing gear constitutes a person as a "climber" and the mountain as "climbable" (Rosenberger and Verbeek 2015, 19).

If the human animal is inseparable from its technicity, what about *bodily experiences* that are not directly mediated by technologies? Ihde and colleagues do not discount these experiences; rather, embodiment is central to understanding the relations of humans and technologies (Ihde 1990, 17). The phenomenological apparatus of humans, body-perception, is in Ihde's term a constant by which the fundamental relationship or relations to technologies occur. There is not a sharp divide between technologies and humans but a nuanced and variable intertwining. Ihde makes this clear in discussing bodily experiences of the environment. When it is cold and wintry, we can experience the wind and freezing temperatures, but we can also "choose" to mediate the cold with a winter jacket that substitutes cold air for bodily warmth. In this example, bodily perceptions are not absent; rather, the experience of the environment has been mediated through the "cocoon" of clothing. This cocoon could easily be other cocoons like buildings, tents, cars, subways, and so on. Our embodied experience of the presence of technologies is a matter of mediation rather than separation (Ihde 1990).

Phototrope by Pauline van Dongen, as discussed in the prologue to this chapter, is one such mediating "cocoon"—a human-thing embodiment experienced in the practice of running (Van Dongen 2019). The bodily experience of running is not absent but is foregrounded and experienced as the commingling of the heat and humidity of our human body and surrounding air, and the interactions of the movement of skin, synthetic fabric, and prismatic foils. The human-thing embodiment of the running garment amplifies the human running form into something that is highly visible at night on dark roads and pathways—sheltered by light as much as by the synthetic fabric worn on the body. *Phototrope* mediates the experience of urban running at night by transforming the runner into a visible component of the landscape that supports the embodied experience of running at night rather than separates the runner from it.

This phenomenological or embodied understanding of technology is rooted in Heidegger's example of the hammer in *Being and Time* (Heidegger 1962). This example is perhaps the most well-known philosophical discussion of technology. Heidegger describes how a technology, like a hammer, is not understood conceptually but understood through bodily praxis or through the act of hammering. Technologies are situated and embodied. In this way, a hammer is understood not by staring at it but by hammering, in which it becomes an extension of the arm. The hammer itself withdraws to seemingly become invisible as nails are driven into wood. Heidegger referred to this as *ready-to-hand*.

In the event that a hammer stops working (perhaps it breaks, or it goes missing in the midst of work, or you are distracted while hammering), the hammer then emerges as a conceptual entity. In Heidegger's sense, it stands against your intention to hammer or, in his words, becomes *obstinate*,

Things Are Interconnected and Transformative   103

obstrusive, or *conspicuous*, what he characterized as *present-at-hand*. Most interestingly, it is the hammer as "breakdown"—taken out of the practice of hammering and work—that reveals through absence the practice of hammering or the embodied nature of the technology. We can say the same is true of *Phototrope*. For example, imagine you are halfway through a ten-kilometer run and the lights of *Phototrope* fail or the synthetic fabric begins to noticeably chafe against your skin. The enabling world of the illuminating lights, comforting garments, running shoes, safe running paths—what Verbeek refers to, using a similar example of a failing word processor, as the "entire mutually referring network"—falls apart (Verbeek 2005, 79–80). The garment *was* a seamless part of your running world but in this situation, it obscures by bringing attention to itself rather than the running. However, once the lights work again or the chafing stops, the world of that particular 10K run reconstitutes and your running pace picks up and all is forgotten.

The hammer or running garment is fundamental, alongside us in unthinking ways as we go about our business of hammering or running. As *ready-to-hand*, it shapes the practice and the "network" or "world" of hammering, or in the case of *Phototrope*, running. In this way, technologies are constitutive—they make us and this world. Ironically, this is only revealed in an "objectively present" fashion when this world is destroyed and when the technology becomes *present-at-hand* (Verbeek 2005). Winograd and Flores (1987), discussed in relation to *ontological design* in chapter 1, used Heidegger's embodied view of technology as a critique of cognitive and rational thinking in computing science. Verbeek sees in this early work of Heidegger the initial building blocks for a postphenomenological understanding of technology. For Verbeek, Heidegger's example reveals technology as concrete human-made entities that give humans access to reality and the shaping of it (Verbeek 2005, 80).

Ihde draws on Heidegger's phenomenological concepts of ready-to-hand and present-at-hand. However, in elaborating on the ways technology mediates, Ihde sees severe shortcomings in Heidegger's concepts. *Ready-to-hand* in Ihde's view is only one of many relations to technology—namely, an embodied relation. And *present-at-hand* "blocks" the understanding of another relation to technology that Ihde labels *hermeneutic*, as in reading a thermometer to know the temperature of something. As part of its functioning hermeneutically, a thermometer presents itself as present-at-hand to be interpreted (Ihde 1990, 80). Further, a technology can have what Ihde describes as an *alterity* relation that is a dialogue with a "quasi-other," like an ATM machine or a mobile map application that queries you on where you want to go and if you need directions. In either case, a dialogue with a machine, to use Heideggerian terms, is almost always *conspicuous* and at times *obstinate* or *obstrusive* despite the "user-friendly" design. Ihde challenges the binarism of Heidegger's concepts and even more so its narrow and limited conceptualization of technologies.

For Ihde, technology mediates through different relations that reveal the variant ways in which technologies are present. In this way, he argues against the vaunted "transparency" or desire to have "total transparency, total embodiment," to integrate technology fully, "to truly 'become me,'" which is implied in the idea of ready-to-hand (Ihde 1990, 75)—that is, to have the power of technologies without technologies. Technology always mediates and is always present. As a result, it is transformative. Glasses allow aging eyes to read, supplemental oxygen systems allow climbers to breathe at high altitude, and insulated Gore-Tex jackets keep those in cold climes warm and dry in subzero temperatures. But in mediating this way, technologies do not disappear or become invisible. Ihde characterizes the persistent presence of things as a limiter on their transparency or a feature of their mediating capacity: "The actual, or material, technology always carries with it only a partial or quasi-transparency, which is the price for the extension of magnification that technologies give. In extending bodily capacities, the technology also transforms them. In that sense, all technologies in use are non-neutral" (Ihde 1990, 75). This transformation of technologies or non-neutrality is neither inherently positive nor negative. The transformations have trade-offs. When amplifying by giving extended sight, as with a telescope, the same technology reduces by restricting the view nearby. Reading glasses make seeing far difficult and supplemental oxygen systems make it difficult to speak by covering your face.

The *New Faces, New Identities* project by Saúl Baeza makes explicit the transformative exchange between technologies and humans (Baeza Argüello et al. 2021). As discussed in the prologue, the wearable prostheses (figure 4.3) extend the ability to maintain privacy by creating new and multiple identities to be read by facial recognition systems. Interestingly, wearable prostheses make public the technological intentionality of the systems or how such systems *see* human faces. It is important to say that the degree to which technologies maintain a presence or do not become transparent, or cannot be fully integrated, are challenged by Verbeek and others. The broader idea of *cyborg intentionality*, for example, takes into account technologies fused with or implanted in human bodies, or *hybrid intentionality*, in which technologies are incorporated into a new human form as with cochlear implants or psychotropic drugs or nonhuman intentionalities (De Preester 2011; Rosenberger and Verbeek 2015; Verbeek 2008), some of which is evident in Baeza's *New Faces, New Identities*. For now, in the context of mediated intentionality, technologies are always present in ways that are distinct and non-neutral.

Van Dongen's *Phototrope*, by design, takes advantage of its ongoing presence through the programmable LED ribbons that emit light. This separates it from other garments as a *wearable* or *techno-fashion* in which digital technologies are part of the garment in ways that transform the runner by making her visible at night and are able to receive simple messages for the running group to guide running goals or desired pace. In the case of the light, the presence and non-neutrality of *Phototrope* is explicit. However, even in the case of its garment technologies, the synthetic fabric, the cut, and tailored assembly are always present and non-neutral, though less explicitly. The fitted garment is present, even though it aims for a high degree of quasi-transparency, because it fits like a second skin, weighing as little as possible and absorbing the least amount of moisture from sweat and humidity like human skin. Despite this, the garment, without consideration for the digital technologies, transforms the runner by extending physical comfort despite the stresses of running, by sufficiently concealing the naked body to maintain social norms, and by expressing an identity of athleticism and performance that makes a runner feel good. And so, in a material way through different technologies, *Phototrope* is always present and shaping the situation.

Phototrope's persistent presence engages multiple relations of technology in postphenomenological terms (Ihde 1990; Rosenberger and Verbeek 2015). As van Dongen points out, it is experienced through shifting perspectives that transition back and forth between wearing and being seen as wearing the garment. Attention and interpretations shift from an *embodied relation* that is the quasi-transparency of wearing and running in the garment to a *hermeneutic relation*, in which a runner reads the changing lights of another runner's *Phototrope* to interpret the desired pace and cadence of the group set by the running coach. This hermeneutic interpretation already assumes an *alterity relation* (Van Dongen 2019), as the garment and the programmable system can be perceived as a *quasi-other*, as Ihde (1990) would describe it. Baeza's *New Faces, New Identities* equally assumes multiple simultaneous relations. To come full circle in this interpretation, mediating technologies or things are co-constitutive, and so the shaping is bidirectional. *Phototrope* takes on the embodied relation of a running garment or techno-fashion only in it being worn and run in. It communicates messages to other runners by being part of a running group and is visible as a quasi-other to the runners and visible to pedestrians, cyclists, and drivers by becoming part of the nocturnal landscape. A runner transforms the assembly of synthetic fabrics, LED ribbons, prismatic foils, stitching, and welded seams into the running garment we call *Phototrope*, which in turn co-shapes the given reality of the runners and their world of running.

The reader may have noticed that I used the word *thing* in the previous paragraph. Up to this point I have been discussing technologies in the context of postphenomenology. I now turn to how these ideas of technology inform the idea of things.

What Technologies Tell Us about Things

In this book's first chapter I offered several starting points for what I mean by things. The relevant starting points at this juncture of the discussion are that things are made by and with humans; things are a part of our different human subjectivities, uniquely extending and shaping who and what we are in profound ways, like a prosthetic arm; and things are interconnected to other things and humans in assemblages that make them unstable and constantly changing and difficult to see as a whole. I build on these points in this section.

I also stated in the first chapter that I approach the notion of things conceptually and concretely. The term *thing* offers a dual role of encapsulating abstract concepts and embodying particulars. So, let's begin with a conceptual understanding of things. Through the discussion in this chapter, I have chosen to start with a postphenomenological understanding of technologies. I include technologies within the term. One reason for this is that things can be said to be composed of different technologies. For example, *Phototrope* consists of digital and garment technologies. In a sense, things can be seen as a *gestalt* of technologies in a designed form since technologies rarely appear to us in a raw or singular form but come designed. Another reason is that Ihde conceptualizes technologies as the concreteness of "technological artifacts" (Verbeek 2001), like the "Artillery" Bow with Thumb Ring (Ihde 1990) or Verbeek's example of Sven Adolph's ceramic heater (Verbeek 2005). And so whether postphenomenology really referred to things all along, as "concrete technological artifacts" or as entities composed of different technologies, I feel we can say that things can be conceptualized in the same manner that postphenomenology conceptualizes technologies.

While this is a simple substitution of the word *thing* for technology, it is worth restating the points on technology discussed earlier using the word *thing*. Based on the discussion of technicity and mediated intentionality (the first of three supporting philosophical concepts of the definition of things as illustrated in figure 4.11), we can neither think about things or humans without invoking one or the other. When thinking about things, they cannot be separated from humans for the fact that a given thing is part of the world through its relations to humans. For example, empty roads without the presence of humans are still understood as a surface for human transport. And humans as "prosthetic creatures" are seen to be acting or interpreting the world through their relations to things. The ability to run ten kilometers through a neighborhood is reliant on the roads that form that neighborhood. In this way, things are irreducible beyond human-things or if you like, thing-humans. Arguably, this can be extended more comprehensively to animal-things, in which humans and nonhuman animals are the same. A nest or a broken path to a den serves as a thing, but I will stay with the narrower focus of human-things.

In the discussion of Ihde and Heidegger we can see that embodiment is central to understanding things. Building on Ihde, the varying forms of embodiment and embodied positions create a range of "human-thing relations": from intimate embodiment on, or within a body, to a quasi-other to being immersed in a background of things in the environment (Rosenberger and Verbeek 2015; Verbeek 2008). Things are interconnected with humans as thing-humans in ways that are situated and that give rise to different relations between them. Given mediated intentionality, things mediate actions and perceptions, resulting in things being non-neutral or shapers of how humans are in the world. Relatedly, the intentionality of technological mediation is co-constitutive, meaning that things help to form the "subjectivity" of humans and the "objectivity" of their world. For example, *Phototrope* constitutes the wearer as a runner and the nocturnal landscape as runnable.

Conceptually speaking, how are things different from artifacts? As a point of reference, artifacts pursue and hold human-centered commitments and assumptions whereas things are postanthropocentric. To recall from chapter 3, artifacts are embedded in complex use and practices, meaning that artifacts are constituted as *something* for human use and progress. A novel computing system in the workplace is analyzed for its ease of use, productivity, and positive impact on the work practices of employees. The interrelatedness of things with humans is much more radical. Where *artifacts* are a product of human use, *things* go well beyond, being a tool *for* humans. Things are *commensurate* with *being* human, in that things shape human actions and perceptions in ways that are co-constitutive or form humans and things together. A novel computing system in the workplace as a thing is seen to be transformative for those who use the system, such that they become fundamentally different humans, in turn altering the environment and the very nature of human activity.

Artifacts are, conceptually speaking, highly flexible in that they refer to multiple forms and temporal states. In this way the term is used for broad categories of computer hardware to specific types like the newest mobile phone. And temporally, artifacts are considered simultaneously as a present entity and a future iteration, as in a design prototype that is equally viewed as the version in the present and its future, more finished iteration. Things, by contrast, are unequivocally embodied; they are concrete as matters of materiality and situatedness. This limits things to the immediate and the particular. The concern with things is what is before us in the present. For example, if in the immediacy of a thing like *Phototrope*, the wearer imagines beyond the mediated experience to consider what a future version of *Phototrope* might be like, the imagined version is dramatically diminished as a thing if it could even be considered a thing. *New Faces, New Identities* is equally present as it is only when a particularly shaped prosthesis and face together are *recognized* through the software that the wearable prostheses become a thing.

This embodiment of things is not limited in scale or even to what is tangible. For example, drawing on Paul Dourish's account of the materialities of virtual computing and entities like digital networks (Dourish 2017), the Internet as a thing mediates interconnectivity through the specific network my computer is connected with at any given time. This can happen through a particular Wi-Fi network that is either part of an institutional

Things Are Interconnected and Transformative 109

or home network (the two are dramatically different) that in turn is networked to particular nodes or transit exchange points in the Metropolitan Area Network for Vancouver when I am at home or in Surrey when I am at work at Simon Fraser University. The specificity of a network is as much a political as a technical arrangement. When I am at work at the Eindhoven University of Technology in Eindhoven, where I am a part-time professor, I inhabit the Internet as a Dutch resident or European Union citizen granted any number of privacy and data rights that are not afforded me when I am in Canada. The Internet as a thing is the specific and current human and nonhuman arrangement that manifests the "Internet" in a given situation.

To elaborate further, the immediate and particular nature of things has them constituted through performance and embodied situations. This is in contrast to the nomadic practice of objects discussed in chapter 3, in which objects are seen as transcendent, governed by principles beyond themselves, such as Rams's ten principles of good design (Rams 1995). This relates to the last feature of artifacts, in which they embody conceptual claims about humans. Things by contrast do not embody claims about humans. Rather, in the various relations with humans, things arise from intentionality. In this way, things are not symbolic; they are performative.

Considering things concretely, you might ask what is the difference between *Phototrope*, a running garment with reflective material, or a runner wearing a headlamp? All are reasonable choices for running at night. In simple terms, each can be a thing that constitutes the wearer as a runner and the nocturnal landscape as runnable. The differences between things are qualitative and measured by the degree to which a thing emphasizes one or more of the assumptions of designing a thing. A headlamp on a runner has an embodied human-thing relationship in being worn on the head, and for the wearer it achieves a large degree of quasi-transparency like eyeglasses. The light itself is clearly transformative in lighting the darkened path or trail wherever the runner is looking. But like other things, it is non-neutral in negative ways, as it is a hindrance in running groups or face-to-face contact since it blinds others. Runners' garments with reflective material are similarly embodied by taking on most or all of the human form. The transformative aspect of reflective material is, relatively speaking, more passive than *Phototrope* and the running lamp, depending on a light source from elsewhere. *Phototrope* highlights its transformative aspects by illuminating the runner and providing messages through illumination patterns (Van Dongen 2019). This emphasis on its mediating qualities explores a range of human-technology or human-thing relations that I discussed earlier: embodiment, hermeneutic, and alterity. *Phototrope* also situates itself as both worn and observed, moving beyond an individual human-thing configuration of the runner's headlamp to more of an assembly of human-things.

In the prologue, I discussed *+Lichtlijn*, produced by HIG Traffic Systems (Ricker 2017) and installed at the intersection of Goudseweg and Vrije Nesse in the Dutch town of Bodegraven (see figure 4.4). Reportedly, *+Lichtlijn* has come under some criticism from the Veilig Verkeer Nederland (Safe Traffic Netherlands) for rewarding bad behavior or "mobile phone addiction" (Scully 2017). Such concerns with addiction and technologies aside, *+Lichtlijn* can be viewed as a thing that is characteristic of interconnectedness.

The extent of interconnectedness of *+Lichtlijn* makes it an *assemblage* of humans and nonhumans, meaning it is an ensemble of heterogeneous elements that function together (Deleuze and Parnet 2002). From a thing perspective, we can unpack the assemblage of *+Lichtlijn* as follows: A person with a mobile phone, let's say a *Google Pixel* phone, at the intersection of Goudseweg and Vrije Nesse is interconnected as *mobile phone user + Google Pixel + +Lichtlijn*. Our mobile phone user, Google Pixel, and *+Lichtlijn* are not isolated but are in an assembly of sidewalks, bicycle paths, roads, rain, temperature, painted traffic lines, municipal policies, and moving cars. And those drivers of the cars need to know when to stop to allow pedestrians and mobile phone users with their Google Pixels or Apple iPhones to cross the street. From a distance, the driver can see traffic lights well positioned at the side of the road and horizontally mounted up high across the road. And so, I can add to what is assembled at the intersection a driver, and let's say the car is a *Hyundai Kona*, approaching the intersection of Goudseweg and Vrije Nesse as *driver + Hyundai Kona + street traffic light*. However, the human and nonhuman arrangements do not stop here, so to speak. For in the Netherlands, almost all traffic lights have a signal dedicated to cyclists installed at the appropriate height for a person on a bicycle. I can add that a cyclist, riding a classic Dutch bicycle, at the intersection of Goudseweg and Vrije Nesse is a *cyclist + Dutch bicycle + bicycle traffic light*. Lastly, a pedestrian, braving the incessant rain blowing across the flat Dutch landscape from the North Sea patiently awaits the light to change is the last addition to the assemblage as a *pedestrian + raincoat + pedestrian traffic light*. In this

Things Are Interconnected and Transformative 111

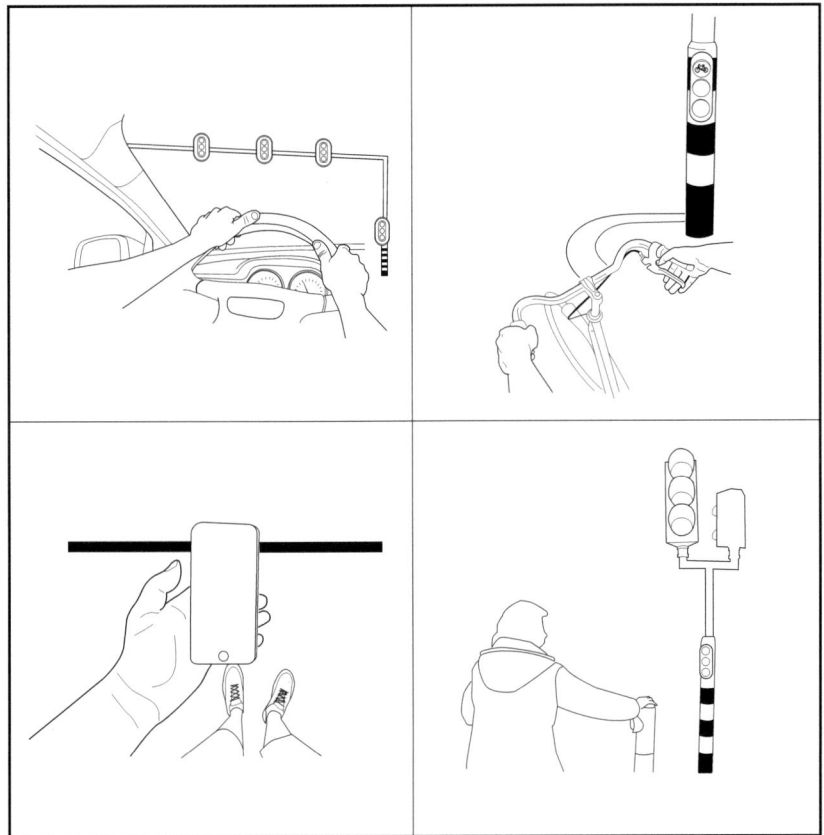

Figure 4.11
The assemblage of human-things at the intersection of Goudseweg and Vrije Nesse.
Source: Doenja Oogjes.

context, the novelty of *+Lichtlijn* fades away. It is simply part of an already-existing ensemble of interconnectedness as illustrated in figure 4.11, such that the intersection of Goudseweg and Vrije Nesse includes the following: *(mobile phone user + Google Pixel + +Lichtlijn) + (driver + Hyundai Kona + street traffic light) + (cyclist + Dutch bicycle + bicycle traffic light) + (pedestrian + raincoat + pedestrian traffic light)*.

Some may see similarities between my schematic representations of humans and nonhumans and schematics of human-technology relations often found in postphenomenological writings (e.g., Ihde 1990) or the schematic networks of human and nonhuman actors of Actor Network

Theory (e.g., Latour 1992). However, here I want to simply focus on the assemblage of human-things and how things can only be considered in a world of interrelated things and humans. What this assemblage of things at the street intersection shows is that the human animal, which is *a* focus for designing things, is not separable from things or its own technicity. And so, like in the case of *+Lichtlijn*, it makes sense to design for the interconnectedness of humans, Google Pixels, Hyundai Kona cars, Dutch bicycles, and raincoats as well. Evidently, as in the example of traffic lights for cars, we have been doing this for some time. Equally, the reflective materials of a runner's garment or the illumination of *Phototrope* are designed as much for the runner as they are for the driver of the Hyundai Kona or the cyclist at night, and we can see that these things, including *New Faces, New Identities*, are designed as interconnected with the technicity of the urban environment. And so, these distinct thing-humans like runner-*Phototrope* shed light on the broader connections with other human-things like driver-car, as face-prosthesis sheds light on public surveillance.

Assemblages are not equal or fair distributions of human-things (Bennett 2010). It is clear that at the intersection, the driver-car is the dominant human-thing and that all other thing assemblies are designed around this dominance. Viewing the assembly of *mobile phone user + Google Pixel + +Lichtlijn* as a matter of technology addiction overlooks the larger assembly that the *mobile phone user + Google Pixel* is a part of. It is a set of larger relations in which driver-car poses an immediate existential threat to our mobile phone user—far greater than an addiction to Instagram—of being run into by the driver + car. The traffic light system of car signals, bicycle signals, pedestrian signals, and mobile phone user signals are militating against the dominance and dangers of the driver-car. And if we look at the materialities of the larger assembly at the intersection of Goudseweg and Vrije Nesse, the car-thing again dominates, as not only a consumer of materials and resources but also as a generator of carbon dioxide (CO_2) and nitrogen dioxide. It would also be an oversight to look at this assemblage as a given or as static. That is, through interventions, perhaps by design, political action, governance, or some combination, the dynamics and power relations can shift dramatically. It was the *Stop de Kindermoord* movement in the Netherlands in the 1970s that led to the first city-wide infrastructure of cycling paths that are now largely taken for granted across the whole country (Van der Zee 2015). Some twenty years ago, the socialist mayor of

Things Are Interconnected and Transformative 113

Pontevedra asked the question: "How can it be that private property—the car—occupies the public space?" and so banned cars from the city center and imposed severe traffic restrictions elsewhere. CO2 emissions dropped by 70 percent (Burgen 2018). It is now becoming commonplace for large European cities to create low-emission zones that shift the balance among human-things such that whole assemblies, like those at the intersection of Goudseweg and Vrije Nesse, could become obsolete or unnecessary (Jones 2018). While I am writing this book, the COVID-19 global pandemic—a massive nonhuman commingling—has usurped countless assemblages of human-things; the surrendering of car infrastructure to pedestrians to allow for two-meters physical distancing between people is creating a collapse in carbon output that sadly will, in all likelihood, be temporary.

I have taken a closer look at interconnectedness in the design of concrete things and, as a result, how things are transformative. Verbeek argues that a theory of mediation should be able to tackle all experiences, including the transcendental or religious: "A good starting point can be to focus on the relations between technology and religion, more specifically on the ways in which technologies help to shape or transform human experiences of transcendence—of what is beyond the grasp of human understanding and manipulation" (Verbeek 2016, 200). In the prologue to this chapter, I discussed the *Prayer Companion* by Bill Gaver and the Interaction Research Studio. Gaver and colleagues discuss the *Prayer Companion* as a "resource" for cloistered nuns that, by balancing appropriation and interpretation through the design, shows how computation can "support" spirituality (Gaver et al. 2010). In this sense, the *Prayer Companion* is viewed as an artifact in ways that I discussed in chapter 3. Similar to my analysis of +*Lichtlijn*, I will discuss *Prayer Companion* as a thing, especially looking at how designing the thing aimed to transform or mediate prayer.

Gaver and his colleagues provide a thorough description of the lives and background of the nuns and life in the convent (Gaver et al. 2010). The Poor Clares are an enclosed order. They are a Roman Catholic order founded in 1212 by St. Clare of Assisi and St. Francis of Assisi. As cloistered nuns, they live within the enclosure of the St. John's Convent that encompasses more than six acres of grounds. The sisters have taken vows of poverty, obedience, and chastity. Their daily lives follow the same routine of celebrating daily mass, reading scripture, preparing Eucharist wafers for churches around the county, maintaining the convent and the gardens, and growing and preparing their food. Time is set aside each day for personal prayer, though it is commented that prayer, or to be "utterly in God's presence," is easily woven into the tasks and routines of the day (Gaver et al. 2010, 2057). The prayers of the nuns must be relevant or "pertinent" to the world, even though they are cloistered. To help in this regard, the nuns received news from radio broadcasts, the diocese, Catholic news agencies, or at the time of the arrival of *Prayer Companion*, the cloister received its first personal computer with Internet access.

Those in the Interaction Research Studio quickly focused on the technicity of prayer for the cloistered nuns. Influencing the prayers were the various media sources for the news and media available to the nuns:

> We realised that this question cut to the heart of their prayer activity, their role in the community, and the ways they are affected by the outside world. It soon led to the playful speculation about media bias in their prayers, and we wondered if we could design devices that would allow them to draw on a wider range of information sources as a resource for their prayer. (Gaver et al. 2010, 2058)

The subsequent design of the *Prayer Companion* intervened on this very question of diversity of media sources and channels. The design interventions of *Prayer Companion* were to have a form and presence that would fit the surroundings of the convent and the nuns' daily lives and structure the sources of information in ways that shaped the prayers and prayer activity of the nuns. In this way, the *Prayer Companion* was interconnected with the prayers of the nuns and helped shape them (figure 4.6).

The designers chose three strategies for sourcing and displaying information to transform the prayers. The first was to use the RSS feeds from a diverse collection of twenty-five websites.[2] These feeds included those that represented news sources familiar to the nuns already, as well as a wider range of international sources and local sources. The designers also pulled content from wefeelfine.org, a site created by Sep Kamvar and Jonathan Harris that harvests content from blog entries of sentences that begin with the phrase "I feel" and "I am feeling." Lastly, the designers programmed the *Prayer Companion* so that every twenty minutes a number of "special" behaviors would occur, including displaying content only from wefeelfine.org or local news or repeating an item over and over. Additionally, the speed of the scrolling text would either be increased or decreased. The hope was that these unusual behaviors would pique interest, disrupting the normal reading of the text that might become too commonplace (Gaver et al. 2010, 2060).

Things Are Interconnected and Transformative 115

The response of the nuns after ten months of living with the *Prayer Companion* was one of temporary incorporation into their prayer life. The intervention of the wefeelfine.org content was met with amusement that gave way to annoyance to the point that the designers lessened the percentage of content from that site. The "I feel" phrases often felt trite to the nuns and in many ways not "actionable" in terms of prayer, though on occasion it made them think of those who had written the phrases (Gaver et al. 2010, 2062). The *Prayer Companion* became an alert system for news that they could follow-up on in other ways. For example, Gaver and his colleagues reported the following:

> The device was the first to inform them that a young woman from the local university had gone missing and they followed the story as it developed. Sister Matthew had been out in the garden attending to her snapdragons when she noticed helicopters flying overhead. She assumed they must be part of the search for the missing girl because she had read on her way out that they were now treating the case as a murder investigation. (Gaver et al. 2010, 2062–2063)

Gaver and his colleagues advocate for Ludic design as an approach for designing technologies. In Ludic design, the aim is to design for exploration, surprise, and improvisation rather than utility alone (Gaver et al. 2004). Given this, looking for causal or measurable impacts of the design choices or reasoning for *Prayer Companion* are not only near impossible but not at all desirable. In a holistic sense, the success of *Prayer Companion* is that it became in many ways incorporated and part of the prayer life of the nuns. Beyond the functional aspects of mediation or transformation by things (i.e., collecting data from the Internet), the transformative effects of *Prayer Companion* are holistic to the point of being difficult to quantify and separate. *Prayer Companion* became a part of prayer life that is still connected with the various websites, the newsletter from the diocese, the radio, and the Internet assemblies for prayer that all come together in a composite mediation to specifically shape the prayer life of the nuns. One way to consider *Prayer Companion* is that it was designed for the human-thing assemblies of the cloistered nuns as much as the nuns themselves. Relatedly, the nuns were at "pains" to remind the designers of the following:

> That they will not come to any conclusions about the value the Prayer Companion has to them for several years. "A month is nothing to us," they explained. In a year, or two years, then they will have an idea. They may yet decide, for instance, that it intrudes upon their seclusion and give it up as a wonderful but inappropriate distraction. (Gaver et al. 2010, 2063)

The *Prayer Companion* is a good example of how a thing is transformative. Its effects, especially beyond the functional mediation, are evidenced by it becoming part of the embodied praxis and assemblies of spiritual life and prayer. The thing becomes part of the "entire mutually referring network" and shapes prayer from within an evolving technicity in ways that are performative and holistic. The designers' interventions are explicit and purposeful, yet the degree to which they contribute to the "success" of the *Prayer Companion* is a matter of partial knowledge. And further, the *Prayer Companion*'s transformative perch, as the sisters constantly reminded the designers, evades any immediate conclusive value and is subject to time and the changing dynamics of life in the cloister. Further, the *Prayer Companion* as any other thing in a human-thing assemblage is always subject to removal or dropping away from the assemblage or, in the case of the convent, expulsion as a mere "worldly distraction."

However, things like the *Prayer Companion* may fall out of one assembly only to "reassemble" in another assembly of human-things and, more broadly, assemblies of humans, nonhumans, and things. In seeing +*Lichtlijn* or *Prayer Companion* as things, a different intentionality from that of artifacts is revealed. The irrevocable interconnectedness with humans means that things often reassemble continuously even when they "fail" or fall out of their initially targeted program, whether its traffic management or prayer. Things never go away until they are purposely disassembled, recycled, or decomposed, and even then, they may continue in their residue to be transformative. It is a matter of course that things will be enlisted into other assemblages. Artifacts, by comparison, hold a narrower view of their relationship to humans and other artifacts. Specifically, it is a relationship of interaction between humans and artifacts that is the sole concern; anything else is more or less a matter of context or unintended consequences. Further, the relationship with artifacts is essentially binary: An artifact is either accepted or rejected by humans. With things, the direct interaction between humans and things is only one part of a greater concern since things can never be severed from their interconnectedness with humans. Even in its most relegated form as waste or pollutant, a thing remains connected and part of new and broader assemblages that can accumulate and even remake the planet. For example, as discussed in the prologue to chapter 4, what is called the *Great Pacific Garbage Patch* that lies between Hawaii and California is 1.6 million square kilometers of plastic nearing the size of a small continent. It is an assemblage of buoyant plastics, ocean currents, marine life, and ultraviolet solar rays that shape and reshape the assemblage.[3] Multiple such garbage patches exist, and while distant from human activity they are each no less an assembly of humans, nonhumans, and things. In the era of the Anthropocene, human-things such as human-produced radiation, chicken bones, or plastics have reshaped the geological record such that it is clear that humans and nonhumans co-shape the thin strip of habitable space across the planet. As an artifact, "waste" that is no longer of human use falls out of view to be out of sight and out of mind. The importance of things is to keep them in constant view as they become enrolled in different assemblies throughout their life cycle. However, what is equally important are the continual effects and consequences of designing things that result from the broad and ongoing interconnections and assemblages of humans, nonhumans, and things.

The Characteristics of Things That Are Interconnected and Transformative

In this chapter, I discussed two features of things: *Things and humans are interconnected* and *things are transformative*. The nomadic practice of things opens design to a postanthropocentric view in which humans are decentered, such that human and nonhuman animals and things share the center. And so together the commitments of posthumanist philosophies inform the idea of *things*. The results of the discussion in this chapter are a set of characteristics of what I mean by *things*.

Mediating Things
Informed by postphenomenology, the mediating intentionalities in effect with technologies are building blocks for developing *things*. This gives us two defining characteristics. Firstly, things transform human actions and perceptions, as illustrated in this chapter, from hammering a nail, to running at night, to walking across town with a mobile phone. In reality, this characteristic extends to all actions and perceptions that constitute us as human animals. Secondly, and in ways that underscore the pervasive and central role of the transformative characteristic, things are *commensurate* with *being* human. Things shape humans and vice versa, such that things influence who we become as human animals. In turn, humans influence how things become what they are in a given moment. In this way, things

are irreducible beyond human-things or thing-humans. The transformative quality of things in the context of mediated intentionality is neither inherently positive nor negative. *Phototrope* embodies these characteristics well as a thing that mediates a nocturnal runner and running landscape in ways that assume variant relations, including *embodied, hermeneutic,* and *alterity*. Yet through stubborn persistence and scale, the continual mediating of things can cascade even in residue form into assemblages of toxic waste and human-thing shaping at a geological and planetary scale.

Embodied and Immanent
The co-constitutive nature of human-things can be said to be performative, which points to things as embodied and immanent. Things in this sense are immediate and are only meaningful when experienced within an embodied and material situation. This contrasts with artifacts that manifest in the present and in the future as well as materially and conceptually. The immanent nature of things is in contrast with the symbolic or transcendental quality ascribed to objects, or the temporal plasticity of artifacts to be both present and future as described in chapter 3. In understanding and describing things, it is best to keep in close proximity to the concreteness of things as matters of materiality and situatedness. Heidegger's hammer and *Phototrope* speak to the embodied dynamics of hammering and running that constitute things and the respective worlds of hammering and running. This embodiment and immanence is also in effect at the predominantly nonhuman assemblies and reassemblies of human-things at a scale difficult to experience from a human perspective, like the *Great Pacific Garbage Patch*.

Assemblages
The transformative effects of things can be said to be holistic and therefore difficult to quantify and separate. Human-things interconnected together do not act alone but become parts of larger assemblages. The *+Lichtlijn* is designed for humans, mobile phones, and traffic lights that in turn belong to an assemblage of traffic management for other human-things like the driver and car. *Prayer Companion* is part of an assembly of interactive technologies and producers of news, social media, and art. Further, *Prayer Companion* can be said to be as much designed for the human-thing assemblage of cloistered nuns and the various news channels as the nuns themselves.

The dynamics and even precarious nature of assemblages play out in many ways. With +*Lichtlijn*, the human-things are not of equal status—for example, the car-driver dominates and predominantly shapes urban environments. However, assemblages, while deeply interwoven into our world, cannot be assumed as a given. Intervening concerns, values, new human-things, practices, or political or market agendas can render whole assemblies as unwanted or unneeded. Also, while I have discussed how the very nature of becoming a thing arises from an interconnectedness with humans, things like +*Lichtlijn* or *Prayer Companion* can fall out of or be removed from an assemblage but likely become part of another assemblage and so never lose their interconnectedness. Regardless of the outcome, purposeful design by designers of things is a necessity for things to exist. Yet this purposefulness is conditioned by the dynamic of constant interventions, appropriations, and situatedness that makes designing things uncertain, partial, and relational.

In summary, the features of things discussed in this chapter, on the one hand, give a great deal of power to designing things in that things are inseparable from and constitutive of what it is to be human. On the other hand, the features reveal that partial knowing is inherent to things and is manifest within assemblages of human-things and the dynamics of evolving technicity of the world. And so, to hold this assumption is to acknowledge that to design things is holistically powerful, though the role of the designer is limited and operates with partial knowledge and agency. In chapter 5, I will elaborate on the second and last installment of describing things through the features of *things are relational* and *things are vital*.

Chapter 5 Prologue: Tilting Bowl, Being the Machine, Obscura 1C Digital Camera, Morse Things, Burgundian Black Collaboratory, and Mineral Accretion Factory: Underwater Table

In this prologue, I describe a number of design research projects that I discuss again in chapter 5 to help me elaborate on the relationality and vitality of things. Projects like my own *Tilting Bowl* (Wakkary et al. 2018) and Laura Devendorf and Kimiko Ryokai's *Being the Machine* (Devendorf and Ryokai 2015) reveal how things embody different meanings as a consequence of their different embodied relations to the world. This relationality can both stabilize and destabilize norms, as is also the case with the *Obscura 1C Digital Camera* by James Pierce and Eric Paulos (2015), also discussed here in the prologue and in the next chapter. These projects uniquely use strategies of defamiliarization to emphasize their relationalities. I also discuss another work of mine known as *Morse Things* (Wakkary et al. 2017), a research partnership called the *Burgundian Black Collaboratory* led by Claudy Jongstra and Jenny Boulboullè (Erichsen 2019), and the *Mineral Accretion Factory* by the School of Art of La Réunion (Énon 2019) to support investigations of the phenomenological intentionality and vitality of things.

Tilting Bowl

The *Tilting Bowl* is a ceramic bowl that unpredictably but gently tilts multiple times daily (see figure 5.1). The *Tilting Bowl* was designed by myself and my colleagues at the Everyday Design Studio at Simon Fraser University. We adopted what we call a material speculation approach to design research in designing the *Tilting Bowl*. Material speculation is the design of a *counterfactual artifact* that is experienced and lived-with on an everyday basis over time as a way to ask certain types of research questions (Wakkary et al. 2015). A counterfactual artifact is a realized functioning product or system that intentionally contradicts what would normally be considered

Figure 5.1
The *Tilting Bowl*.
Source: Henry Lin.

logical to create given the norms of design and design products, like a ceramic bowl that tilts. This countering of norms opens the possibilities to empirically investigate multiple alternative existences (or "what ifs") as lived-with realities of the counterfactual artifacts. In addition to our material speculation approach, we recruited trained philosophers who have the competencies (critical thinking, ethical training, philosophical vocabulary, etc.) to help us speculate, reveal, and describe human-technology relations with the *Tilting Bowl*. We believe speculation of this nature requires the bringing together of lived-with experiences and philosophical work. We refer to this additional methodological approach as *co-speculation*. Co-speculation is the recruiting and participation of study participants who are well positioned to actively and knowingly speculate with us, in our inquiry, in ways that we cannot alone.

We produced six identical versions of the *Tilting Bowl* for long-term deployments in the homes of our philosopher participants. The *Tilting Bowl* is similar to any other ceramic bowl in that it is food safe and washable, but it cannot be used in a microwave or washed in a dishwasher. The battery lasts seven to nine months on a single charge. The tilting of the bowl is of varying degrees, raising the artifact by as much as 9.5-millimeters or hardly at all. A small wheel is attached in an offset manner from the center to a motor. The motor rotates at varying fractions of turns or duration each time it activates. The combination of the time of rotation and varying distances from the outside rim of the wheel to the motor shaft determines the height and amount of tilt each time. Over time there are enough opportunities to see the bowl tilt, but more often than not the experience is of hearing the motor and noticing the tilt after the fact. In various studies, we deployed the *Tilting Bowl* for anywhere from three months to over two years with a number of trained philosophers. In chapter 5, the *Tilting Bowl* helps to elaborate on relationality—in particular, how a thing like the *Tilting Bowl* assumes different meaning through its different relations to the world and in the process can be seen to stabilize and destabilize normative assumptions.

Being the Machine

Being the Machine by Laura Devendorf and Kimiko Ryokai (2015) is a digital fabrication system that guides makers in building three-dimensional forms out of everyday materials. The system, modeled after 3D printers, distributes control and agency of the making process between humans, materials, and a machine in order to explore hybrid fabrication. Hybrid fabrication, or what Devendorf would later refer to as *coproduction*, is existing craft practices combined with automated digital processes like 3D printing (Devendorf and Rosner 2017). Devendorf and Ryokai (2015) aim to expand the design space of human-machine fabrication by inserting humans between the machine processes and the materials. They argue that their explorations open a space for meditation and reflection that leads to preferred or personal modes of making within digital fabrication.

Being the Machine is composed of a laser pointer moved by servo motors that can pan and tilt. The laser and motors are attached to a tripod and extending arm. G-Code instructions of a 3D model are translated into position points for the servo motors to move the laser pointer. G-Code is a computer language that instructs machine tools on how to make something and is commonly used to instruct and position the printhead of a 3D printer. Unlike a 3D printer, the laser pointer guides the actions of a person to manipulate or shape material into the position and form suggested by the laser dot (see figure 5.2). The person advances the system to the

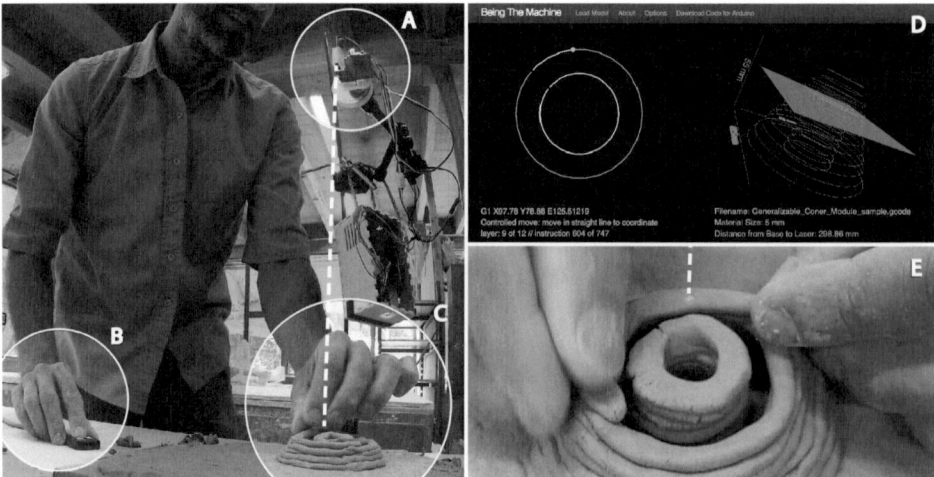

Figure 5.2
An overview of *Being the Machine* (Devendorf and Ryokai 2015). (a) A laser guide draws a point on a 2D plane. (b) A user pushes Next and Back buttons on a wireless key fob to move the laser point to the position of the next or last G-Code instruction. (c) The user moves her materials to follow the path of the laser. (d) The G-Code visualization software allows the user to see the paths of her model in two and three dimensions. (e) A close-up view showing what users see (a laser dot) when building their model.
Source: Courtesy of Laura Devendorf.

next position with a wireless controller. Also, unlike a 3D printer, the user can make a form with any materials they choose (see figure 5.3). *Being the Machine* is portable and can be installed and used almost anywhere. Devendorf and Ryokai (2015) studied its use by fourteen makers of different backgrounds and expertise in their homes, studios, public spaces, and outdoors.

Similar to the *Tilting Bowl*, *Being the Machine* shows how, in this case in the deconstruction of a 3D printer, the thing and the user acquire new meanings in relation to each other rather than either being fixed or stable. Further, these meanings and the making of the forms themselves are an immanent process that emerges from literally becoming the 3D printer.

Obscura 1C Digital Camera

The *Obscura 1C Digital Camera* by James Pierce and Eric Paulos (2015) is a work that addresses small-scale experimental production and distribution

Figure 5.3
Examples of the different forms produced and the different materials used with *Being the Machine*.
Source: Courtesy of Laura Devendorf.

of a *counterfunctional device*. The device is a functioning digital camera enclosed in concrete (figure 5.4). The idea of counterfunctionality is that through direct opposition or inversion of expected functions, new values or functionality may emerge. This understanding helps to further the discussion in chapter 5 about the role things play in stabilizing or destabilizing normative conventions. Pierce and Paulos suggest that a way to design for counterfunctionality is to identify positive features, restrict or remove these features, then find ways to design around the absence or curtailment of these features (Pierce and Paulos 2015).

The counterfunctional device was produced, packaged, and distributed in ways that it could be experienced by "everyday audiences" (figure 5.5). A succinct description appears on the packaging for the device:

> *Obscura 1C Digital Camera* captures photo, video and audio recordings. In order to access the media files recorded, you must physically break apart the concrete enclosure to reveal the micro SD memory card buried inside. Obscura inhibits access to its contents to offer a digital experience based on uncertainty, patience and surprise.

Several cameras were distributed through a number of ways: handing out cameras to those who expressed an envisioned use of the camera, Craigslist ads listing the device for free or for sale, anonymous mailings to individuals, community bulletin boards, and what is known as "droplifting," the reverse of shoplifting in which a product is left in a retail store.

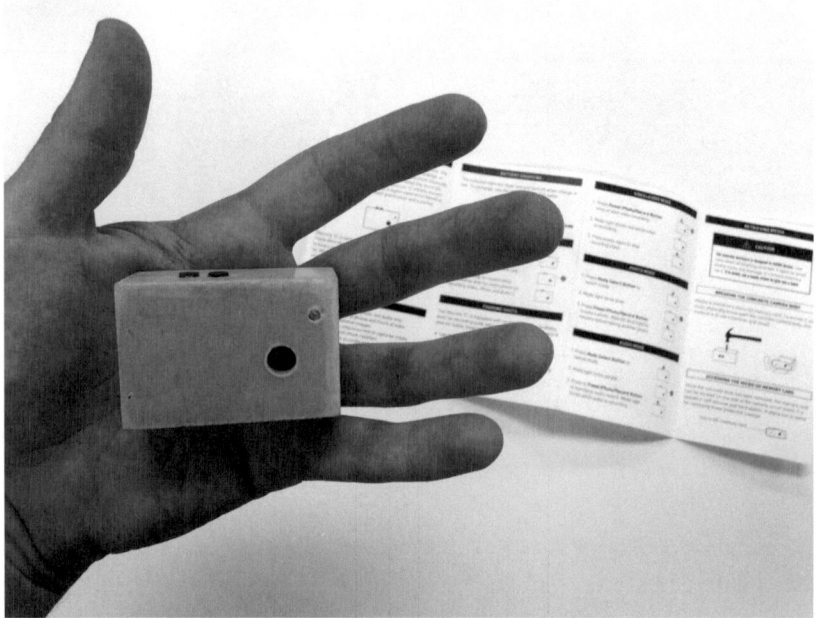

Figure 5.4
The *Obscura 1C Digital Camera* and manual.
Source: Courtesy of James Pierce.

The *Obscura 1C Digital Camera* helps to elaborate on the discussion in chapter 5 on the vitality of things. The concrete casing and its eventual destruction create an anticipation or trajectory of action for the thing. It also shows the non-neutrality of things that can either stabilize or destabilize norms, as this counterfunctional artifact does with digital photography.

Morse Things

The *Morse Things*, also a design research project of the Everyday Design Studio, are sets of ceramic bowls and cups that communicate only to each other over the Internet (figure 5.6) (Wakkary et al. 2017). Over time, enabled through different machine learning algorithms, *Morse Things* increasingly connect with each other to achieve a level of "awareness" of not only each other but that a network of things exists. There is no digital interaction with people.

Figure 5.5
The *Obscura 1C Digital Camera* packaged for distribution, including SD card, operating manual, and counterfunctional cameras brochure.
Source: Courtesy of James Pierce.

The *Morse Things* mostly sleep (computationally speaking) and wake at random intervals during the day at least once every eight hours. Upon waking a Morse Thing will send and receive messages to and from another Morse Thing. The messages sent by each Morse Thing are in Morse code and simultaneously expressed sonically and broadcasted on Twitter (figure 5.7). The *Morse Things* can be used like any other bowl or cup for eating, drinking, and containing items, with the exception (similar to the *Tilting Bowl*) that they cannot be put in the dishwasher or microwave. We designed and fabricated six sets of *Morse Things*, each including a large ceramic bowl, a medium bowl, and a cup. The form of each Morse Thing is made of ceramics shaped around the embedded electronics. Each Morse Thing consists of a Wi-Fi microcontroller, sleeping module, amplifier circuit, speakers, and battery. An Internet server coordinates the messages sent and received by a Morse Thing and runs the machine learning program.

The *Morse Things* project is an inquiry into a thing-centered view of the Internet of Things (IoT), which is the networking together of Internet-enabled

Figure 5.6
A set of *Morse Things*: a Morse Thing router and instructions.
Source: Henry Lin.

products to create services. It also adopts a material speculation approach (Wakkary et al. 2015). In this way, *Morse Things* are counterfactual Internet-enabled artifacts for the home in that their digital capabilities are at the service of things rather than people. Their human functionality is of an everyday nature that already exists in homes, shifting the question from what they *do* to how they *are* in our homes. In particular, we wanted to investigate the gap between things and us that will become more pronounced through an increase in Internet-enabled home products. This gap results in somewhat of a conundrum: We simultaneously cannot understand what it is to be a thing yet would not be able to function in or comprehend our lives without things. In various studies, we deployed the *Morse Things* across many households to live with for six weeks to six months (figure 5.8).

In chapter 5, the *Morse Things* open the discussion to the phenomenological intentionality of things and how they not only direct themselves uniquely at the world but can also be seen to "experience" the world

Tilting Bowl, Being the Machine, and Obscura 1C Digital Camera

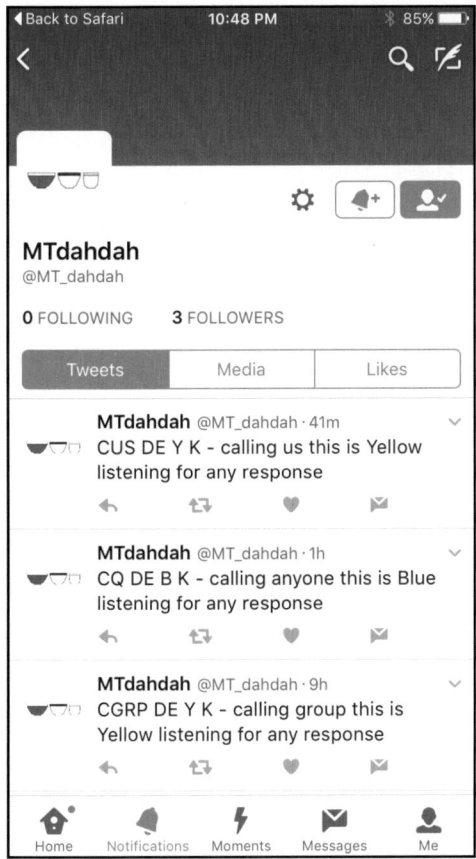

Figure 5.7
The Twitter account of a set of *Morse Things*.

distinctly in relation to humans, offering insights into the qualities of agency that things may hold.

Burgundian Black Collaboratory

The *Burgundian Black Collaboratory* researches the recipes and techniques of Renaissance-era Burgundian blacks, a color widely seen in Flemish and Italian portrait painting. It is a collaboration between the European Research Council project ARTECHNE (Utrecht University and University of Amsterdam), the Belgian Museum Hof van Busleyden in Mechelen, the Dutch contemporary artist

Figure 5.8
Morse Things in the homes of study participants.

Claudy Jongstra, the University of Antwerp, and the research laboratories of the Cultural Heritage Agency of the Netherlands (RCE) (Utrecht University 2019). The group finds, translates, and puts into practice black dye recipes from Flemish and Italian master dyers including the Venetian Plichto by Rosetti, who was among the first to assemble and archive dye recipes. While the collaborators aim to reconstruct the recipes, they actively "rework" the formulas and methods, given that the recipes are often vague in instructions and measurements. A central value of the collaboration is its embodiment of experimentation with the crafting of the dyes and dyeing processes.

Burgundian black was seen as the highest-quality black to be worn and sold to the merchant class and aristocracies in Europe in the fifteenth and sixteenth centuries (see figure 5.9). It was a product of imperial powers that combined materials from their worldly empires with imported and local artistry that together displayed a height of mastery of resources, knowledge, and wealth. It can be said to have represented a peak in wool and dyeing technologies and techniques. Recipes were recorded though kept secret

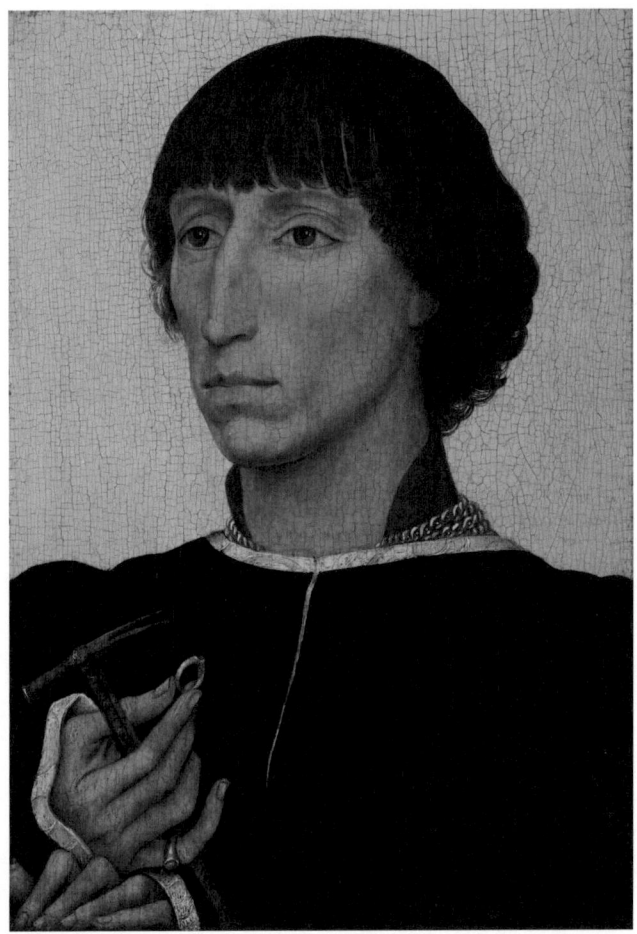

Figure 5.9
Franceso d'Este, son of the ruler of Ferrara in Burgundy, adorned in Burgundian black.
Source: Rogier van der Weiden (ca. 1460).

within different guilds that also exacted the highest degree of control and oversight over the blackness of the black and the quality of the materials and dyeing.

The *Burgundian Black Collaboratory* and, specifically, a visit to Claudy Jongstra's studio add immensely to the discussion in chapter 5 on the vital materialism of things in which things and matter hold a form of agency that is distributive, directional, and often opaque.

Mineral Accretion Factory: Underwater Table

Mineral Accretion Factory is a design and production system of objects and furniture by David Énon of the ESA Réunion (École Supérieure d'Art de La Réunion) on the island of La Réunion in France. The system is based on the artificial reef production process of the Symbiotic Process Laboratory that was developed by Wolf Hilbertz and Thomas J. Goreau and used to restore coral reefs. The *Underwater Table*, like other furniture made by the Mineral Accretion Factory, uses a process of immersing a steel structure in seawater to allow marine growth to adhere to the structure (see figure 5.10) (Énon 2019). A low-voltage supply is connected to the steel frame to allow for a redox reaction to take place in which minerals accumulate and form over the steel. This chemical reaction creates a bond of calcium carbonate over the steel that continues to grow, like the limestone that forms the exoskeleton of coral. The material continues to grow and eventually hardens as other minerals and marine life accrete as well to form a composite. After two to three years

Figure 5.10
The *Underwater Table* at approximately one year of growth.
Source: "Mineral Accretion Furniture" by David Énon, licensed under CC BY 4.0.

the structure is sufficiently robust and no longer requires the electric voltage to accrete.

Énon and his colleagues have experimented with different techniques for creating structures, powering the structures, and ultimately retrieving and "finishing" them. In the case of the *Underwater Table*, he suggests freezing it to destroy the microorganisms and the marine smell. The aim of the Mineral Accretion Factory is to model and create an ecosystem for production that requires little human labor and has little impact on the environment. Énon states:

> It is a low-tech and slow tech system that respects the biological rhythms and production capacities of the earth. If the factory becomes the sea, there is no local involvement (building to be built, car park, access road, dustbins, heating, air conditioning . . .). The ground hold here is virtuous since it contributes to the reconstruction of the coral reef and accompanies the development of marine fauna and flora. (Énon 2019, 10)

The Mineral Accretion Factory is an ongoing process in researching and modeling "slow tech" and "wildtech" and explicitly relies on nonhuman vitality as a productive and co-collaborative force.

Chapter 5: Things Are Relational and Vital

Much of the discussion in this book is committed to the idea of relationality. Relationality is central to the idea of nomadic practices that I've been using to frame and articulate what I mean by design. This reveals the potential to see design as variants, constituted in different ways by different designers *in relation to* the different *somethings* designed. I've discussed how the design of things transforms what it means to be human and is co-constitutive, which means things equally shape humans as humans shape things. And so, who or what is in control? In this chapter, I expand on these thoughts by discussing the remaining two characteristics introduced in chapter 1. Firstly, that *things are relational*, meaning they are not fixed, highly interpretive, multistable, and ultimately political. Secondly, *things are vital* in ways that are a shared intentionality between things and humans, and *aliveness* in the form of agentic capacities that flow across and through humans and nonhumans.

In this chapter, I focus on the second of the three philosophical concepts supporting the idea of things, which I refer to as *assembly of vital matter* (see figure 5.11). These concepts draw on multistability (Rosenberger 2014), vital materialism (Bennett 2010), and agentic capacities (Coole 2005, 2013) that describe how things are relational, seen as situated or belonging to assemblages and so not discrete. Things are also seen to have agentic qualities and intentionalities that contribute to their own making and the making of other things.

The Relationality of Things

Supporting the notion of relationality, philosophically speaking, is the concept of *relational ontologies* (Bennett 2010; Braidotti 2013; Ihde 1990). A relational ontology is the idea that either subject or object is defined in

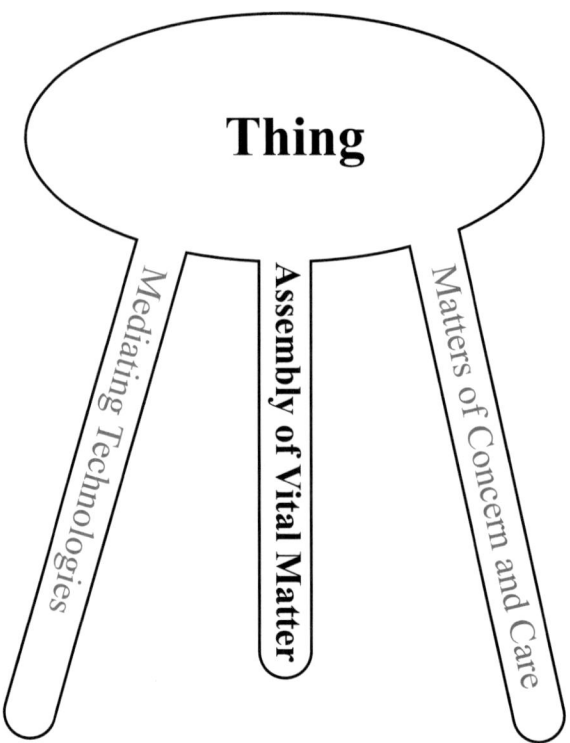

Figure 5.11
The philosophical concept of *assembly of vital matter* that supports this part of the discussion of things.

relation to the other, and as a result subject and object cannot be split and separately understood or defined (Rosenberger and Verbeek 2015). A key aspect is that as either subject or object shifts, so does one or the other. To further make this point, Ihde argues, an objectivist view that separates and stabilizes, for example, human, technology, and world would be "nonrelativistic" and would obscure the human-technology relations or the human-thing relations I discussed in chapter 4 (Ihde 1990, 97).

In the prologue to this chapter, I described the *Tilting Bowl*, a project of my Everyday Design Studio that was a material speculation inquiry into human-technology relations that we conducted with philosophers. To materially speculate is to ask a what-if question through the design of a thing (Wakkary et al. 2015). As I described in the prologue, the *Tilting*

Things Are Relational and Vital

Bowl is a ceramic bowl that periodically and unpredictably tilts. We asked several philosophers to live with the *Tilting Bowl* to help us uncover philosophical aspects of our relations to technology in everyday contexts. In our inquiry, it was plain to see that the different philosophical identities of our participants shaped their accounts of or opened them to being shaped by the experiences of the *Tilting Bowl* (Wakkary et al. 2018). The philosophers consciously or unconsciously brought their particular viewpoints to bear in articulating their reflections. Together, these views raised issues of essence, autonomy, and tolerance, among other issues. These interpretive positions ranged from Husserl's phenomenology to political philosophy, and these explicit framings could be understood as variant interpretations or "hermeneutic strategies" (Rosenberger and Verbeek 2015). Ihde (1990) used the term *cultural variances* or multiple cultural stabilities of structuring the world, which in the case of the *Tilting Bowl* arise in the different concepts, classifications, and vocabulary of the various philosophical approaches of our philosopher participants. While these examples point to trained perspectives acquired through education, hermeneutic strategies can also be less declarative, more individual, situated, and constant as a matter of day-to-day living. In this respect, interpretive strategies are central in a relational reality.

In the *Tilting Bowl* study, our participants, who we also referred to as co-speculators, since we asked them to actively speculate with us on experiences of the *Tilting Bowl* (Wakkary et al. 2018), were asked about times when they explained the *Tilting Bowl* and the study to friends and coworkers. These encounters with others helped externalize what and how our participants were thinking about and experiencing with the *Tilting Bowl*. In addition, these explanations forced a self-reflection on how the philosophers' embodied relations with the *Tilting Bowl* changed. It positioned them and the *Tilting Bowl* more explicitly as part of a research study as well as something they lived with. For example, one of our participants, Franklin, explained that when he encountered skeptical responses to the *Tilting Bowl*, he felt the need to defend it and the study to a certain degree: "I defend the project to a point and then I say, it's not my study." Over time, he defended the study even less, especially as he came to view the *Tilting Bowl* as "normal" and not as strange or weird as others perceived it. At this point in his relationship with the bowl, he found himself defending his position of indifference or normalcy with regard to the *Tilting Bowl* rather than the study itself:

> Others (guests, friends) had a much easier time remembering the bowl's strangeness because they had never forgotten it. And when confronted by their appreciation of that strangeness, the absence of such an appreciation of my own itself appeared strange to me. I would be struck by how strange it was that I no longer recognized the bowl as strange. Of course, to recognize that an attitude is strange is not necessarily to change that attitude, and after a few flickering moments of recognizing the strangeness of the bowl, it would once again seem normal; but the sense that that sense of normalcy was strange would linger. . . . It is a form of self-doubt or self-uncertainty to find yourself a stranger to your own attitudes. (Wakkary et al. 2018, 9)

This account of shifting positions, Franklin's reflections on how the relationship between him and the *Tilting Bowl* change and how the bowl mediates his world, is relative to the perspective or embodied position that forms him as subject at any given time. Unsurprisingly, this relational dynamic led to "self-doubt or self-uncertainty." Despite the simplicity—even triviality—of the tilt, it is this straightforward action that shifts the reflections on what is "normal" about the bowl. The tilt *defamiliarizes* existing relations with things, suspends them for reflection, opening them for consideration and reconsideration. The many viewpoints and alternatives of even something as mundane as a fruit bowl emerge as an unavoidable condition. This account echoes Braidotti's idea of *defamiliarization* or *disidentification* and, in turn, extends the potential of the experience in consequential ways that are no less at play even in the reflections on the "trivial" (i.e., what is a ceramic bowl that tilts):

> The post-anthropocentric shift away from the hierarchical relations that had privileged "Man" requires a form of estrangement and a radical repositioning on the part of the subject. The best method to accomplish this is through the strategy of de-familiarization or critical distance from the dominant vision of the subject. Dis-identification involves the loss of familiar habits of thought and representation in order to pave the way for creative alternatives. (Braidotti 2013, 88–89)

The purposeful estrangement of "familiar habits of thought" and "representation" opens to creative alternatives that are ontological and political in nature. As such, relationality of things plays a role, a non-neutral role, in the positioning of the subject as "Man" or the repositioning of the subject. The *Tilting Bowl* uses the strategy of a *counterfactual artifact* as discussed in the prologue. This countering of the norms of design artifacts is how we incorporate *defamiliarization* or *disidentification*. In returning to the *Tilting Bowl* study, two of our co-speculators/philosophers who lived

Things Are Relational and Vital

together, Desmond and William, created a "trap" or a makeshift surveillance system to alert them when the *Tilting Bowl* tilts or had tilted. They put a small metallic pot in the bowl so that if it tilted, the pot would move and make a sound. For added measure, they leaned a piece of paper against the ceramic bowl that would tip over in the event of it tilting (see figure 5.12). However, later in the study, they relayed how they became concerned with this act of surveillance. They came to see themselves as desiring mastery and control over the *Tilting Bowl*. In seeing their relationship with the counterfactual artifact in *quasi-other* terms, they became very uncomfortable. William stated: "Think about that politically. That's the way refugees are treated sometimes—the same kind of surveillance, with the bowl, the same suspicion, exactly."

That this shift in understanding the *Tilting Bowl* ultimately became political would not be a surprise to Braidotti:

> Deleuze would call it an active "deterritorialization." Race and post-colonial theories have also made important contributions to the methodology and the political strategy of defamiliarization (Gilroy, 2005). I have defended this method as a disidentification from familiar and hence normative values, such as the dominant

Figure 5.12
A "trap" or surveillance system to alert when the *Tilting Bowl* tilts.
Source: Doenja Oogjes.

institutions and representations of femininity and masculinity, so as to move sexual difference towards the process of becoming-minoritarian. (Braidotti 2013, 89)

It may seem that the relationality of things defies norms or destabilizes them, especially in instances of designing counterfactual artifacts or incorporating defamiliarizing/disidentification strategies in which relationality is emphasized. However, it is important to recognize that it is a matter of *emphasizing* the existing relationalities of things rather than *creating* relationality or relativism among otherwise stable entities. By this I mean, that the tilt merely brings into view the idea that all things are relational; it does *not cause* the relationality. And it is in the face of these changing relations that norms are constantly established and constructed. Furthermore, normative values are intricately constructed through our relations to things and each other. In this way, we can also unravel or destabilize norms through as trivial an action as tilting a ceramic bowl. This unraveling opens to alternatives or, more radically, a multiplicity of alternatives that, as Braidotti (2013) suggests, aim toward "becoming-minoritarian." This notion is grounded in Deleuze and Guattari's "becoming-minor" as an ethical action and related to their concept of nomadism discussed in chapter 2, to avoid dominance or becoming the majority (Deleuze and Guattari 1987).

Franklin and his father Mark debated the degree of concern one should accord a nonhuman entity like the *Tilting Bowl*. Mark relayed how he had formed an attachment to the *Tilting Bowl*, considered it as part of the family. Franklin struggled to see the *Tilting Bowl* in those terms. He was concerned with the limits of assigning human values or quasi-human values to nonhuman entities. His worry was about the ease with which an artifact as strange as the *Tilting Bowl* was accepted as normal and how its very otherness was made a virtue: "I want to complicate that a little bit by saying there's some things we shouldn't come to see as normal . . . and it does make me question. I mean, the bowl is a bowl, right? But I mean in a grander scale, it does make me question [that] if we can get used to this . . . what else are we used to that's stuff that we shouldn't be used to—stuff that we should have a problem with. . . ."

Two points arise from Franklin's problematizing of "acceptance." Firstly, as I cited earlier, he later in the study came to "accept" the *Tilting Bowl* as no longer strange (contradictions and shifting viewpoints should not be surprising when it comes to relationality!). Secondly and more importantly, he makes the point that there is a need to assert or mind the bounds of what is normal or what could be made into a virtue, as a matter of vigilance. There is a surprising fragility of norms owing to relational ontologies. This in turn gives rise to the political realities or politics of dominance in exercising and maintaining normative values of which things play a central role, whether by reifying values, explicitly aiming to create conformity through things, or designing for exclusion. Yet it is not so simple, as both the relationality and non-neutrality of things can also provide a counter tension or destabilizing of fixed positions, as the *Tilting Bowl* suggests.

The postphenomenological response to the relationality of things is in the notion of *multistability*. This refers to the idea that any technology can be put to multiple purposes and can be meaningful in different ways to different users. Multistability refers to the multiple understandings a thing may hold dependent on the embodiment of the observer or user (Ihde 1990). Similar to Franklin's "flickering" and changing views of the *Tilting Bowl*, Ihde illustrates multistability by citing the experience of optical illusions and how when we imagine different viewpoints of the same illustration, our perception of the illustration dramatically changes while the illustration has not physically changed (see figure 5.13). For Rosenberger, multistability has two main features: (1) Multiple relations are always possible with a technology, (2) but the potential relations are limited by the material particulars of a technology, such as its "physical composition" (Rosenberger 2014, 377). Multistability adds to the discussion of relationality that I've been discussing in this chapter. It articulates clearly that the meaning of things is a matter of variant interpretations of experiential, situated, and embodied positions.

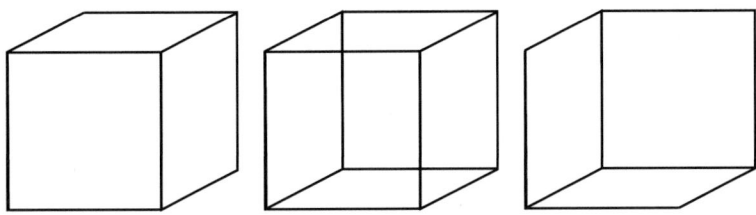

Figure 5.13
The optical illusion called the Necker Cube (middle) and its perceptual variations (left and right).

Multistability is also seen as a response to the non-neutrality or transformative nature of things. As Rosenberger and Verbeek state, this very question of non-neutral technologies or things is partly a dilemma:

> How should we understand the way that technology at once in part determines our choices and actions, and yet at the same time itself remains open to our manipulation and interpretation? How is technology both something we design and use for our own purposes, and also something that influences, restricts, leads, inclines, or controls us? (Rosenberger and Verbeek 2015, 25)

In the prologue, I discussed *Being the Machine*, a portable digital fabrication system that guides people to make physical forms rather than simply fabricating or printing the forms on their behalf (Devendorf and Ryokai 2015). The idea and design of *Being the Machine* is informed by Tim Ingold (2011), who argues against what he sees as a *hylomorphic* view of making, in which ideal forms are manifest through inert matter. Hylomorphism originates with Aristotle, who saw things as primarily representations of the mind from which passive matter could be shaped to reproduce. In opposition, Ingold argues that making is non-hylomorphic, a combination of active materials and ongoing forces in which a shape or form emerges as a matter of process and flow. Inspired by Ingold, Laura Devendorf and her colleagues saw in non-hylomorphism the "framing of materials as entities to be harnessed and adapted" rather than facilitators of preexisting ideas of form (Devendorf et al. 2016, 173). The process they created aimed to bring attention to the emergence of form making with lively matter (see figure 5.2). *Being the Machine* also emphasizes the relationality of things. If we look at it as a thing, the "machine's" relationship decenters the user as central in the making or in full control. Devendorf and Ryokai see trust and control as key determinants in the experiences of *Being the Machine*. Designing the machine "to act on the user rather than materials directly" (Devendorf and Ryokai 2015, 2485) creates a relationship whereby the user is orchestrating not fully controllable dynamics rather than commanding the machine to act on its behalf (Devendorf et al. 2016). Devendorf and Ryokai report that the various makers and users of *Being the Machine* experienced different "machines" or interpreted them differently, some even seeing the machine as a creative collaborator. In many respects, the loss of predictability is a gain in surprising and unexpected insights and expressions. *Being the Machine* is multistable and bound to our particular subjectivities while also shaping and positioning our notions of self.

Relatedly, it can be argued that our subjectivities are "saddled with a socially and historically situated perspective from which things appear with meaning and relevance" (Rosenberger 2014, 386). In this sense, in a human-thing relation there are neither "innocent" things nor "detached and disinterested" human subjects (Rosenberger 2014, 386). In relationality or multistability, we can assume that our viewpoint is embodied and enmeshed in this world, perspectival, subject to failure, limited in knowing, prone to bias, and blinded by privilege. And so any variant meaning of things can be seen as political. Things are open to constant shaping or fixing toward normative values in ways that are not always apparent. We encountered this in chapter 4, in the discussion of the assembly of human-things at the traffic intersection of Goudseweg and Vrije Nesse, in which the human-car is more dominant in its shaping of other human-things. Through the lens of multistability, Rosenberger describes the convergence of design and policy that together enacts programmatic norms of what is public urban space that excludes the unhoused or homeless. Specifically, he focuses on what he refers to as *callous objects*—the design of public devices such as garbage cans, ledges, fences, and signage that discourage or severely restrict undesirable stabilities or uses (Rosenberger 2017). Others have referred to this phenomenon as *unpleasant design* (Savičić and Savić 2013) or *hostile architecture* (Kohlstedt 2018).

One such callous object is the public bench—specifically, what Rosenberger calls a "sleep-prevention bench" (Rosenberger 2014, 2017). The public bench like other things is multistable. In Rosenberger's analysis of multistability, he calls our attention to the idea of a *dominant stability*. The dominant stability of a bench is for sitting, such as a bench at a bus stop. The bus stop bench appears as a "transparent embodiment relation" such that an able-bodied daily commuter can readily sit on it. Additionally, Rosenberger invokes his concept of *sedimentation* to further elaborate on dominant stabilities. In this case, through "force of habit" or "resiliency," a particular stability can become "deeply sedimented" to the point that our daily commuter sits at the bench unthinkingly each morning (Rosenberger 2014, 376). As we would expect, there are other stabilities of a public bench. One that offers a different embodied relation is the bench as a place to lie down and sleep, especially if you are homeless or unhoused or, for that matter, not well or simply tired. The bench-as-seat is dominant whereas the bench-as-bed is an alternative stability. At this particular intersection of dominant and alternative stabilities, the callous object emerges as an enforcement of policy through concrete and material adjustments that fix the dominant or desired stability by erasing the alternative or undesired stability. Enacted from positions of authority or dominance, callous objects are effective and well-designed solutions to foreclose undesirable alternatives. The "sleep-prevention bench" is a redesign of a bench with uneven surfaces or protrusions that prevent someone from lying across the seat of the bench. More often than not, these additions are minimal, decorative, even playful, thus hiding or distracting from the callous nature by which things are diminished in their multiplicity to enforce a dominant stability (see figure 5.14).

Rosenberger's analysis of multistability brings together Latour's theories of Actor Network Theory (ANT) with postphenomenology that situates the postphenomenological notion of multistability within a network of human and nonhuman actors.[1] In ANT terms, the protrusions and interrupted

Figure 5.14
Public benches as *callous objects* in London (top left), New York City (top right), New Orleans (bottom left), and Philadelphia (bottom right).
Source: Courtesy of Robert Rosenberger; photos by Robert Rosenberger.

Things Are Relational and Vital   145

surfaces would be seen as *material inscriptions* that carry out the delegated task of preventing people from sleeping on the benches (Akrich 1992). What multistability brings to this discussion is how things can be at the ready, so to speak, to enforce one stability over another. For example, bodily and perceptual considerations reveal how stabilities are structured by transparency in embodied relations and the degree to which one becomes accustomed to the embodiment relation over time, or *sedimentation*. Rosenberger describes how stabilities can be formed or changed through such *bodily comportment and habits*. A second form of structuring that he refers to is stability's *role within a program*, in which the multistability of a thing assembles different associations for different actors that can lead to different programs of action (i.e., one for those at the margins versus one for those at the center). And thirdly, there are physical alterations or adjustments that make a particular stability more readily available and dominant; alternatively, a thing can be tailored to shed light on other stabilities. Rosenberger referred to this feature as *concrete tailoring* (Rosenberger 2014).

Callous objects point to a program of concrete tailoring to enforce and exclude in order to fix norms and maintain dominant stabilities at the expense of a marginalized group. Conversely, as stated earlier, related counterfactual and defamiliarization/disidentification strategies can create counter tensions to norms or explicitly enact a program critical of norms or dominant stabilities. In the prologue to chapter 5, I described the *Obscura 1C Digital Camera* by James Pierce and Eric Paulos, which can capture photos, videos, and audio recordings and is encased in concrete. As a result, in order to access the digital captures of the camera, the camera enclosure must be physically broken apart. As the authors state, the camera "inhibits access to its content to offer a digital experience based on uncertainty, patience, and surprise" (Pierce and Paulos 2015, 2103). *Obscura 1C Digital Camera* is a literal concrete tailoring of digital cameras that unravels our embodied use and habits with similar devices to make way for a different program of "counterfunctionality" in which inhibited and limited use, along with absent functionality, are seen as desirable. The work emphasizes this alternate stability and suggests its desirability in comparison to dominant stabilities or interpretations of digital devices as immediate, accessible, and in our control.

Rosenberger's analysis of multistability offers a structure to the relationality of things without being foundational. Multistability helps answer the earlier question of how we can simultaneously design and use things for our purposes while things themselves shape, limit, or control us beyond our aims or intentions (Rosenberger and Verbeek 2015). While things cannot be reduced to being a single and independent entity, we can temporarily shape them to our purposes in and through the concrete materializations of design. These material manipulations (that can include manipulation of software or virtual features as well) interact with probable habituation and embodiment. Further, these material configurations are neither stabilizing nor destabilizing on their own; rather, their material configurations and sedimented use wittingly or unwittingly "enroll" things into programs of dominance, such as the bench-as-seat, or alternative programs, such as bench-as-bed, bench-as-table, bench-as-stage, bench-as-ladder, bench-as-roof, bench-as-hiding place, bench-as-memorial, bench-as-perch, and so on. These programs enroll multistable things along with other human and nonhuman actors—commuters, the unhoused, city officials, police, policies, bus shelters, parks, grieving families, work lunches, and so on—as a product of multistability. This relationality positions things within struggles of political dominance and countermovements, territorializing and deterritorializing, habitual sedimentation, and counterfactual/defamiliarizing strategies aimed at fixing, emphasizing, or revealing stabilities. It is in this way that things and their relationality shape us, shifting in and out of possibilities in ways that offer a multiplicity of abilities and restrictions only limited by the embodiment of things and us. And so, in the relationality of things, we can never take one stability over another for granted despite our best or worst efforts.

The relationality of things is always open to critical speculation and new collective imaginings. As Braidotti (2013, 89) explains, "Feminist thinkers like Moira Gatens and Genevieve Lloyd (1999) argue that socially embedded and historically grounded changes require a qualitative shift of our 'collective imaginings,' or a shared desire for transformations." Relatedly, in discussing the suppression of the political dimension of things as a matter of conformity and enforcement, what Rosenberger (2017) calls "political occlusion," he quotes Linda Martin Alcoff, who refers to ways of seeing and challenging norms through "contradictory perceptions" and "multiple forms of the gaze" (Rosenberger 2017, 56).

This brings us back to the opening example of the *Tilting Bowl* that was explained in this chapter's prologue as a *material speculation* (Wakkary et al. 2015). Material speculations adopt these contradictory and multiple ways of looking in the form of counterfactual or defamiliarizing strategies to not only analyze the relationality of things but to creatively investigate the multiplicity of things. Counterfactual artifacts like the *Tilting Bowl* sit on the *actual* side of the boundary between actual and possible worlds, or purposely inhabit the liminal space between dominant and alternative stabilities, in this sense making visible new ontological perspectives. A counterfactual artifact not only opens up speculation on the thing but on its conditions as well. When encountering a material speculation, potential reasoning would include asking not only "what is this thing" but also "what are the conditions for its existence" (e.g., the systemic, infrastructural, behavioral, ideological, political, economic, and moral reasons for being). Material speculation probes the relationality of things and the conditions bound to them. Following Braidotti (2013) and Alcoff (2006), there is an opening to consider things in their collective multiplicity (extending beyond a matter of dominant or alternative) or a minoritarian stance in which things can help to shape.

The assumption that things are relational establishes things as having the following features: Multiple stabilities are always in effect with things; the possible stabilities are limited by the material configurations or particulars of things; and stabilities are interpreted and situated within human-thing assemblages and their programs. The interpretive positions from which stabilities of things are understood, acted on, or simply assumed, are as unfixed and dynamic as the things themselves.

The Vitality of Things

In explaining what I mean by a thing, I started with the idea that things and humans are fundamentally interconnected. Things are a part of our different human subjectivities, uniquely extending and shaping who and what we are in profound ways that are transformative, like a prosthetic arm, a concrete camera, a facial prosthetic, or an illuminated shirt. Things are also transformative alongside humans in relation to other things in networks or assemblages that make them dynamic, open to change, and difficult to see as a whole, like traffic signals at an intersection or the ever-changing assemblies of plastic residue swirling within the Pacific Ocean. So far in this chapter, I have discussed the relationality of things that defy the notion of a thing as a fixed single entity; rather, a thing is open to a multiplicity of relationalities and interpretations. In the remainder of this chapter, I will discuss the last feature in the nomadic practice of designing things—*things are vital*. I will describe the way things have a certain aliveness through forms of intentionality and agentic capacities. This liveliness of things emanates from the way they direct themselves at the world in particular ways and the inherent forces that are part of their matter, form, and the assemblies they become enrolled in.

In chapter 1, I introduced the idea of the vitality of things by drawing on Jane Bennett's analysis of the massive power failure in the Northeastern United States and Canada in 2003. As discussed, the Northeast blackout of 2003 showed a distributed agency across the assemblage of the electrical power grid in which humans and nonhumans could be seen as equally contributing to the blackout. The power grid is viewed as an assemblage in which "very active and powerful nonhumans: electrons, trees, wind, fire, electromagnetic fields" (Bennett 2010, 25) form part of a system that can be seen to be functional but not without breakdowns as with a power failure. Despite this, the fullness of knowing how a system like an electrical grid operates (which includes how it ceases to operate) is limited, yet it can reliably (most of the time) be put to the purpose of distributing power. The power failure or how the system failed revealed this notion that a thing—and we can call the electric grid a thing—operates or has a life to it, so to speak, and much of that life happens in ways that we can only get glimpses of or partly understand and predict in detail. As Ihde argues, technologies (or things) can never completely disappear to become fully transparent to us, but it is also clear that things never fully appear to us. We can say that things partly disappear or withdraw from our perception, as is evident in Ihde's *embodied relation* (Ihde 1990) or Verbeek's *hybrid intentionality* (Verbeek 2008), or that there is a "leaky distinction" between organism and machines (Haraway 1985) or "viscous porosity" between humans and environment (Tuana 2008). Philosophically, I will trace this idea of vitalism in things through the co-constitution of us and things, in which things withdraw from us because of their own intentionality toward the world, to a more radical monistic view of co-constitution that is better described as mutual becoming, in which humans and nonhumans are flows of matter in assemblages that can be incoherent, porous, dynamic, and contingent. All tracings point to a decided intermingling of human and nonhuman vitalism.

In the chapter 5 prologue, I discussed another material speculation called *Morse Things*, a set of Internet-enabled ceramic bowls and cups that are decidedly simpler than an electrical grid but that send messages designed to find other *Morse Things* on the Internet. Like most of our studies and in keeping with a material speculation approach, we asked several people to live with and speculate on the experience of the *Morse Things*. In one study, we asked technologists, artists, and designers, because we believed they had the experience and abilities to represent or imagine a perspective of life as a thing. We also asked our participants to design or create concepts of other things that could live with and interact with the *Morse Things* as another way of getting at a thing perspective. In many respects, a human-centered approach to design aims to close the gap between humans and technologies in order for technologies like the Internet of Things (IoT) to better serve human needs. Yet, what might a human-centered approach hide with respect to the relations we have with technology? Our adoption of a thing-centered approach in the *Morse Things* project began with this question. Stated in the positive, what might be revealed in the relations we have with technology through a thing-centered approach to IoT? In this way, the study focused on revealing the gap between humans and things rather than closing the gap.

Similar to the *Tilting Bowl*, the *Morse Things* are counterfactual, engaging relations to things by way of defamiliarization. So, on the one hand, the things as bowls and cups readily became part of the sedimented use of eating, drinking, storing items, and so on, like any other cup or bowl. However, this sedimentation is unsettled by the occasional sound of Morse code messages being sent to seemingly no one or no "thing" in particular and without any relation to human actions. The Morse code messaging mirrors the opacity or partial transparency of the vitality of things. Morse code is incomprehensible to most people, but it is learnable. With *Morse Things* we translated the messages for Twitter, but even with the translation of a given message, the fuller apprehension of the message and what the *Morse Things* are at that given moment is still only partial. As a result, there is the sense that something is going on with the *Morse Things*, what we can call a form of intentionality, and specifically what Verbeek sees as a technological or *composite intentionality*.

In chapter 4, I discussed at length the form of *mediated intentionality* as a matter of the transformative nature of things, in which it can be said that human intentionality works through things or technologies (Ihde 1990;

Verbeek 2008). In this chapter, with respect to the vitality of things, I draw on another form of intentionality, *composite intentionality*, as described by Verbeek that arises when technological intentionality and human intentionality are combined. For example, radio telescopes create visualizations of distant stars by seeing radiation that we cannot see. For Verbeek, composite intentionality makes accessible "ways in which technology 'experience' the world" (Verbeek 2008, 393). In *Morse Things*, we can clearly see technological intentionality at work in that the emphasis is on how the *Morse Things* "experience" the world as connecting with other things on a computational network.

In the case of the *Morse Things*, this form of intentionality is in large part by design. For example, the ostensible goal of the *Morse Things* is to express a thing-centered perspective through the animations of algorithms fed by the actions of the *Morse Things*, independent of any human interaction or human data. In this way, the aliveness of the *Morse Things* appears as glimpses of the intentionality of algorithms and network technologies, emphasized by the less than scrutable sounds of the Morse code messages. In contrast to Verbeek, the *composite intentionality* in this case is problematized or made more complicated. That is, the bringing together of human intentionality and technological intentionality in the *Morse Things* is not so easily resolved or clearly focused. The liveliness of the *Morse Things* (technological intentionality) is intermingled with norms of use of cups and bowls (human intentionality) in ways that don't easily align. This disjuncture created a range of reflections by our study participants. Within this unsettled composite intentionality, reflections shifted to an uneasy tension or even embrace of the idea that much about the *Morse Things* was unknown to them or *felt* unknown. This partial knowing and glimpses of aliveness gave the *Morse Things* a partial autonomy that was expressed through comparisons to other things, companion species, and people. For example, the *Morse Things* were seen to be like lost socks:

> Those are things that are in our homes and they are just, they're there. I suppose that's why I went to that space because, although we think of bowls as functioning in a particular way—we put things in it—as another type of entity that has a digital life, it wasn't functional. It was like the lost socks. We have an object that actually functions, physically, but we have an object that is just there.

Morse Things were also described as being like cats or teenagers in a household, in that a pet owner or parent does not quite know what's going on with either the companion or kin species and this not knowing is accepted as being okay: "And there is something kind of nice about not knowing, . . . but with a bowl, that's where it sort of gets strange."

In our studies, the participants were keenly aware that the *Morse Things* were designed to bring out the "strange" in things. As one participant succinctly stated: "You are playing with our assumptions." Similar to the *Tilting Bowl*, the counterfactual and defamiliarizing strategies are ways to emphasize or reveal aspects of things that are present but often overlooked. Just as the *Tilting Bowl* emphasized the relationality of things rather than causing it, the *Morse Things* emphasized the vitality of things rather than causing it. In this way, all things are vital. In a funny twist, the surprise at the indifference of the *Morse Things* is a result of the emphasizing or amplifying of its liveliness through making present its technological intentionality or the animation of the ceramic bowls and cups through algorithms and sound. That typical ceramic bowls or cups appear to us as indifferent or "unknowing" in the world is not at all a surprise since they are seen as inanimate. However, it would be a mistake to see aliveness exclusively as things animated or having technological features (in the digital or computational sense) that in some way mimics human agency (*callous objects* are a good example). The *Morse Things* aimed to emphasize the particularities of the vitality of nonhumans. The study as a result highlighted both shared and not shared vitality between humans and nonhumans like IoT ceramic bowls and cups, pets, and lost socks. Accounting for the lost socks in this list of things takes us beyond animated forms, technologies, and companion species as vital things.

Another way to refer to vitality is what Diana Coole (2005) describes as *agentic capacities*, which is a redefining of agency that Coole derives from phenomenological intentionality in which agency is embodied and extends into the world. Like Merleau-Ponty (1962), she rejects, as a matter of phenomenological intentionality, the idea that agency is best described as human autonomy and moral reasoning. Coole's view is that agency is grounded in our bodily lifeworld that is messy, imperfect, and emergent and therefore impossible to contain. In this way, she argues that agency is better defined as a spectrum of agentic capacities (Coole 2005). Bennett's idea of vibrant matter extends the idea of agentic capacities to include nonhumans or "vital materialities and the human and nonhuman assemblages they form" (Bennett 2010, 30). This is evident in her analysis of the 2003

Northeast blackout. For Coole and Bennett and others, matter itself (not just the form that matter takes) is seen as "a co-constituting force" (Wingrove 2016, 461). Coole would refer to the ceramic Morse Thing, the teenager, or the lost sock as a "provisional concentration of agentic capacities that acquire more or less coherence and duration, depending on their context" (Coole 2005, 135). In this light, vitality is equally at the level of matter that can be formless and at the level of matter that has taken a form like a cat or ceramic bowls. Further, vitality is also at the level of the social arrangement of matter and forms like assemblages of humans and nonhumans, for vitality (or agentic capacities) courses through matter, forms, and assemblages.

And so, vitality is not exclusive to forms or shaped entities. Ingold argues that theorists such as Latour tend to focus on the "agency of objects" at the expense of considering the "vitality of materials," describing the world as being at a constant boil, simmering in endless transformation like an active kitchen or alchemist's lab (Ingold 2011, 213). The making of things occurs in the practices of builders, gardeners, cooks, alchemists, and painters who know better than to impose form on material but aim to gather diverse materials to combine and redirect the flow and movement in anticipation of what might emerge, as Ingold noted:

> For makers have to work in a world that does not keep still until the job is completed, and with materials that have properties of their own and are not necessarily predisposed to fall into the shapes required of them, let alone to stay in them indefinitely. (Ingold 2010, 93)

For Bennett, matter also holds a formative power that is integral to all matter:

> Instead of a formative power detachable from matter, artisans (and mechanics, cooks, builders, cleaners, and anyone else intimate with things) encounter a creative materiality with incipient tendencies and propensities, which are variably enacted depending on the other forces, affects, or bodies with which they come into close contact. (Bennett 2010, 56)

To the classical designers, this is a familiar description of designing with materials. Donald Schon famously characterized "designing as a conversation with the materials of a situation." Design for Schon is a matter of indeterminacy and uncontrollable forces as a product of its embodied and situated nature in which a designer engages in a reflective conversation with "materials of a situation" that "talk-back" to the designer (Schon 1984, 78–79). Relatedly, Lars Spuybroek talks about "the sympathy of things," in which there is a deep correspondence between objects, matter, and us (Spuybroek 2012). In this "sympathy," there is a feeling of things in the way they orient themselves toward each other, as in the way a hinge "likes" a door by the way it mimics its flatness by lying against it (Spuybroek 2017).

Bennett articulates vibrant matter as "quivering, evanescence, or an indefinite or nonpurposive suspense. This vibratory vitality precedes, or subsists within, or is simply otherwise than, formed bodies" (Bennett 2010, 55). Drawing on Deleuze and Guattari (1987), she sees the vitality of matter and things as not quite spatial or bodily, meaning that we mistakenly view aliveness or vitality as bodies that act and move in space (i.e., are visibly animated). Returning to the spectrum of agentic capacities, animated bodies in space, like the ceramic cups and bowls of the *Morse Things*, are only one modality of vitality. Bennett wants to equally emphasize the formless or invisible of what the monist philosopher Spinoza calls "unformed particles" or that Deleuze and Guattari call "bodies without organs" (Bennett 2010, 55). This philosophical grounding of vibrant matter in monism is practical and purposeful in a posthuman context by freeing matter from disembodied reasoning and human mastery:

> The aim here is to rattle the adamantine chain that has bound materiality to inert substance and that has placed the organic across the chasm from the inorganic. The aim is to articulate the elusive idea of a materiality that is *itself* heterogeneous, itself a differential of intensities, itself a life. In this strange, vital materialism, there is no point of pure stillness, no indivisible atom that is not itself aquiver with virtual force. (Bennett 2010, 57)

The vitality of ceramics was naturally in force in The *Morse Things* and *Tilting Bowl*. For example, ceramics in clay form has a plastic memory because of its material composition and structure. The plastic memory in clay is a characteristic of a clay-water interaction in which once a force is removed it may return to its shape. As a result, clay has the tendency to "physically remember" both intentional and unintentional changes to its form or plastic shape, even after the shape has been corrected. This plastic memory releases during thermal change, which occurs in the firing processes that can cause the ceramic to unexpectedly deform or crack (Andrade, Al-Qureshi, and Hotza 2011). Aside from such obvious deformations, ceramics are constantly changing shape or deforming in ways that happen very slowly and temporally at a nonhuman scale. Similarly, glass also changes over time, remaining viscous, but again at an incredibly slow and imperceptible rate. However, such matter as clay, as embodied in the world, goes beyond material properties to become lively enactments with other bodies, matter, and forces. For example, "clay could act 'dusty' when a miner first digs it out of the ground, 'plastic' when mixed with water, and 'rigid' when exposed to high heat in a kiln" (Dew and Rosner 2018, 3).

Seeing *Morse Things* as lively enactments can begin with the sound of Morse code messages, generated by voltage changes in a circuit that vary slightly with the current flow from the battery. The electric signals are sent to a vibration speaker or transducer that creates the sounds by vibrating or resonating through the ceramics and any other materials the ceramics are in contact with, like the surface of a table or someone's hand. This material form of the *Morse Things* determines the "proclivities" of the sound of the Morse code message that defies replication and repeatability (Ingold 2011). Additionally, there can be a materiality to the machine learning that structures the intervals, duration, and character counts of the messages as a result of rules, rewards, and assumptions programmed into the algorithms. These algorithms perform over the Internet enacting the IoT, a promised vitalism of services and data. While in the home, the perceived liveliness of a particular Morse Thing, whether the Morse code is heard often or not, can in either case endear itself to a person living with it or perturb a nearby cat.

In the spring of 2019, I visited the studio of the textile artist Claudy Jongstra in Spannum in Friesland in the Netherlands.[2] Jongstra is known for her fashion design and large-scale artworks made of wool. As I discussed in the chapter 5 prologue, she is part of the *Burgundian Black Collaboratory* researching and "reworking" historical recipes of what is known as Burgundian black. Natural dye practices have largely faded since the use of synthetic processes in the late nineteenth century to the point that, as Jongstra says, "we are so distant from these making practices that we don't know anymore."[3] In Jongstra's hands, the "reworking" of the medieval recipes begins with the translations from old Flemish and Italian recipes, which have instructions like "pray four to six times as a way to keep time," and engaging in a deeply embodied and lived set of practices of growing and sourcing materials, felting, and processes for dyeing. In Jongstra's case, she raises the Drenthe Heath sheep for her wool and grows the vegetables and plant matter for the dyes. While visiting her studio, she explained and demonstrated her making of Burgundian black dye. She used walnut shells or alder bark to prepare the wool or silk for dyeing in what's known as mordant. The dye itself was made from either fermented Asian indigo or locally grown woad leaves to create an indigo bath. The indigo dyed wool was overdyed with a red dye made from the root of a madder plant grown in her nearby garden (see figure 5.15). Depending on the weather and humidity, fermenting the indigo takes about three months if watered every three to four days. She explained that the madder plant root is a much longer affair. The root itself is typically best when it is at least three to five years old, though upwards of eleven to twelve years old is not uncommon and is desirable. The root itself is then dried for at least two years. Jongstra pointed out that it makes a difference if she uses water from a well, rain, or the sea, and even the flow of the gas for heating the indigo bath can create slight variances and differences of shades of black. She quietly explained that "everything that seems irrelevant is relevant" as she slid felt wool into an indigo bath.

Figure 5.15
Asian indigo, root of a madder plant, and fermented woad leaves used in the Burgundian black dye produced by Claudy Jongstra's studio. All plants were grown locally in her garden near the studio.

Jongstra's Burgundian black dyed wools are lively enactments of matter that have followed and stretched through human time to defy the idea of matter as having mere material properties. Burgundian black at one time held the vitality of elite power and the assemblies of imperial wealth and politics, while at the same time it was reliant on the vibrancy of fermented indigo leaves, mordant, water, and twelve-year-old woad roots.

The agentic capacities or vitalism I have been discussing, informed by Bennett, Coole, Braidotti, and others, is not attributable to a self-contained agent or subject; rather, it is distributive and unreliably purposeful and often incoherent. Braidotti sees vitality as reinstating to matter its "self-organizing capacities" (Braidotti 2012, 16); Coole suggests that agentic capacities appear as a "chiaroscuro," illuminated in parts while other parts are lost in the dark (Coole 2005, 126); and Jongstra sees the most irrelevant as relevant.

Aiming to make distributed agency in vibrant matter, a "swarm of affiliates," more intelligible, Bennett creates a range of characteristics of agency that includes *efficacy*, *trajectory*, and *causality* (Bennett 2010, 31). These characteristics are useful in elaborating on the vitality of things. *Efficacy* can be understood as the ability to create something new through agency. However, the type of agency discussed here is distributed and does not have a subject as its root cause, so efficacy is seen more in its "contours" (Bennett 2010, 32). The need is to identify the "swarm of vitalities" at play and the kind of relations between the different vitalities. Not unlike composite intentionality between humans and machines, human actions can be seen to be part of the swarm of vitalities that are "always in competition and confederation with many other strivings"; in other words, human vitality or agentic capacity is one among many vitalities that are working both in contradiction to and in concert with each other. While humans may be involved, it is being together with nonhumans as interwoven effects that may result in less definitive outcomes than we desire. The combined distributed agency or efficacy has the "power to make a difference," though one "possessed by nonhuman bodies too" (Bennett 2010, 32). The *Morse Things* display efficacy in the Morse code messages that originate with execution of programming code, voltage changes, and resonance of material surfaces, even translations in Twitter, but then merge together with other sounds, movements, or tweets to become interpreted alongside other lively enactments of a given moment.

Things Are Relational and Vital

The second aspect of distributive agency is *trajectory*. Here Bennett describes assemblages as having a drive that gives direction without suggesting "purposiveness." Trajectory is the directionality or movement toward somewhere, even if that somewhere is "obscure or even absent." In traditional agency, this is understood as purposiveness or being goal directed; however, Bennett sees in agency more of a direction than a destination. Citing the philosopher Jacques Derrida, trajectory is a "promissory note" that will never be redeemed. For Derrida, this "straining forward" is a phenomenon of life, or as Bennett writes, "things in the world appear to us at all only because they tantalize and hold us in suspense, alluding to a fullness that is elsewhere, to a future that, apparently, is on its way" (Bennett 2010, 32). Trajectory is evident in the *Tilting Bowl*, as the study's participants (myself included) waited on and even desired the next unpredictable tilt of the bowl. The *Tilting Bowl* becomes defined by the expectant time between tilts. The trajectory of the *Obscura 1C Digital Camera* is in the material of concrete and its form as the enclosure. It anticipates and promises a moment of its own destruction as "patience and surprise" (Pierce and Paulos 2015), something more than its actual end (see figure 5.16). *Photobox*, a design that I discussed in chapter 2 equally emphasizes a trajectory of digital data that is felt as "anticipation" (Odom et al. 2014).

The third and last characteristic that Bennett adds to vibrant matter that is here applied to things is the most elusive: *causality*. This causality is not the type of billiard ball or pool ball causality, in which events are directly attributable to prior events or what is known as "cause and effect." For Bennett, causality lacks this kind of efficiency since it is emergent, affecting in ways nonlinear and fractal. Further, causality in distributed agency is the process by which cause and effect intermingle, even doubling in on themselves in complex feedback loops that are impossible to trace, let alone predict. According to Bennett, "emergent causality places the focus on the process itself as an actant, as itself in possession of degrees of agentic capacity" (Bennett 2010, 33). By way of illustration, Bennett cites Hannah Arendt's distinction between "origin" and "cause" in understanding the rise of totalitarianism. Determining the actants or elements that give rise to totalitarian states is more readily a matter of complex and heteronomous origins rather than definitive causes. The resulting forms or "prints" of *Being the Machine* have their origins in the intentionality of the "machine,"

Figure 5.16
A smashed-open *Obscura 1C Digital Camera*.
Source: Courtesy of James Pierce.

the performers, the material, the place of making, time of day, ambient temperature, and so on, rather than each of these in discernible degrees being the cause of the form produced.

The *Obscura 1C Digital Camera*'s concreteness emphasizes the vitality of all things. It defamiliarizes the digital camera, creating a new efficacy and, as we discussed, a trajectory that directs the thing to a moment of its destruction but naturally continues on in some new form afterward. It offers a causality or origin for the photos taken with the camera should they ever be freed from the concrete form. The *Underwater Table* from the *Mineral Accretion Factory*, discussed in the prologue, capitalizes on or "crystalizes" the vitality of things, revealing how the table grows from the seeming purposelessness of marine and mineral growth. The very trajectory is required to become a form that is resilient enough to be a table. Its origin lies in the injection of low-voltage current in the rebar substrate structure, but this cannot be mistaken for the cause of the final form. The vitality of the *Underwater Table*, which is literally alive as coral growth, raises the real ethical question of whether it should be removed from the ocean to cease living and become a table for human use.

The Characteristics of Things That Are Relational and Vital

The features that I've discussed in this chapter and in chapter 4 (*things are interconnected, things are transformative, things are relational,* and *things are vital*), come together to describe things. These features are interdependent and build on each other and inform each other. For example, the notion that things are relational is dependent on the assumption that things are interconnected. At the conclusion of chapter 4, I gave a set of characteristics of things that are interconnected and transformative that included *mediating things, embodied and immanent,* and *assemblages*. Here I round out the effort by describing characteristics of things that build on and include these previous characteristics.

Multiplicity of Things

Things are commensurate with being human and shape human actions and perceptions. However, the way they shape is relational, multistable, and situated, bound only by the materiality or embodiment of things and humans. In this way, interpretation or interpretive strategies are central to human-things. The relationality of things means things can give way to a multiplicity in which a public bench is both an urban amenity and policy enforcement. The multiplicity of things is an unavoidable condition that even emerges in the triviality of the tilt of a ceramic bowl. This relationality extends the transformative nature of things such that each situated interpretation remakes or repositions the subjects within human-things. In this way, things alter us as they themselves shift in their relations, consequences, and effects. *Being the Machine* held a multiplicity of human-thing alternatives that co-constituted maker and machine as perfectionists, collaborators, creatives, or rule makers.

Things Are Not Innocent

The multiplicity of things is not neutral, and so things can both stabilize and destabilize. Things in assemblages intricately construct normative values as one set of alternatives and can also unravel or destabilize norms to open to other sets of alternatives. The underlying multiplicity means that differently interpreted stabilities of things can provisionally fix or shape realities in ways that are not apparent, are difficult to decipher, and are more interrelated than causal. The sleep-prevention bench contributes to the marginalization of the unhoused or homeless in ways that do not cause homelessness but certainly have the effect of enforcing a certain political dominance over public space. However, through critical speculation and collective imaginings, things can offer contradictions to norms that qualitatively shift human-thing assemblages toward one trajectory or another of desired transformations.

Distributed Agency

Distributed agency of things refers to the agentic capacities that transverse a spectrum of matter, human-things, and assemblages. As a consequence, this agency is not attributable to a self-contained agent or subject; rather, it is distributive across matter in ways that are best characterized as efficacy, trajectory, and causality. What I earlier described as the technicity of things can now be seen to also be part of the more expansive vibrant matter. In vibrant matter, things are not just bound up in being human, but the very vitality that forms things is distributed across animals (human and nonhuman), things, and matter. The vitality of Burgundian black at one time was a part of the assemblages of imperial wealth and politics while interdependent with the matter of fermented indigo leaves, mordant, well water, and decades-old madder roots. In *Morse Things*, the resonance of ceramics, electric voltage, algorithmic rules, and IoT networks surface a vibrancy and sense of agency in the things. Our plastic bags and packaging swirling within the oceans break down into toxins and plastic particulates to become part of the seawater and nonmetabolizable edible matter for marine life. This distributed, perhaps even spectral agency of things emanates before, after, and during the life cycle of matter in ways that are difficult to pinpoint and take different forms of agentic qualities.

Part III: Designer

Chapter 6 Prologue: Living in a Prototype, Greenscreen Dress, Supersurface, and Children Village

In this prologue I discuss design and design research cases that enlighten and inform the discussion that follows in chapter 6, on the designer of things as a biography. I begin with two autobiographical design research investigations (Neustaedter and Sengers 2012), *Living in a Prototype* (Desjardins 2016; Desjardins and Wakkary 2016), and *Greenscreen Dress* (Mackey et al., "Blending Clothing and Digital Expression," 2017; Mackey et al. 2020). These investigations are longitudinal and situated first-person inquiries into the Internet of Things (IoT) and wearables. The prologue also includes architectural examples, separated by decades that help develop the understanding of the agentic capacities that bind the designer of things to things that are designed. These include Superstudio's *Supersurface* (Branzi 1984) and Aleph Zero/Marcelo Rosenbaum's *Children's Village* (Wainwright 2018).

Living in a Prototype

Living in a Prototype is a design research inquiry by Audrey Desjardins that engages the complexities and relationalities of making, transforming, and adapting the space one lives in (Desjardins 2016; Desjardins and Wakkary 2016). In detail, the study is a two-year autobiographical design research project of converting a Mercedes Sprinter van into a camper van. During this period, Desjardins and her partner reconfigured the space in a cargo van to allow activities like cooking, eating, sleeping, and entertaining during their biking and skiing trips. The research offered the opportunity to reflect, critically and in depth, on how people imagine, design, make, and repair an environment they live in. The core goal of the investigation is to interpret insights from this project in order to explore different approaches and to revisit concepts at the center of notions like home automation, smart homes, and the IoT. Toward that end, the study emphasized the role of the designer in autobiographical design, in which designers design for themselves, a do-it-yourself (DIY) or maker culture, in which the line between the user and the maker is blurred.

Autobiographical design is defined as "design research drawing on extensive, genuine usage by those creating or building the system" (Neustaedter and Sengers 2012, 514). Neustaedter and Sengers (2012) argue that successful autobiographical design occurs when the system being developed fulfills a genuine need and is lived with over a long period of time, and the designer is the user of the system. They also argue that autobiographical design research can support fast tinkering, which is the testing of real systems beyond concepts, and provide detailed and experiential understanding of the system and reveal the larger effects of a system. Relatedly, DIY enthusiasts and makers share the common practices of designing, appropriating, and transforming existing products to better fit their own needs, lifestyle, or aesthetic tastes.

In this investigation, Desjardins (2016) refers to herself and her partner as the *maker/user*, a term that invites the reader to consider a user to be simultaneously using and making (or remaking) a thing or a space, hence combining the two actions into a unique identity. In fact, the study emphasizes the interweaving of the autobiographical designer with a maker/user, because the designer embodies both the making aspect as well as the living-with aspects of the maker/user. In this way, the relationalities between designer, maker, user, dweller, materials, technologies, and environment interestingly co-mingle and co-shape the ever-changing space of the camper van (see figures 6.1 and 6.2). In chapter 6, *Living in a Prototype* anticipates in microcosm what I will describe as the *biography* of the designer in which things created cohabit the same lifeworld as the designer.

Living in a Prototype engaged with and became part of the DIY community, especially on the DIY platform *Instructables*. Desjardins and her partner documented the conversion and created DIY tutorials for the different aspects of the conversion. During the time of the research, the tutorials had close to 180,000 views and as of this writing has just over 1,000,000 views.

Greenscreen Dress

Greenscreen Dress is an exploration of wearing garments with digital display capabilities or what is known as dynamic fabric (Mackey et al., "Blending

Living in a Prototype, Greenscreen Dress, Supersurface, and Children Village 165

Figure 6.1
The van in *Living in a Prototype*.
Source: Courtesy of Audrey Desjardins.

Figure 6.2
Different possibilities for configuring the table and bed (left); a "prototype" kitchen in use (right of middle); field testing the dining table and seats (upper right); experimenting with hooks in the ceiling (lower right).
Source: Courtesy of Audrey Desjardins.

Clothing and Digital Expression," 2017). The study, led by Angella Mackey, brought together a combination of research methods including autoethnography, autobiographical design (Neustaedter and Sengers 2012), and material speculation (Wakkary et al. 2015) as a way to speculate on and experience the daily wearing of dynamic fabric. Mackey wore a variety of green garments every day for ten months and used a chroma key ("greenscreen") mobile application to turn the garments into digital displays through augmented reality (see figures 6.3 and 6.4). This approach, on a practical level, addressed the lack of readiness of embedded technologies in wearables that could be worn daily. However, during the course of the study, the actualities of the experience opened the researchers to new understandings and definitions of dynamic fabric (Mackey et al. 2020).

The study began as a speculative inquiry into the sociocultural understandings of the emerging technology. The main question being asked was, *What would it be like to wear dynamic fabric in everyday life?* To that end, Mackey's autoethnographic accounts detailed a range of experiences that included the role of social media in realizing and expressing the fashion of the garment; the evolving understanding of wardrobe as virtual patterns,

Figure 6.3
The *Greenscreen Dress* and augmented reality mobile application.
Source: Courtesy of Angella Mackey; photo by Rachel Rietdijk.

Figure 6.4
Sample images of the *Greenscreen Dress* on Instagram.
Source: Courtesy of Angella Mackey.

photographs, and videos that led to an extended understanding of textiles as digital material; and the extension of the space of her identity into the physical and virtual (Mackey et al., "Blending Clothing and Digital Expression," 2017; Mackey et al., "Designing and Wearing Dynamic Fabric," 2017). And so, in the process of materializing and living with the *Greenscreen Dress* and having placed the greenscreen system so deeply into her life, the researcher found that many aspects originally perceived as simulations of dynamic fabric became perceived as real and authentic. From that point onward, the inquiry moved to explore the hybridized nature of dynamic fabric, which opened up an understanding of digital materiality in fashion (Mackey et al. 2020).

In chapter 6, I build on *Greenscreen Dress* as another radically situated example of designing things that contribute to the concept of *biography*.

Supersurface

In chapter 3, I discussed Superstudio, an Italian architecture collective that coauthored the manifesto for the *Italian Radical Design* movement in 1966. Superstudio was founded in Florence, Italy, by Adolfo Natalini and Cristiano Toraldo di Francia. In a 1971 lecture at London's Architectural Association, Natalini expressed Superstudio's disavowal of architecture and design:

> If design is merely an inducement to consume, then we must reject design; if architecture is merely the codifying of bourgeois model of ownership and society, then we must reject architecture; if architecture and town planning is merely the formalization of present unjust social divisions, then we must reject town planning and its cities . . . until all design activities are aimed towards meeting primary needs. Until then, design must disappear. We can live without architecture. (Lang and Menking 2003, 167)

This "rejection" of design in reality became a radical departure into new territory for design that is critical, ironic, and challenging. Superstudio disassembled architecture into being immaterial while reassembling it as totalizing. What emerged were forms of critical utopias. For the 1972 exhibition *Italy: The New Domestic Landscape* at the Museum of Modern Art in New York,[1] Superstudio created an installation called *Supersurface: An Alternative Model for Life on Earth*. The installation was a six-foot cubic room of mirrored tiles that repeated itself endlessly (figure 6.5).

The critical utopia of *Supersurface: An Alternative Model for Life on Earth* is an erasure of architecture. It is aimed at a political liberation from capitalism, a reclaiming of one's autonomy and labor through a new vision for design: "the final attempt of design to act as the 'projection' of a society no longer based on work (and on power and violence, which are connected with this), but an unalienated human relationship" (Ambasz 1972, 242). Superstudio described its work as "evasion design" in which architecture was used as "obstruction" (Branzi 1984, 55). Within the cube was a terminal, several objects connected to the terminal, foliage, and other matter. These objects also repeated themselves endlessly as reflections. The installation was accompanied by a film—a series of photo-collages of natural and urban landscapes that are wholly or partially covered in an infinite, totalizing architectural grid system (figure 6.6). The designers describe *Supersurface: An Alternative Model for Life on Earth* as "a network of energy and information extending to every properly inhabitable area" (Frassinelli et al. 1972, 242)

Figure 6.5
Supersurface: An Alternative Model for Life on Earth, installation by Superstudio for the *Italy: The New Domestic Landscape* exhibition at the Museum of Modern Art (MoMA) in 1972.
Source: Superstudio and Museum of Modern Art.

that is devoid of consumer objects and production, free of human labor, open to the nomadic wandering of inhabitants in which people "live *with* objects and not *for* objects" (Frassinelli et al. 1972, 245).

Supersurface symbolizes unbuilt architecture that strives to be more in tune with the terrain and nomadic forces of the earth, including people. In chapter 6, this work helps to elaborate on the full-scale and real-time nature of things that make both designer and thing immanent and distributed.

Children Village

Children Village is housing for approximately 540 students of the Canuanã school in northern Brazil designed by the architectural firm Aleph Zero with designer Marcelo Rosenbaum (figure 6.7). The Canuanã school is a boarding school by necessity since it is located in a remote agricultural region that is

Figure 6.6
A photo-collage by Superstudio as part of *Supersurface: An Alternative Model for Life on Earth*, commissioned by MoMA.
Source: Superstudio and Museum of Modern Art.

difficult to reach, requiring lengthy trips by horse on unpaved roads (Wainwright 2018). As a consequence of the remoteness, the materials are local and mostly earth, bricks, and timber. The complex is intended to have a low-impact environmental footprint. In concept, it is a small village or cluster of buildings made of perforated breathable walls arranged to allow airflow and circulation for passive air cooling. The sleeping areas are rooms of six students assembled around courtyards and other structures including elevated walkways, play areas, learning centers, and reading spaces. The courtyards include

Living in a Prototype, Greenscreen Dress, Supersurface, and Children Village 171

Figure 6.7
The *Children Village* for the Canuanã school in northern Brazil, designed by the architectural firm Aleph Zero with designer Marcelo Rosenbaum.
Source: Leonardo Finotti.

local savannah, tropical species, and a pond with small fish (figure 6.8). The courtyards, in addition to being gathering places, reduce heat and control the humidity. They also collect rainwater and return the overflow to the nearby Javaés River.

The architects describe the *Children Village* in the following way:

> A thin, white metallic roof supported by a lightweight wood structure following a regular grid of 5,90m by 5,90m embraces the villages and common spaces. Beyond protection from sun and rain, the roof and grid set compose an intermediary space between the outside and inside, behaving as a great veranda that marks the vast horizon and frames views of the exterior and interior vegetation. The choice for glued laminated eucalyptus wood in the structural elements came from its versatility, pre-fabrication and sustainable characteristics, in response to the necessity of accelerating construction speed and minimizing hassle to the school's functioning. Likewise, stabilized earth blocks composed of local soil were chosen as the means of construction for its elimination of long distance transportation and optimal thermic properties. The material was used as enclosure in form of apparent brick walls as well as brick latticework to provide ventilation and protection to the washing areas. The brick performed technically but also

Figure 6.8
A courtyard in the *Children Village*.
Source: Leonardo Finotti.

aesthetically, much in the way the locals have been doing for a long time. Ultimately, the design for the new villages aims to increase the children's self-esteem, individuality, sense of belonging, responsibility for the environment and overall academic performance, through the dialogue with local knowledge and constructive potential. Thus, a dialogue is created between vernacular techniques and a positive model for sustainable housing. ("Aleph Zero" 2018)

In chapter 6, I discuss how *Children Village* is an example of the radical practicality in seeing things as cohabitants materially and temporally.

Chapter 6: The Designer as Biography

This chapter marks the beginning of part III of the book, with the focus shifting to the designer in the nomadic practice of designing things. In the discussion of things that occupied part II of the book, it was hopefully clear that the entanglement of humans and nonhumans underpinned the defining features of things. Things emerged as the sharing of intentionalities and agencies, the configuring of each other in assemblages, and the co-shaping of the worlds that are a part of this entanglement. The posthumanist commitments that have propelled the discussion to this point precede us to set the stage for the designer of things. And as if the reader needs reminding, this stage or foreground is shared with nonhumans. And like other nomadic practices, the *intentionality toward something* (see chapter 2) mutually constitutes the designer and the something designed. In the designing of things, the designer cohabits the world of the things designed and shares in the entanglements and distribution of agencies between humans and nonhumans. In this way, the designer of things cannot be seen to be exclusively human. So, how to describe or critically imagine the designer of designing things when freed of the assumption that a designer is exclusively human? To answer this question, a place to start is where I left off in the last chapter: the vitality of things. This vitality, a distributed agency, is a good starting point for seeing the *designing-with* or the sharing of the foreground with nonhumans that, so to speak, are as equally creative or agentic in the designing of things. The designer of things is the bringing together of agentic capacities across humans and nonhumans in ways that create things.

In my description of the designer of things, I don't plan on offering a complete and total view of the designer since that would replace my commitment to situated knowing with fanciful constructs of objectivity. That would also willfully ignore that such a view is simply not available. The vitality the human/nonhuman designer shares with all vitality is that it is largely opaque since it is distributed, nonlinear, and dramatically heterogeneous, or as Bennett states, vitality is a "nonlinear, nonhierarchical, non-subject centered mode of agency" (Bennett 2010, 33). And so, I will offer different ways to understand the designer of designing things rather than define it. This description is propositional, to be understood more in sensemaking terms than as a description of something already known or that could possibly have a readily available contour.

To that end, I propose three notions to make sense of the designer. To begin, I discuss the overarching concept of the designer as *biography*, an identifiable human and nonhuman life force (a creative entity) that constructs and inscribes itself into the world. The notion of a biography makes it clear that the *good* in designing things is the cohabiting of the designer and thing in a shared world that is accountable for what it inscribes and leaves behind in the world. Next, I also describe the designer as *force*, referring to the different agentic capacities across the assembly of the designer that helps to design things. Lastly, I describe the designer as a *speaking subject*—that is, the unique human role that is present in increasing *intensities* and at the *origins* in the designing of a thing.

Designer as Biography

I have at times described things and humans in this book as human-things to underscore their integral relationship. In this sense, a *designer* in its most basic form is an interconnected human-thing. A good example is the "hammerer" in Heidegger's analysis of the embodiment of tools, which I described in chapter 4. In Heidegger's example, the hammerer is a cobbler making shoes (Heidegger 1962); the cobbler is the designer entity of the combination of a human and a hammer. A human can be integral with a hammer, or a hammer can be integral with a human; in either sense, they together shape and assemble matter. A programmer or a team of programmers writing code cannot be conceived without a programming language, a programming environment, and the software and hardware required to make the program legible and manipulable. The same is true of an architecture team that uses parametric software and computer hardware to plan a building. However, here I want to push the entity of a designer further than what might be interpreted as a human and tool configuration.

The Designer as Biography

In chapter 3 and its prologue, I discussed Dieter Rams's *Braun Pocket Receivers* as exemplary cases of the nomadic practice of designing objects. To remind the reader, I argued that to design *objects*, as opposed to things, is to create products or conceptual designs that manifest idealized human values like beauty, longevity, or anti-consumerism (Wilson 2018). In the case of Dieter Rams, he argued for principles of good design that every object should aspire to incorporate (Rams 1995). Further, in the context of designing objects, Rams himself is exemplary of the traditional notion of the designer as a discrete agent that is exclusively human—the opposite of a designer of things. However, can Rams be separated from nonhumans used in his role as a designer? More specifically, was Rams not equally a human-thing interconnected with drafting pencils, drafting tables, thermoplastics, prototyping tools, and prototyping materials when he set out to design the *Braun Pocket Receiver T3* (see figure 3.2)? Can Rams be separated from Braun, the product company that employed him? Is Rams not part of the material science research, the portfolio of Braun products, corporate direction and strategy, design team employees, engineers, equipment, studios, buildings, sales force, distribution systems, suppliers, manufacturers, and partners like the Ulm School? If Rams were a designer of things, he would not stand alone.

One might counterargue that Rams, like all designers, is simply contextualized, embedded in a context that informs who he is as a designer. However, a designer of things is *radically situated* rather than simply contextualized. The difference is that to be radically situated describes how the designer is integral to the assemblages that make a thing and the thing itself. In this sense, the designer is not an independent human agent in the foreground of activities while related but separate nonhuman entities are relegated to the background. The human designer, like all other humans, is relational, meaning interconnected and interdependent with things and the larger assemblies that form. This is important as it signals that the human aspect of the designer cannot act independently of its nonhumanness. And further, this interdependence is extant; in large part it assumes a nonhuman temporality in which Rams is inseparable from the *Braun Pocket Receivers* or the *Braun MPZ 22 Citromatic* and will continue to be long after his life is over. Dieter Rams, if he were to be a designer of things, is bound up materially and temporally in the assemblies of Braun in ways that dictate that no other Dieter Rams designer could emerge.

I use the term *biography* to describe how the human/nonhuman designer of things is radically situated. Etymologically, the word is composed of *bios* (meaning life) and *graphe* (meaning writing)—the writing of life. I use the term postanthropocentrically. By *biography*, then, I mean the configuration of human and nonhuman life forces (*bios*) that irreversibly inscribes (*graphe*) itself by creating things in the world it cohabits. This understanding of *bios* is informed by Braidotti's concept of *zoe* (Braidotti 2002, 2012), a term that envisions the life or vitality of animals and nonhumans, in contrast to *bios*, which is laden with a privileging of life as human or anthropocentric. Braidotti decenters this anthropocentric hold by arguing for a *zoe-centered* understanding of life that is a form of *bios egalitarianism*—a way of *thinking-with*, in which the "dynamic and generative force" (or life force) centers on both humans and nonhumans (Braidotti 2016, 384). In this respect, the notion of the designer of things as a biography is intended as *zoe-centered*, such that an alternative term could easily be *zoegraphy*. Regardless, the notion of a biography is to make the designer of things accountable for what it designs into the world and what it leaves behind.

The term *biography* emphasizes that the designer is radically situated, in intra-action, or entangled within human and nonhuman lives, together with the things they produce. In the prologue to chapter 6, I described *Living in a Prototype* (Desjardins and Wakkary 2016), in which Audrey Desjardins and her partner reconfigure a camper van (see figures 6.1 and 6.2). One way to consider *Living in a Prototype* is that it is an exercise in the type of radically situated designer of things that forms a designer as biography. Specifically, it is an investigation into the evolving mutual constitution through design of a thing, the "camper van." The human-thing consists of the "campers" (namely, Desjardins and her partner) and the Mercedes Sprinter van. Desjardins calls herself and her partner the "maker/user" to signal that they design the van as they inhabit it in ways we (including me as coauthor) called "reciprocal shaping" (Desjardins and Wakkary 2016, 5278)—she and her partner shape the van, and the van simultaneously shapes them. In other words, the more the van is configured into a particular "camper van," they in turn are configured into a particular type of "van camper." Desjardins and her partner, like Rams, are bound up in the assemblies of nonhuman and human-things that comprise the designer biographically. Desjardins and I referred to the design of the camper van as *autobiographical design*, building on the concept by Carman Neustaedter

The Designer as Biography

and Phoebe Sengers (2012) as explained in the prologue to this chapter. Desjardins elaborated further on autobiographical design, arguing that it is a central strategy in different approaches to designing (Desjardins and Ball 2018) rather than a marginal or ancillary approach as originally framed (Neustaedter and Sengers 2012).

A good example of this central use of autobiographical design is Angella Mackey's *Greenscreen Dress* (Mackey et al., "Blending Clothing and Digital Expression," 2017; Mackey et al., "Designing and Wearing Dynamic Fabric," 2017), also discussed in the prologue to this chapter. Mackey engaged in a material speculation (Wakkary et al. 2015) that allowed her to investigate the experience of wearing dynamic fabric in her everyday life. In her study, she adopted an autoethnographic analysis of her daily wearing of a green dress and green garments for ten months using a chroma key ("greenscreen") mobile application to transform her garments into a dynamic and changing digital display. Autobiographical design is a central strategy as the very idea of what is dynamic fabric arose out of Mackey living-with the *Greenscreen Dress*.

Autobiographical design, in the extended sense of being central to designing of things, is the antecedent form of designer as biography, in that it radically situates designing into the biography or life of the human and nonhuman designer. It also inextricably connects the things designed to that biography by making clear that things created cohabit the lifeworld of the designer. Thinking of the designer as a biography points to a particular ethos of designing things. This ethos is to fully know that to design while cohabiting this biosphere is to be inseparable from the thing that is designed.[1] This means that to design is to add something new to the biography of the designer that created it. The new interconnection or addition to the assemblage through design creates a togetherness between the biography and the things designed:

> An important reason for needing a new grounded, embodied, and embedded subject has to do with the second half of the crucial sentence: "we" are in this together. What this refers to is the cartography as a cluster of interconnected problems that touches the structure of subjectivity and the very possibility of the future as a sustainable option. "We" are in this together, in fact enlarges the sense of collectively bound subjectivity to nonhuman agents, from our genetic neighbors the animals to the earth as biosphere. "We," therefore, is a non-anthropocentric construct, which refers to a commonly shared territory or habitat ("this"). (Braidotti 2012, 121–122)

I am not using the term *biography* to describe a collection of past events of a given life. I am also not using the term to explain outcomes of that life. Rather, I use the term *biography* to be accountable for the life constructed in part through the thing designed. In this way, the designer and thing share a biography and so are inseparable. In addition to being nonanthropocentric in its meaning, this form of accountability calls for understanding a biography as becoming or immanent. This means that a biography is an ongoing process of inscribing and reinscribing itself. In describing the autobiographical design process of *Living in a Prototype*, Desjardins and I described the reciprocal shaping as a constant dynamic that has no end or that the camper van (and van camper) is "invariably unfinished."[2] In this sense, a biography is a material process that is concrete and grounded in a particular lifeworld while always in the process of forming the biography. The theorist Manuel DeLanda describes the historical processes at work in an assemblage that relates to biographies. Biographies include the historical processes within an assembly of a designer, making clear that a biography does not simply appear but is formed and reformed historically as an ongoing process:

> All of these entities are assemblages, their defining emergent properties produced by their interacting parts, and therefore contingent on the occurrence of the requisite interactions. The historicity and individuality of all the assemblages forces us as materialists to confront the question of the historical processes which produced or brought into being any given assemblage. (DeLanda 2016, 140)

DeLanda describes the biographical aspects of assemblages as "historical processes" and as having "individuality." DeLanda's discussion of the "historicity" and "individuals" in assemblages is a part of his unpacking of Deleuze and Guattari's ideas of assemblage (DeLanda 2016). Here, he draws on Deleuze's concept of *individuation* (Deleuze 1995). For Deleuze, individuation is a process of "undergoing" to become an individual or it is the dynamic of forming or coming into being. In this respect, a biography is an extant and ongoing process of living that folds and unfolds. The end of this process is the end of the biography, though the biography typically lives on much longer in its nonhuman aspects than human aspects.

In summary, the idea of biography shows the designer of things to be a configuration of human and nonhuman life forces (*bios*) that become irreversibly inscribed (*graphe*) in a cohabited world by creating things. In this way, the designer of things and the things it designs share a biography. They are forever entangled together within the lifeworld they helped form

The Designer as Biography

and cohabit. The concept of a biography is intended to make the designer of things accountable for what it designs into the world and what it leaves behind—hopefully ensuring that any judgment of the value of a designer is not separated from the lifeworld it contributed to through designing. Biographies are of the present, informed by actions of the past but always in the process of forming, even once its human aspects have ceased to exist.

Designer as Force

I have described the designer of things as a biography of shared vitality between humans and nonhumans. Delving deeper, a designer as biography is animated by the human and nonhuman life forces that design things. To better describe this force, I draw on the discussion of agentic capacities from chapter 5—specifically, Bennett's description of agentic capacities as qualities of *efficacy* and *trajectory* (Bennett 2010, 31). Efficacy is the creative force of agency, the ability to create new things; trajectory is the direction of the force, a movement or progression without suggesting "purposiveness."

With this in mind, I would like to revisit the discussion in chapter 4 of the traffic intersection of Goudseweg and Vrije Nesse that I described as an assemblage of human-things. This traffic intersection—namely, the traffic lights, pedestrian lights, bicycle lights, bicycles, mobile phones, cars, drivers, pedestrians, cyclists, and mobile phone users—has its own agentic capacities. This agency can be said to have made concrete or brought into reality the +*Lichtlijn*, the mobile phone user traffic light. The vitality and agency of things contributed to the design of +*Lichtlijn* in the role of a designer as force. Here the designer as force appears through the agentic capacity of efficacy that helped to create something new—in this case, +*Lichtlijn*. The designer as force also manifests in the directionality of an assembly, a trajectory that contributes to making new things, though without suggesting a purpose or reason. I earlier described how the direction of the evolving assembly of the traffic intersection of Goudseweg and Vrije Nesse makes +*Lichtlijn* seemingly inevitable, like a natural occurrence. In chapter 5, I described how the agency of trajectory revealed itself in the concrete material of the *Obscura 1C Digital Camera* (Pierce and Paulos 2015). The brittleness and thinness of the concrete promised its future destruction.

The trajectory and efficacy of agentic capacities are linked together. For example, the digital matter of information is durable, replicable, and recyclable such that the transactional data of an online book purchase can be reassembled from financial records into a profile of consumer preferences and consumer patterns. The trajectory of these profiles and patterns is to drive recommendation systems to encourage more purchases while, at the same time, the efficacy of digital data or digital matter suggests new possibilities. In this way, the same data as profiles and patterns seem to iterate and design themselves to take the form of consumer profiles for targeted advertising or criminal profiling or emerging forms of data surveillance, like epidemiological surveillance in which government agencies track viral spread through transactional and location data (Halbfinger, Kershner, and Bergman 2020). The force of digital matter also sets it on a trajectory of mass accumulation and storage that takes news forms in the sense of efficacy—for example, a physical infrastructure of lands and buildings form acres of data centers storing exabytes of data (one exabyte equals one million terabytes) and consuming billions of kilowatts of electricity. The force of the designer can both challenge and improve lifeworlds.

Digital matter in another form, the "poke" on Facebook, is a highly ambiguous and purposely pointless function in which one Facebook user can simply "poke" another user in a way that contains no message other than signaling the poke "itself." Seok and colleagues saw in this ambiguity an unfinishedness or what they called a *non-finito* product that encourages users to create their own meanings for what a poke communicates (Seok, Woo, and Lim 2014). The poke was introduced in 2007. It began as a prominent interface feature and has since migrated throughout the interface to its current state of being well buried as a sub-feature but not removed. Its migration throughout the user interface is a result of the interactions of digital matter of data and algorithms over the last decade or more. Digital matter has an intentionality—it directs itself to the world as manipulable and programmable. It can be readily manipulated and combined with other interface functionalities, like poke. It is programmable to be responsive to inputs of data from human interaction or nonhuman processes. Digital matter in the form of interfaces can then be created or altered by other digital matter, such as the behavior data from billions of online users[3] that fuels the machine learning and other artificial intelligence algorithms to direct and, in effect, design the interface.

Earlier, I referred to Deleuze's concept of individuation (Deleuze 1995) to explain how biographies are in a constant process of forming or coming

The Designer as Biography

into being. Deleuze's idea was heavily influenced by the philosopher Gilbert Simondon (Bowden 2012). In addition to the broader concept of individuation, Simondon saw in technical objects, or what I have called things, a particular process of individuation that he referred to as *concretization* (Simondon 2017). A technical object originates as a primitive invention that iterates to become more refined and concretizes or comes into being in ways not foreseen by the human inventor. The refinements are driven by the technical relations between nonhuman components more so than human creativity or decision making. A given part or change in a part simply requires another specific part to keep the whole functioning. Simondon calls this form of iteration the "condensing" of the technical object in a way that intensifies or creates new functionalities while simultaneously simplifying and reducing the object to essential components or relations. In this way the technical object or thing evolves almost on its own. The Facebook user interface is an example of concretization in that it is a result of a myriad of nonhuman relationships of algorithms and data. This idea is also useful in understanding the force of the designer of things.

While concretization involves complex human and nonhuman interactions over time, Simondon's focus is on the level of the technical object or the nonhuman relations in which components synthesize and exchange roles to condense to become more "self-sufficient" and less extraneous (Iliadis 2015), such as the shifting of "poke" as an interface element of the Facebook interface. In addition to condensing, another critical aspect of concretization is what Simondon refers to as seeking support from the technical object's surrounding environment for intensifying and streamlining its functionalities. He refers to the external environment as the technical object's *milieu*. This interchange with its milieu is essential to the technical object since parts of the environment become a part of it, like the interfacing of heterogeneous elements in a natural system. Simondon describes the Guimbal hydropower turbine as an example of the importance of milieu in concretization (Simondon 2017). The turbine is submerged under water so that the flow of water created by the dam spins the turbine that in turn generates electricity. The same water cools the turbine to maintain the desirable operating temperature and, in doing so, becomes a component of the turbine. The "offloading" of functionality allowed the turbine to be designed more compactly and without an internal cooling function. Further, the reliance on the milieu is such that the turbine only functions if immersed in water (Iliadis 2015). Similarly, the Facebook user interface supports user interactions, yet it is the data produced by those interactions that is needed to direct the hierarchy and architecture of the different user-interface components. And traffic intersections like Goudseweg and Vrije Nesse rely on humans pressing a button in place of sensors and actuators to notify the system that they want to cross the street.

Simondon's notion of concretization is radically nonhumanist. The technical object "iterates" but does so as a matter of its existence or being rather than in the sense of a human designer iterating on an idea or prototype. The "evolution" of the technical object is not a matter of adaptation through human use that is central to the idea of designing artifacts. Rather, it evolves through nonhuman interactions of relations and the interaction of a thing with its environment. There may well be a human agent involved but more than not the directive is the relations between nonhuman agents, like precisely fitting a machine part with another. While centrally technical in its focus, concretization is an argument against the separation of culture and technology (Simondon 2017). Concretization sees technological things as dynamic in ways that lose their culturally imposed notions of artificiality to approach natural modes of existence like evolution and adaptation. In this respect, Simondon's ideas are a precursor to notions of natureculture (Haraway 2003) or technicity (Ihde 1990) that are key assumptions of posthumanist thought.

The designer as force has one other quality: It operates at what Latour calls "scale one"—at full scale and in real time (Latour 2011, 3). The effects of defamiliarization of the *Tilting Bowl*, as discussed in chapter 5, in some cases required being lived with over multiple years or a fullness of time (Wakkary et al. 2018). The autobiographical design of *Living in a Prototype* (Desjardins and Wakkary 2016) was at full scale in real time. The autoethnographic speculation of the *Greenscreen Dress* was a ten-month exercise of daily wearing (Mackey et al., "Blending Clothing and Digital Expression," 2017). Dwarfing these examples, Facebook operates at a scale of over 2.7 billion users in a real-time social experiment. Trinity, the first nuclear detonation, was a "scale one test" of the vitality of atomic energy. Latour refers to the climate crisis as a "scale one" experiment that is happening to all of us. It is an experiment that requires a full collective ceasing of carbon outputs in order to stop (Latour 2011, 3). That is, agencies and intentionalities emerge at full scale and in real time such that it is impossible to represent

The Designer as Biography

or effectively prototype or simulate. In Lewis Carroll's 1889 novel *Sylvie and Bruno*, the character Mein Herr tells of a map of his country that is on the scale of a mile to the mile. When asked if it has been used much, he replies that it has never been used since the farmers objected, saying it would block the sun and ruin their crops. This points to the difficulties in representing the designer as force or modeling and predicting its effects.

In the prologue to this chapter, I described Superstudio's "microevent" called *Supersurface: An Alternative Model for Life on Earth*, an installation for the exhibition *Italy: The New Domestic Landscape* at the Museum of Modern Art in New York in 1972 (see figure 6.6). It metaphorically tackles design as force at "scale one" and the challenge of its own representation. The installation is an eight-foot cubic room of mirrored tiles that creates a *mise en abyme* or a hall of mirrors that infinitely reflects itself and the room's contents. The visual effect destabilizes what is seen while also creating a totalizing visual surface in the form of a grid. Other representations of the work occurred in film and collages. The grid flows over and through the landscape as a "network of energy and information" (Ambasz 1972, 242). *Supersurface: An Alternative Model for Life on Earth* replaces the static hierarchies of organization and their permanent structures in buildings, roads, and cities with a type of nomadism of social structures of movement. It is designed for the constant gathering and dispersal of humans, animals, and things. For Superstudio, buildings are simply membranes that separate outside from inside to control the need to move and assemble. Architecture is replaced by flows of energy or vitality: "The next step is the disappearance of this membrane and the control of the environment through energy (air-cushions, artificial air currents, barriers of hot or cold air, heat-radiating plates, radiation surfaces, etc.)" (Ambasz 1972, 244). *Supersurface: An Alternative Model for Life on Earth* is a radical gesture that can be linked to what Braidotti refers to as the anti-humanist movements of the 1960s and 1970s that inherited the legacies of fascism, Soviet communism, and late-stage capitalism—movements that sought new epistemologies, social theories, and a more radical politics (Braidotti 2013, 17). The work is seen as a critique of capitalist labor and consumption that points to a world of anti-labor (see, by comparison, Elfline 2016). The installation is speculative design at its potent best, radically problematizing assumptions while creatively generating alternative realizations. While the Eurocentric and gendered biases of the time require some overlooking, it is an expression of seriously considering design in its totality in the face of the totalizing force of consumer capitalism, the most dominant of "scale one" social experiments.

Superstudio literally aspires to designing with energy and forces through generating airflows and radiating heat, explicitly embracing the vitality of matter in design and the designer as force. As a result, it becomes clear that a thing that continues to evolve and have agentic capacities blurs the boundaries between the designer and what is designed. The designer as force complicates this divide, and this is implicitly the case with the designer as biography, in which the things become part of the designer. *Supersurface: An Alternative Model for Life on Earth* captures well the ambiguity between what is designing and what is designed. The totality eludes representation. Rather, it implies a force of human and nonhuman elements at a "scale one" that is dynamic and evolving.

The *Children Village* by the architectural firm Aleph Zero with designer Marcelo Rosenbaum that I discussed in this chapter's prologue (see figures 6.7 and 6.8) is a more prosaic though critically imaginative example of the designer as force and biography. Designed as an open veranda, the structure relies on airflow and pond water for cooling, not unlike Simondon's concretization example of the Guimbal turbine's reliance on water flow for cooling (Simondon 2017). The use of local materials like eucalyptus (introduced to Brazil in the early 1900s) and nearby soil to form earth blocks holds an agentic trajectory that is similar to how the concrete material of *Obscura 1C Digital Camera* (Pierce and Paulos 2015) held the promise of its future destruction. With *Children Village*, the trajectory points to its ultimate decay and dissolution back into the matter and locale it started with. What is often referred to as sustainable housing now takes on the form of a designer as biography. The thing designed cohabits or *lives-with* the lifeworld of the designer, taking care of what it will leave behind in what constitutes the biography of Aleph Zero and *Children Village*. There is in this biography a much-unheralded humility as a result of distributed agencies across humans and nonhumans.

In summary, designer as force can be seen through the lens of Bennett's distributed agentic capacities of design as efficacies and trajectories that contribute to the creation and designing of things like mobile phone traffic systems, destructible digital cameras, changing social media interfaces, and architecture (Bennett 2010). The designer as force can also be seen in Simondon's concept of concretization, in which a technical object evolves

The Designer as Biography

and condenses into an essential set of technical relationships that also integrates aspects of its environment or milieu for additional functionality. The agentic capacities of efficacy and trajectory alongside the notion of concretization hopefully paint a clearer picture of how nonhumanness operates and animates the designer of things as a force. And lastly, designer as force means design happens in real time and at full scale or, as Latour described, "scale one" (Latour 2011), which makes even more clear the ambiguous distinction between designer and what is designed.

Designer as Speaking Subject

So far, I have articulated different ways of describing the designer of things. The discussion has focused on the nonhuman aspects of the designer. I now turn to the human aspects of the designer. Unsurprisingly, humans come with different intentionalities as well as unique agentic capacities in comparison to nonhumans that contribute to the designer of things. Key among these differences is language, and so a uniquely human aspect is the designer as *speaking subject*. In a human and nonhuman assembly of the designer of things, it is humans who speak for and among mute things and matter. As such, the speaking subject has the power to express claims of purposefulness and desires on behalf of the designer of things.

It is understandable, as the reader, if the human role in the designer of things seemed to get lost in all the attention I have given to nonhuman agency. However, I purposely began the discussion of the designer with an emphasis on the nonhuman as a way to establish the relationality and interdependence of the human subject as designer. And so, as I now turn to focus on the human role, it is clear that this role shares the stage with nonhumans. This stage is a posthuman stage or a posthuman world in which a human designer is understood as a posthuman subject. This uncovers a key motivation of the book: to understand the world, specifically the world of designing, as a *posthuman subject*. Braidotti sees human subjectivity as an expanded and relational self that is technologically mediated (Braidotti 2013, 61). The posthuman subject, or more accurately a theory for posthuman subjectivity, as Braidotti argues, is a nonanthropocentric worldview in which the central element of existence is shared by humans with nonhumans. In this posthuman context, the designer proceeds with humility. It is a humble role as it shares agency with nonhumans and matter. This humility also stems from the awareness that a designer is part of a biography that cohabits a world with the things it has designed. There is a sense of this in the autoethnographic reporting embedded in autobiographical design in the work of *Living in a Prototype* and *Greenscreen Dress* (Desjardins 2016; Desjardins and Wakkary 2016; Mackey et al., "Blending Clothing and Digital Expression," 2017; Mackey et al. 2020). Both Desjardins and Mackey, as speaking subjects, account for their experiences of things in ways that are knowingly contingent and provisional.

There is also a deeper understanding that the life of things exceeds the life or the presence of the designer, especially the designer as speaking subject.[4] As Bennett succinctly declares, "This material vitality is me, it predates me, it exceeds me, it postdates me" (Bennett 2010, 120). As an extended and relational self, humans become part of the collection of agentic capacities within humans and nonhumans. And within this collection or "confederate," there are competing and cooperating agencies at play (Bennett 2010). In a multispecies world, it is unavoidable that one identifies with one's species if for no other reason than survival. Our survival plays a role in the cooperation and competition of the different agencies that, if only marginally, hold a particular place for human agency in the world of humans and nonhumans:

> Since I have challenged the uniqueness of humanity in several ways, why not conclude that we and they are equally entitled? Because I have not eliminated all differences between us but examined instead the affinities across these differences, affinities that enable the very assemblages explored in the present book. To put it bluntly, my conatus will not let me "horizontalize" the world completely. I also identify with members of my species, insofar as they are bodies most similar to mine. I so identify even as I seek to extend awareness of our interinvolvements and interdependencies. The political goal of a vital materialism is not the perfect equality of actants, but a polity with more channels of communication between members. (Bennett 2010, 104)

Human "interinvolvements and interdependencies" qualifies what is meant by survival. So even as Bennett argues that the need to bring purpose to the world or "regard the world instrumentally" is unavoidable and necessary for human survival, survival in this sense is as a posthuman subject (Bennett 2010, 77), expanded and relational, or *survival-with*.

Bennett in the quoted passage raises the issue of the necessity for communication between humans and things in order for a "polity" to form, meaning a political structure and process inclusive of nonhumans. At the heart of this question is the difference between humans and nonhumans within the existing languages of power. In this respect, nonhumans have little voice, or as Bennett states, there is a gap between humans as speaking subjects and mute objects (Bennett 2010, 108). In this respect, the intelligible purposes of the designer defaults to the speaking subjects, the humans in the designer assembly. As such, human purposes influence all aspects of the assemblages as "the bearer of an exceptional kind of power" (Bennett 2010, 34). This is not to argue that design is exclusively a human activity; the New Caledonian crows described in chapter 4 might argue against such a claim if they could (Jelbert et al. 2018). Rather, my focus is on the unique power, as speaking subjects, that humans bring to the assembly of the designer of things. The power is to express claims of purposefulness or representations on behalf of the designer that includes the other muted agentic capacities. This is no doubt "an exceptional kind of power." However, it is a power that is subject to being contested and mediated by nonspeaking others. This makes expressions of purpose limited in their power but still powerful within their limitations.

As I said earlier, the survival or design as a form of survival of the posthuman subject includes the survival of nonhumans. This expanded notion complicates survival to the point that it becomes more than an existential concern. Design, represented by the speaking posthuman subject, becomes a matter of equity[5] and politics with respect to who is seen to participate agentically, who speaks on behalf of whom, what is said, and what matters of concern arise in answers to these questions. This constitutes what I mean by posthuman design. The human designer as a posthuman subject takes on what Bennett describes as a "new self-interest" to become the speaking subject that is separate from things and matter while also belonging to, and speaking on behalf of, things and matter.

In summary, when describing the human role in the designer of things, the human designer is seen as a posthuman subject in which subjectivity is expanded and relational. In this context, the unique human contribution to the designer of things is the exceptional power to be the speaking subject among nonspeaking others. Yet this power is open to being contested and mediated. This gives rise to a humility that recognizes that agency is shared with nonhumans and vitality extends to matter. Given the interdependencies of humans and nonhumans, designing things as represented by the speaking posthuman subject becomes a matter of equity and politics.

Designer as Intensities and Origins

The designer of things in this discussion is diverse and dynamic. It is also distributed and expanded beyond humans in ways that make it amorphous and present in different ways. As I discussed in chapter 1, electricity in a continental power grid or massive air movements at the peak of Everest can be a "co-constituting force" that powerfully shapes things, humans, and worlds. I also described how an assemblage of things at the traffic intersection in Bodegraven, Netherlands, evolved to create +*Lichtlijn*. It may be tempting to divide these assemblages along the lines of human-made versus naturally occurring. However, this is a false dichotomy within the posthumanist and nonhumanist assumptions of designing things. Earlier in this chapter I discussed how Simondon's idea of concretization sees technological objects as approaching natural modes of existence rather than being seen as artificial. And in chapter 4, I discussed Ihde's critique of the false opposition between nature and technology (Ihde 1990). Haraway (2003) coined the term *natureculture* to argue that nature and culture are entangled. Both nature and culture are determined and made possible by historical, material, and political conditions such that neither is separate from each other. Nature is not distinct from humans as a non-negotiable reality, nor is it culturally determined; rather, in Haraway's view the two co-evolve. Braidotti sees posthuman subjectivity as functioning within a natureculture continuum (Braidotti 2013, 61). And so while differences clearly exist, there is a co-constitution that makes distinctions difficult to fully delineate.

I noted earlier how the force of the designer acts at "scale one" with full-size and real-time effects, which makes the distinction between things and designers ambiguous. In what way is the designer not simply subsumed within the continuum of ongoing forces of vibrant matter that in turn designs things and reconfigures assemblages? One possibility is to consider and understand *intensities* within assemblages (Deleuze and Guattari 1987). This allows us to see the designer of things as a matter of degrees of presence rather than present or not present. Changes that occur in an assemblage are a result of increasing or decreasing intensities. For example, the difference in speed between no movement, slowness, and quickness are different intensities of speed (Deleuze and Guattari 1987, 381). DeLanda uses the example of heating water to describe the effects of intensity. When heating a kettle of water the temperature increases with each additional

The Designer as Biography 189

degree centigrade in a constant fashion until it reaches a threshold of 100 degrees centigrade, water's boiling point, and the liquid is transformed to steam (DeLanda 2016, 76).

How does this relate to the designer of things? I suggest that a designer of things is composed of agentic forces and a speaking subject (or subjects) that form biographies together with the things it designs. But the designer is present at varying intensities, from negligibly present to actively present. The intensity of a designer is not a fixed characteristic. As water can change states at different thresholds as temperature intensities change, the designer of assemblages can emerge and fade throughout the life of a thing. So, while it is clear that the falling of the stratosphere into the "death zone" of Mount Everest on May 10, 1996, is overwhelmingly nonhuman in its force, we know as a matter of global warming that changing weather is not without human forces, no matter how negligible.[6] Yet, such a negligible intensity of human forces substantially minimizes the presence of a designer of things—especially the designer as a speaking subject. However, in the case of the +*Lichtlijn*, alongside the very potent nonhuman forces that contributed to its making, there is the presence of a human as a speaking subject. The speaking subject expresses, articulates, and rationalizes the purpose for a new traffic light for mobile phone users and helps to convene and further mobilize the designer assembly required to bring the new traffic light into existence. At the Bodegraven intersection, designers emerged at different times, from the design of the first traffic light for cars to the significant addition of +*Lichtlijn*. The difference is an increased intensity of the designer of things as biography, force, and speaking subject, at critical junctures.

The concretization of a technical object for Simondon (2017) has its origins in the primitive invention by the human speaking subject of design. In the ongoing iterations of the technical object, its evolution is unanticipated or exceeds the purpose and vision of the speaking subject. The designer as speaking subject is not the cause behind the design and does not hold exclusive agency over the thing. Drawing on Bennett's description of causality and agentic capacities, the agency of the designer as a speaking subject can be seen as a matter of *origins*. As I discussed in chapter 5, when describing the causality that can result from agentic capacities, Bennett refers to Hannah Arendt's distinction between "origins" and "causes." With agentic capacities, there is no linear cause and effect; rather, agency plays a role at the origins of an effect, which can be quite indeterminate (Bennett

2010, 33–34). In the case of the human aspects of the designer—namely, as speaking subject—the causality or the power to have an effect is nonlinear and fractal, lacking any efficiencies in cause and effect. More so, the different trajectories and effects intertwine and become emergent through complex feedback loops that can neither be untangled or predicted.

Applying the ideas of intensities and origins to examples from the prologue, *Living in a Prototype* (Desjardins and Wakkary 2016) can be seen as an instance in which Desjardins and her partner (the speaking subjects), along with the assembly of tools, materials, and things, increase in intensity to shape a Mercedes Sprinter cargo van into a camper van. This increased intensity is also a moment of origins, in which the speaking subjects give cause to the desire of a camper van. Mackey proposed the *Greenscreen Dress* as an exploratory speculation of future dynamic fabric (Mackey et al., "Blending Clothing and Digital Expression," 2017). The design collective Superstudio is at the origins of *Supersurface: An Alternative Model for Life on Earth*. In each instance, the speaking subject may be at the origins of a thing, but it is by no means the exclusive agent in the design of the thing. The camper van emerges from ongoing co-shaping and reciprocity between the human and nonhuman assembly of the designer of things and the van. The *Greenscreen Dress* in its day-to-day actuality *became* a form of dynamic fabric (Mackey et al. 2020). Superstudio as the speaking subject increasingly withdraws after the point of origin as the "architecture" of *Supersurface: An Alternative Model for Life on Earth* expands and reflects itself in myriad ways.

Ingold (2011), whose work I discussed in chapter 5, sees the world at "a constant boil"—"a vitality of materials" that are always in transformation. Analogous to the designer of things as a dynamic assembly of humans and nonhumans, Ingold describes a world of interacting materials and forces that come to make things. These "heterogeneous materials, enlivened by forces of tension and compression and with variable properties, mix and meld with one another in the generation of things" (Ingold 2011, 210). For Ingold, the generative process is a matter of "worlding" or "throwness," as Heidegger (1962) would describe being in the world. This means being taken up within the vitality of materials, as in the experience of flying a kite wherein kite and kite flyer are "swept up" into the wind and air or the vitality of matter (Ingold 2011, 214).

Extending this idea of flying a kite can be useful in understanding what it is like as the speaking subject of the designer of things. Ingold refused to

The Designer as Biography

see agency in any single entity, whether the kite or the human flyer, such that one or the other is mistakenly seen to be doing the flying and in control of the spiraling, darting, lift, and drop of the kite in the air. This aligns well with flying a kite as a matter of agentic capacities distributed across an assembly of colorful cloth or plastic, string, air, ribbons, arms, running and standing legs, spool, wind, and air temperature that flies a kite. In understanding what flies the kite is to also see by analogy what designs it. The speaking subject as human kite flyer is at the origins or gives the desire to go to the park to fly a kite. Once air bound, the kite is a conspiracy of air, materials, and humans that all together are flying the kite, although none on their own fly the kite. Wind no more directs the path than does the tension and yielding of the anchored weight and strength of a human arm, along with the tension, shape, and flex of materials. The speaking subject of flying a kite, like designing things, gives an original purpose or may speak on behalf of the different agentic actors yet then recedes to maybe reappear again at varying intensities as a part of the assemblage.

For Ingold, the human maker or practitioner is a "wanderer" or "wayfarer" who encounters, intersects, or intervenes in the aliveness of the world to follow it and bend it to an "evolving purpose" (Ingold 2011, 211). In the designer of things, the purpose may in itself be heterogeneous, concretizing in unforeseen ways and assuming biographies that co-evolve on their own. Furthermore, humans in the designing of things are speaking subjects that convene or are conveners of humans and nonhumans, whether it is to fly a kite or design a thing. That is, at the origin or moments of intensities, speaking subjects aspire to stand above the mute things and matter, yet this standing above is always open to rebellion or contestation. The designer of things, as discussed earlier, becomes a matter of polity or the politics of designing things.

In summary, seeing the designer as biography establishes the need for inseparability, a togetherness, between the designer of things and the things it designs. In this way, biographies ensure that any judgment of the value of a designer is not separated from the lifeworld it contributed to through designing things. Hence, the contributions of a designer of things can only be valued by the terms of designing-with that is expansive and relational. Acting with this degree of inclusivity begins with the participation of nonhumans in the assembly of the designer of things, which act as a force that comingles the different agentic capacities of nonhumans and humans in the forms of trajectories, efficacies, origins, and intensities. Further, given the power of language and the muteness of nonhumans, there is an additional role for humans to be the speaking subject of the designer of things. In this role, the speaking subject expresses the purpose and rationale of the actions of the designer of things and also represents nonhumans in how they participate in the designer of things. However, as discussed, this power is subject to being contested and mediated by the nonspeaking others. This opens up to the politics of things or, as Bennett suggests, the necessity for a political structure or a "polity" for humans and nonhumans for matters of participation and representation (Bennett 2010, 104). Biographies speak to the necessity of participation and representation but are less clear on who or what is to be included and what inclusion requires. In chapter 7, I aim to address these limitations by following through on the expansiveness and relationality required of posthuman design and wade into an unbuilding of the practice of design and what I call a *constituency*, or the gathering of the matters of concern and care of things to make them central to design before they are even designed or come into being.

Chapter 7 Prologue: Anti-biographies and Lifepatch

The majority of works I discuss next are counter or negative examples of design that I call *anti-biographies*, in contrast to the biographies described in chapter 6. In design, there is a tradition to make explicit and label examples or strategies that work against the generally understood goals of design. For example, an *anti-pattern*, a term coined by Andrew Koenig (1998), refers to an unreliable and potentially counterproductive software programming routine; a *dark pattern*, as named by Henry Brignull (2011), describes user interfaces designed to deceive users rather than serve them, as in surreptitiously forcing users to buy unneeded insurance when making a purchase online. These counterexamples are identified to warn designers or to "name and shame" designers that are malicious or lack competence. It is in this spirit that I describe the majority of examples in this prologue as anti-biographies and discuss them more fully in chapter 7. The one exception is *Lifepatch*, a do-it-yourself biology (DIYbio) collective based in Yogyakarta, Indonesia. The collective and its different descriptions of its activities help to develop the idea of constituency that is explored in chapter 7.

Anti-biographies

These *anti-biographies* are motivating counterexamples to the *good* of biographies in designing things.

Bag with Handle of Weldable Plastic Material
The ubiquitous plastic shopping bag is the design and invention of the Swedish package designer Sten Gustaf Thulin, who worked for the Swedish packaging company Celloplast. Thulin and Celloplast successfully patented the design in 1965 after filing it in 1962 (see figure 7.1) as the *Bag*

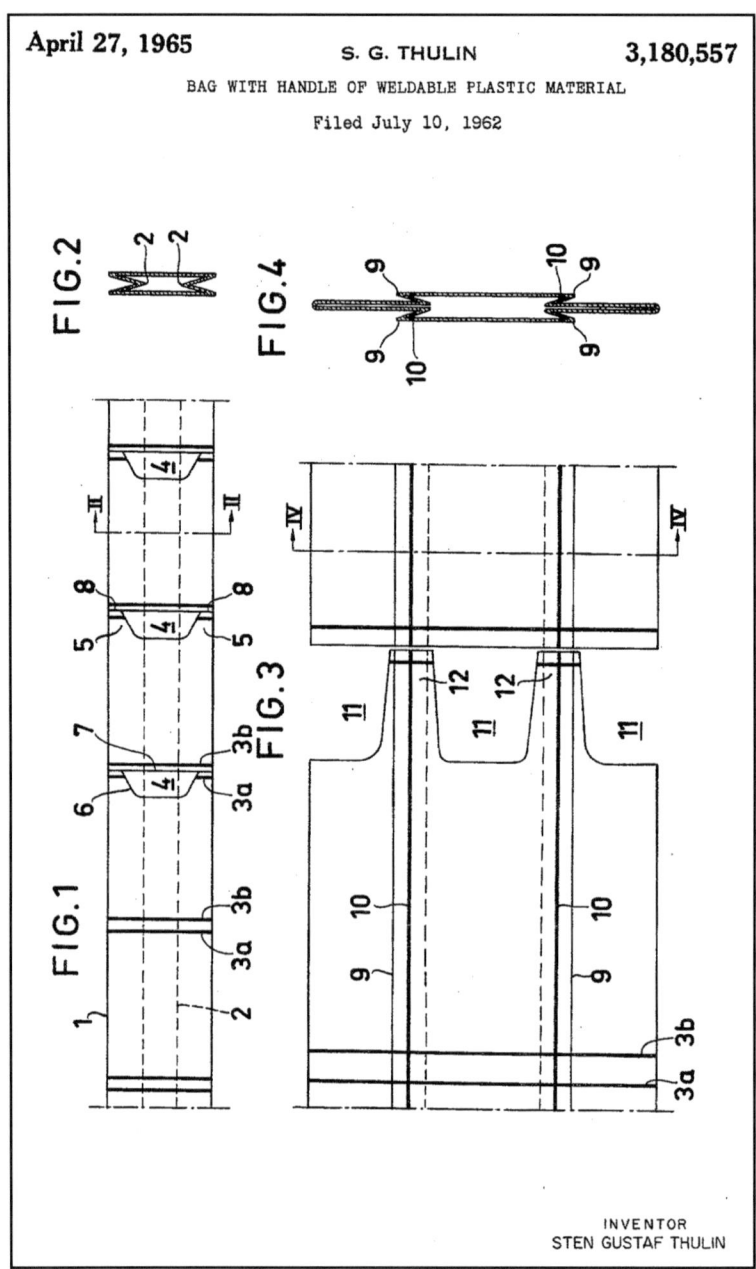

Figure 7.1
The US patent figure for the *Bag with handle of weldable plastic material*.

with handle of weldable plastic material (Gustaf 1965). The design of the bag is simple. It is comprised of a tubular strip of polyethylene plastic folded flat together then folded four times (twice on either side) so that the widest ends of the bag are folded inward, toward the center of the tube (see FIG.2 in the patent image of figure 7.1). The tubular strip is then welded at the desired length at the top and bottom of the bag. Material is then cut away with a die cut to create handles out of the remaining plastic. When unfolded, the tubular strip forms the sides of the bag, the bottom is welded close, and the welded strips at the top form handles.

Celloplast went on to dominate the European market and later brought the plastic bag to North America. In part due to its shape, it was often referred to as "the T-shirt plastic bag" (Laskow 2014). In 1977, the petrochemical corporation, ExxonMobil overturned the patent and began producing its own similar plastic bags. By 2011, it was estimated that 102 billion such bags were used annually in the United States alone (Doucette 2011).

The *Bag with handle of weldable plastic material* arose out of an assembly of humans, materials, patents, and machinery not unlike Latour's description of the development of the Kodak camera (Latour 1990). Polyethylene plastic was first developed accidentally in 1933 in Norwich, England, and would take a number of years to become an industrial-scale material. Celloplast had earlier filed a patent in 1960 in which Thulin along with other colleagues were the inventors for forming packages from tubular strips of polyethylene by similarly folding, welding, and cutting the strips at the desired packaging length to create bags. Thulin's patent for the *Bag with handle of weldable plastic material* created the integrated handles by cutting away material. This design at the level of manufacturing and with industrial production in mind was the hallmark of industrial design. It incorporated aspects of production and manufacturing as well as the design of the product. As a consequence, ongoing and related designs were necessary elements and various machines were patented (Apparatus for separating and sealing bags 1967; Apparatus for stacking bags 1968) that formed the assembly to create, produce, and distribute the ubiquitous plastic bags.

The anti-biography of the single-use plastic bag, as discussed in detail in chapter 7, has led to 150 million metric tons of annual waste and countless legislation to end or reduce its use.

M-16/AR-15 Rifle

The M-16/AR-15 rifle was designed in the late 1950s by the designer Eugene Stoner and the weapons company Armalite. The expressed purpose of the design was to make the weapons easily repairable on the battlefield by swapping out parts rather than servicing the whole weapon. This meant encasing the core functionality of the weapon within modular attachments. This gave rise to custom modifications through what became known as *tactical attachments*. In 1959, the AR-15 patent was sold to Colt Manufacturing, another arms company that developed the weapon into the M-16 for use in the military. The modularity of the design allowed the weapon to be marketed in separate configurations as a military and consumer product. The military version, the M-16, is a fully automatic machine gun. The civilian version, known as the AR-15 is a semiautomatic weapon. The lightness of the weapon, its reliability, and its modularity led to the AR-15 being a commercial success and the weapon of choice in mass shootings in North America.

The modularity of the design of the AR-15 has enabled countless designs of tactical attachment by gun manufacturers and do-it-yourself enthusiasts to evade legislation and continue the AR-15's use as a high-capacity automatic weapon.

Weather Channel Weather App

The Weather Channel Weather App for mobile phones and tablets provides location-aware data about weather. The Weather Channel describes the many features of its app as follows:

> Never get caught in the rain again with this powerful, free mobile app for iPhone, iPad and Apple Watch. Stay informed with reliable forecasts, interactive radar and real-time rain alerts, backed by the most trusted name in weather—The Weather Channel. It's the app users call "awesome" and the "best app on my phone." ("Weather—The Weather Channel" n.d.)

In addition to the range of functions, the app's key features are live forecasts fifteen days in advance and weather alerts:

> Live forecast updates are at your fingertips with The Weather Channel. Get the local weather forecast news delivered directly to your phone or tablet. Prepare with severe weather reports and live radar maps. Extreme weather alerts and forecast information is available wherever you are! Get daily local weather news and extreme weather alerts so you can live life with confidence. The Weather Channel provides accurate reports that help you plan up to 15 days in advance. ("Weather: Forecast & Radar Maps—Apps on Google Play" n.d.)

Anti-biographies and Lifepatch

Chapter 7 discusses how the convenience of the weather app is one example among countless others that deceptively collect personal data as a business model.

Camden Bench

The *Camden Bench* was designed in 2010 by Factory Furniture, a design firm that specializes in street furniture. It was commissioned by the Camden Borough Council for the municipality of Camden in the United Kingdom ("Great Queen Street, Camden" n.d.). The brief for the design was to address various antisocial and criminal behavior that could potentially occur in Camden city center. The bench is concrete and formed in undulating shapes, slight angles, and shallow recesses (see figure 7.2). The undulating shapes as the designers argue allow for comfortable seating for people of different heights but prevents the homeless or unhoused from sleeping on the benches like many "sleep-prevention" benches I discussed in Chapter 5. The changing angles of the surface of the bench are also designed to deter skateboarders from using the bench. The shallow recesses provide enough

Figure 7.2
The *Camden Bench* by Factory Furniture.
Source: "A *Camden Bench* outside Freemasons' Hall on Great Queen Street, London" by The wub, licensed by CC BY-SA 4.0.

space to stow purses and bags without concern that they will be stolen from behind. The lack of crevices or slots prevents the stashing of illicit drugs. The surface of the bench is treated to prevent graffiti and the gluing on of posters and stickers, and it repels dirt to be easier to keep clean. Lastly, the bench can only be moved by a crane, so it is of sufficient mass and volume to act as a security barrier against cars and trucks in the event of terrorist acts.

The *Camden Bench* is the example par excellence of a *callous object*, as discussed in chapter 5. The bench reveals the assertion of human agency over things to enforce an exclusionary public space, as discussed in chapter 7.

Lifepatch

Lifepatch is a citizen initiative in art, science, and technology that was formed in 2012 and based in Yogyakarta, Indonesia. The collective operates with an ethos of do-it-yourself (DIY) and do-it-with-others (DIWO) to foster new approaches to life and work through the creative processes of individuals engaged within their communities (Hatanaka 2016). *Lifepatch* has made a practice of organizing and running fermentation workshops and hackathons. As a result, along with diverse collaborators from citizen groups, community members, scientists, hackers, DIYbio enthusiasts, engineers, academic researchers, and artists, the collective has produced open-source software, hardware, wetware, community projects, citizen science tools, and exhibitions. The members have diverse backgrounds and expertise. For example, the director, "Timbli," formally known as Agus Tri Budiarto, identifies as a scientist, farmer, and yoga master; Andreas Siagian identifies as an artist and engineer; Nur Akbar Arofatullah is a scientific researcher. *Lifepatch* has an active presence in Indonesia with installations at the Biennial Jogja and Jakarta Biennale, and internationally elsewhere in Asia and Europe. In 2015, the collective was awarded the Digital Communities Honorary Mention at Prix Ars Electronica.

Cindy Lin and Silvia Lindtner (2016), scholars from the fields of science and technology studies (STS) and human-computer interaction (HCI), conducted ethnographies of *Lifepatch*. They followed members and their activities through three related projects that included a water sampling protocol, a digital river map, and a wine fermentation workshop in 2012. The projects occurred in Yogyakarta, focusing on supporting community know-how and knowledge of the quality of the water in Yogyakarta rivers. The

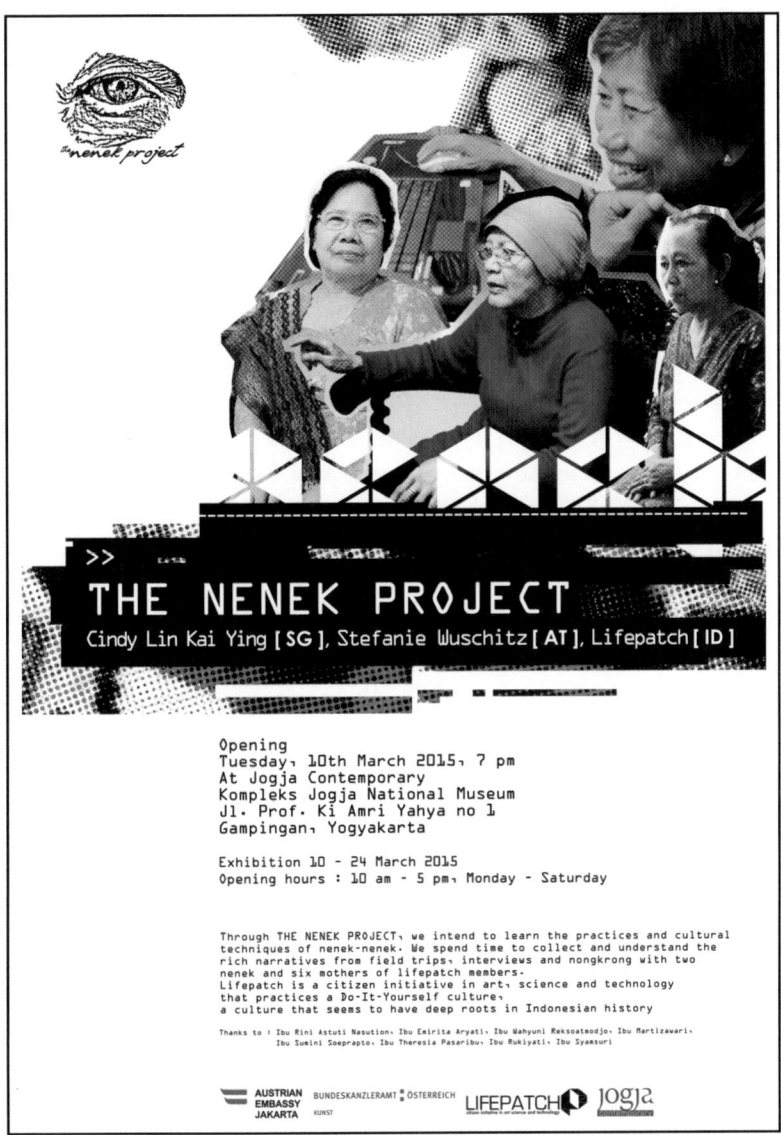

Figure 7.3
A poster for *The Nenek Project*, an exhibition in Yogyakarta by Cindy Lin Kai Ying, Stefanie Wuschitz, and Lifepatch.
Source: Courtesy of Cindy Lin; poster design by Adhari Donora.

DIWO ethos brought together a local community group that lived along the river known as *Kali Code*, biologists from the local Gadjah Mada University, and artists and academics from Lausanne, Zürich, and Bangalore. Lin and Lindtner trace the projects as "boundary objects" that enable diverse stakeholders and representatives to enact a form of cultural, communal, and scientific legitimacy for DIYbio that attracted international collaboration and received international recognition. This in turn extended at the politico-cultural level, a degree of legitimacy for Indonesia as a unique and critical culture for DIY and DIYbio that was socially engaged. Lin and Lindtner subtly argue that *Lifepatch*, knowingly operating within a postcolonial context, played out this transnational "legitimacy" in ways that troubled the Western-centric notions of the "Maker" movement for some and rejuvenated it for others (Lin, Lindtner, and Wuschitz 2019). The authors trace the locales of *Lifepatch* from their professional and familial base in Yogyakarta to their presence internationally. These ethnographies included family members, in particular the mothers of the *Lifepatch* members (see figure 7.3), and described overlapping and unresolved narratives from postcolonial sovereignty and cultural legitimacy to transnationalism and authenticities of the maker movement. The ethnographies bring into relief various issues, from the tensions between innovative democracies of "DIY" and long-standing generational and communal practices of "buat sendiri," or make-it-yourself, that predate DIY and carry on alongside it, to ideals of counterculture that involve different forms of state involvement in DIY and buat sendiri practices.

In chapter 7, I use *Lifepatch* for a detailed exploration of the material arrangements in the form of discussion and things that form a complex, overlapping, and irreducible set of stories of the matters involved in an assembly of those concerned with designing things.

Chapter 7: The Constituency of the Designer

In chapter 6, I described how biographies speak to the necessity of togetherness between designers and things in how they inscribe themselves into the world in ways that are accountable. I concluded the discussion with the need for a political structure for humans and nonhumans to continually ask who participates and who is represented among speaking subjects and mute things that assemble into designers. In this chapter, I explore the challenges and possibilities to create such a political structure for the nomadic practice of designing things—a structure that convenes humans and nonhumans together to discuss design before there is a commitment to assemble a designer and to make things. I call this convening a *constituency*. A constituency is the assembly of humans and nonhumans from which designers of things are gathered to go on to design things and form biographies. It can be seen as an expansive version of what is called design practice. To imagine a structure that is similar to a constituency is to think of bringing together the sociomaterial interdependencies and commitments of designing that include human actors of design (e.g., speaking subjects, stakeholders, audiences, families, partners, sponsors, clients) as well as nonhuman actors of design (e.g., locale, materials, tools, methods, techniques, organizations, institutions, policies, companion species, and other entities that can also be understood more fluidly as cross-assemblies of matters and forces). It is a way to make the cohabited lifeworld palpably present and persistent, like with biographies, though with constituencies it is to make the lifeworld visible before things are designed and even the designer itself becomes a reality.

A constituency is at the ready to assemble into designers of things as needed. To help explain the concept further, I borrow another metaphor from Tim Ingold. The metaphor is a kitchen, and it is also used to describe the world "at a boil" (Ingold 2011). The kitchen, which is "huge," as Ingold describes it, is where "stuff is mixed in various combinations, generating new materials in the process that in turn will become mixed with other ingredients in an endless process of transformation" (Ingold 2011, 213). To attend to a constituency is to attend to a kitchen, to assemble all matters of concern and care before cooking (or designing) and before even a cook (or designer) is present. It is to gather the things like tools, ingredients, skills, recipes, produce, air temperatures, along with the commitments that are open to discussion and contestation like organics, genetically modified (GM) foods, veganism, diets, allergies, and so on. A kitchen as a constituency is the place to gather that is porous with the lifeworld it is within. And so, it should also be seen as a network of relations that extends back in time to preserved foods, an outdoor vegetable garden, grocery stores, and neighboring cooks and other kitchens. A constituency is similarly networked. A cook or a designer is situated and formed within a particular kitchen or constituency. Whatever meals are cooked or things designed are a product of a particular kitchen or constituency.

Constituencies internalize key philosophical concepts, and so at this point of the book, I put the weight on the third and remaining leg of the stool that I have used to define what I call *things* (see figure 7.4). This leg is *matters of concern and care*. It draws from Latour's *matters of concern*—that is, the bringing together of the many associations and attachments that assemble and construct things that are open to discussion and contestations. Matters of concern as a term is intended to contrast with *matters of fact* that make things appear self-evident and indisputable (Latour 2004b, 2004a). For Latour, matters of concern are "variegated, uncertain, complicated, far reaching, heterogeneous, risky, historical, local, material and networked" (Latour 2005a, 23). In essence, matters of concern are contestable and negotiable and hold a plurality of voices whereas matters of fact do not, as they are seen to be indisputable. Yet, things are invariably constructed to be presented as matters of fact. Latour argues that things are "thrown out of the political sphere" and so rendered mute and passive (Latour 2005a, 23). To let things speak is to hear or make visible matters of concern that can also be called *thingpolitics* (Latour 2005a; Puig de la Bellacasa 2017). The aim of constituencies is to allow nonhumans to participate more fully and be represented, ensuring that design "will have to *engage in politics*" and to both form and inform a designer with this commitment (Latour 2004b, 83). That is a world of contestations,

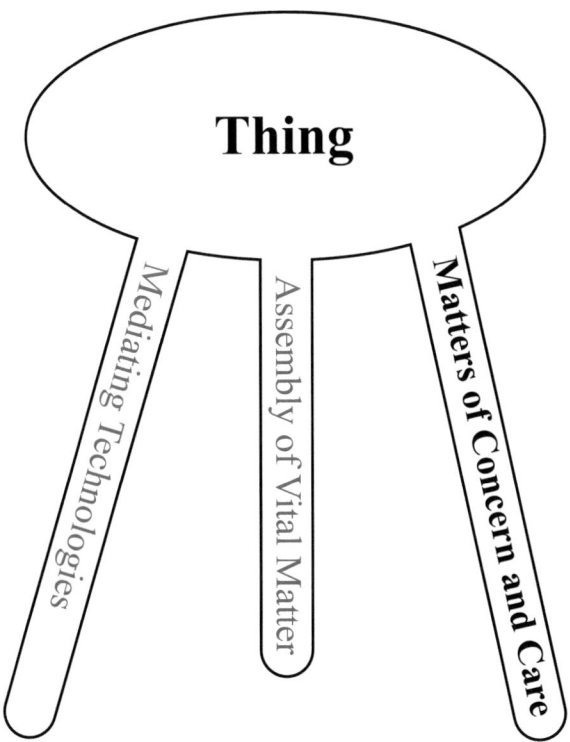

Figure 7.4
The *matters of concern and care* leg of the definition of *things*.

mediations, and affinities, and it is the same messy world that designers and things cohabit.

The other half to this leg of the definition of things is *matters of care*, which is drawn from Maria Puig de la Bellacasa (2017). Matters of care extends Latour's matters of concern to draw out the "affective and ethical connotations" of concerns (Puig de la Bellacasa 2017, 42). Puig de la Bellacasa offers a notion of care and ethics grounded in nonhuman agencies that sees ethics and care as situated—that is, they arise from relations with nonhumans, matter, and things rather than *a priori* or fixed values to be applied:

> The notion of "matters of care" is a proposition to think with: rather than indicating a method to "unveil" what matters of fact are, it suggests that we engage with them so that they generate more caring relationalities. It is thus not so much a

notion that explains the construction of things than it addresses how we participate in their possible becomings. Caring here is a speculative affective mode that encourages intervention in what things could be. (Puig de la Bellacasa 2017, 66)

I build on these concepts to consider not only how constituencies gather and make visible the nonhumanness of the designer of things but how ethics and care emerge through the formation of constituencies. And as Puig de la Bellacasa makes obvious, caring is "a vital necessity of all beings, that nothing holds together without relations of care" (Puig de la Bellacasa 2017, 67). These points are critical in thinking through this last piece of things we could design given the posthuman dimensions of things, design, and designers.

What I mean by politics is simply the discussions, debates, and compromises between humans that arise from the events of living together. However, politics include things. The meaning here is that things are political (Winner 1980) but also, in the active sense, that things gather with humans to engage in politics. This is what Latour calls a "progressive composition of the common world" (Latour 2004b, 247). There is a commonality that brings a world together but one that requires ongoing discussions and debate that are inevitably attached to the things and people that gather. The "common world" is not *the* single world; rather, it refers to *a* world in common, which implies many other worlds formed around other commonalities or *pluriverses* (Latour 2004b, 246). A given constituency of designing things is one such pluriverse. This progressive composition is not the resolution—an impossible nonpolitical world but a creative refuge from which things can be made out of the expansive discussions, debates, and compromises in which nonhumans participate as well as humans. Puig de la Bellacasa adds to an ethico-politics of things, where "caring becomes a thinking pattern" when engaging with things and a care that arises from such engagement (Puig de la Bellacasa 2017, 18).

In the first half of this chapter, to serve as motivation for the idea of constituency, I describe counterexamples to biographies, what I call *anti-biographies*. Anti-biographies are the designing of things that through ignorance or willful denial exclude the participation of nonhumans by radically restricting the concerns or lifeworld of design to matters of the *design problem*, a thin and pure world that is more easily resolvable. The restriction of the participation of nonhumans in the design process leads to the design of things as matters of fact, thrown into the world in which the inevitable

The Constituency of the Designer 205

matters of concern or thingpolitics arise to be dealt with by anyone other than designers. This also leads to a separation of the designer, thing, and lifeworld such that there can be no serious accountability. This separation renounces or abandons the entanglements of designing-with. It retreats to the self-proclaimed privilege of designing without account for the lifeworld that one cohabits—the sharing of the foreground with others that are human and nonhuman. Anti-biographies thrive on the fiction that designers hold a place outside the lifeworlds they help create through the things designed—lifeworlds that are in environmental crisis, ungovernable, open to deceptions of surveillance capitalism, and exclusionary. Anti-biographies are failures of design. Anti-biographies are, in short, anti-life.

Anti-biographies

In the prologue, I described the *Bag with handle of weldable plastic material* that became the infamous single-use plastic shopping bag. The patent by the package designer Sten Gustaf Thulin and his company, Celloplast, marks the origins of the plastic bag. The staying power and ubiquity of the bag is owed to its simplicity, material, production, and distribution. This has led to an incredible stability of use and manufacturing over the almost sixty years since the patent was filed. The steps of design and manufacturing are simple and few: Create a long tube of plastic, apply heat in intervals to create a welded seam, then cut out the handles. The polyethylene plastic was and is inexpensive and readily available in unsurpassable volumes (it is the most common plastic). Thulin's patent was accompanied by patents for machinery to stack and later separate the bags, making mass production and distribution easily scalable. Of course, this "elegance" of design and manufacturing created a product that has led to a global environmental disaster. The "success" of the design has contributed to the plastic bag's multitrillion annual single-use consumption globally,[1] over 150 million metric tons of waste annually,[2] and resiliency to endure for up to 1,000 years (the time required for the polyethylene to break down) only to result in nondegradable microplastics (Stevens 2001). As I described in the chapter 4 prologue, over 80,000 metric tons of plastic has collected in the *Great Pacific Garbage Patch*. Environmentalists estimate over 13 million metric tons are floating in all the oceans,[3] affecting over 700 marine species and attributing to the deaths of 100,000 marine animals and a million seabirds annually.[4] The

Bag with handle of weldable plastic material solved the very particular design problem of human convenience—namely, how to inexpensively manufacture a bag for ten minutes of use, the time it takes to walk from a store to a car in a parking lot (Zhang 2016)—while simultaneously, wittingly or unwittingly, unleashing a "scale one" crisis of devastation.

On the blog site *Disposable America*, hosted by the History Department at the University of Delaware, there is a post on Sten Gustaf Thulin that ends as follows: "It is important to ask the question, did Thulin know his plastic bag would impact the world? In thinking about busy consumers, did he also realize how the plastic bag would change human behaviors and ecosystem health across the globe?"[5] In short, the likely answer is *no*. The ability to separate the design of the thing, the plastic bag, from its irrevocable togetherness in our and Thulin's world is one of many illusions of anti-biographical design. The separation is a trick. In all likelihood, Thulin's reasoning (and that of the firm Celloplast) as the speaking subject is that the design problem is essentially a matter of designing products for consumer capitalism. The lines are drawn such that the task at hand is to create a marketable product that creates profit and satisfies consumers. This is not to blame Thulin or Celloplast, as the issue is consumer capitalism. This anti-biography thrives at the center of the nomadic practice of designing products that I discussed in chapter 3. Almost all implications or considerations are limited to issues of market and costs of production. This radical constraining of the design problem constructs the illusion of control and unfettered agency on the part of the designer—a constraint that is as narrow as it is defiant. Despite the obvious negative consequences, it is easy to overlook just how extreme it is to construct an understanding of design that is so short-sighted and so limited in accountability and action. A further consequence of narrowing the design problem is eschewing any serious form of contestation. As a result, the thingpolitics of things becomes external to designing things. It is taken up by others through political action, regulations, and laws, well after the harm is done.

The M-16/AR-15 rifle, which I also discussed in the prologue, is another anti-biography. The AR-15 is infamous for its use in mass shootings, such as those in Las Vegas, Newtown (Connecticut), Aurora (Colorado), San Bernardino, and other US cities, and recently in Portapique in Canada. A weapon for civilian use that can fire up to nine bullets a second (or 540 bullets a minute) with a tactical attachment is within all reason a caricature,

The Constituency of the Designer 207

though real, of harmful design. Yet the AR-15 is legal and unsurprisingly at the center of gun control battles in the United States. Further, it is the modularity of weapon design that keeps it a legal product. Whether or not this was the intent on the part of Eugene Stoner (the AR-15 rifle's designer) or Colt Manufacturing, the modularity of the weapon's design allows for a deadly cat-and-mouse game between subsequent designers in the form of manufacturers and gun enthusiasts and US federal and state laws to control assault rifles like the AR-15. For every legislation that tries to limit the magazine capacity and reloading capabilities of the machine, a modular hack or tactical attachment arises to get around the legislation (White 2019). The modular design of the weapon established by the designer at the point of origins is used again and again at critical points in the biography of the AR-15. It is a product that through design—the valorization of modularity as an elegant design solution to the problem—has become an ungovernable thing, resistant to contestation by others. The inability to fully regulate such a weapon, as was done previously in the federal assault weapons ban of 1994 (which expired in 2004), is not only a failure of politics but a failure of designers.[6]

In a seemingly benign example though no less an anti-biography, the Weather Channel app (owned by IBM) for mobile phones is designed to be "location aware." This means the app can detect the location of your mobile phone and then provide you the weather forecast for that location on its own. This feature is prominent in other weather apps and all location-related apps like Google Maps. In the field of human-computer interaction, the opportunities of location-based technologies (more specifically, "context-aware computing") have been a subject of research and development for over two decades (Abowd et al. 1997). In these early days, there was a naivete about context awareness as it was seen to be a potential boon for undiscovered user-centered services like guided tours of cities or museums.[7] Over the years, the assembly of technologies, envisioned user services, and market developments has concretized into a pervasiveness of location tracking. Almost every mobile phone freely collects location data, whether through the most mundane and least location-related mobile applications, like Facebook or wine-tasting apps like Vivino, or through essential Wi-Fi networking functions. In exchange for these free apps and services, you freely give over a constant stream of your location data. This data is aggregated and analyzed by companies and sold without your knowledge.⁸ In 2018, the *New York Times* purchased four months of location data from over a million mobile phones in New York City from a data broker company (Valentino-DeVries et al. 2018). From this data, the reporters were able to trace the daily movements of individuals and identify them. For example, the daily movements of Lisa Magrin, a forty-six-year-old math teacher, included her going back and forth to work at a middle school fourteen miles from her home, visits to her dermatologist and the durations of her appointments, hikes, walking her dog, Weight Watchers meetings, and stays with her ex-boyfriend. The data the *New York Times* purchased had data points for her as often as every two seconds or, on average, more than 14,000 times a day. That the data of one individual is so unrelenting and unfathomably detailed is more than enough to give pause. App providers, technology companies, and data brokers claim their interests are in the demographic patterns rather than individual patterns and that the anonymity of the data is protected. Yet, determining the identity of anonymized unique identifiers in the data is as simple as comparing locations with public records such as home addresses and work addresses, which is what the *Times* likely did to determine the identity of Magrin. The coronavirus pandemic showed how quickly such data and technologies can pivot from anonymous epidemiological tracking of populations for adherence to physical distancing, as proffered by Google (Fitzpatrick and DeSalvo 2020), to tools for individual contact tracing by governments that clearly identify the individuals (Lawrie 2020).

The technical underpinnings of location tracking include data from GPS systems, Wi-Fi networks, cell tower data, Bluetooth, and cross-device tracking (Brookman et al. 2017). These networking technologies serve ostensible purposes such as car navigation, text messaging, or personalization, although they also include layered and obscured functionalities (e.g., tracking your location when you connect to a Wi-Fi network) or purposely hidden functionality (e.g., ultrasonic audio beacons at a frequency too high for human ears) (Davies and Rankin 2007). These technologies create multiple layers of different and simultaneous functions, most of which are not evident or even comprehensible to users. Design theorists Johan Redström and Heather Wiltse (2020) refer to these variable functions as *multi-instability*. These technologies are changing what Redström and Wiltse also refer to as things that are, in their view, typically fixed and stable into things that have become unfixed and foster multiple instabilities. They argue that advanced digital

The Constituency of the Designer

technologies can best be described as *fluid assemblages*, such as the Weather Channel weather app. A feature of fluid assemblages is that the presence of the technology before you, the weather app, conceals many hidden layers of functionality and purposes such as location tracking. In this way, users do not know what in fact they are interacting with.

These ideas align well with earlier discussions of the entangled vitality of digital matter, things, and humans (see chapter 6). Here, the qualities of the combined nonhuman and human agentic capacities, in the form of trajectories and efficacies, create new manifestations of digital matter and technologies in ways unseen or opportunistically kept hidden. These forces of the designer are not deterministic, and neither are the speaking subjects of the designer. In an anti-biography, the kite flyer as designer (to use the example given in chapter 6) discovers the concretization of the forces in ways the designer does not control but can opportunistically exploit. This is exactly how Shoshana Zuboff (2019) describes the emergence of what she calls *surveillance capitalism*.[9] By this she means the exploitative, free, and surreptitious mining of human behavior in the form of digital data (like daily routines as daily movements, as in the other example of the Weather Channel app) through cross-device tracking and other ways of data tracking. This freely purloined data is then sold in the marketplace as raw resources or *prediction products* to advertisers, hedge funds, corporations, governments, and others without the knowledge of users who mistakenly believe they are receiving a service for free. Within the confines of the nomadic practice of designing products, blind to the deception, this is seen as either dumb luck, a gift that falls into the designer's lap, or an ingenious and resourceful design solution to an unknown problem!

Surveillance capitalism is the opportunistic use of what Zuboff calls the discovery of *behavioral surplus*. Behavioral surplus was the result of designers and engineers at Google creating the capacity to automatically collect data on the use of their search engine to improve the service—a classic user-centered design approach. However, the technical abilities of the service collected more data and data types than was needed to improve the search service. This was a result of the concretization of the search engine such that it extended beyond its original aims (Simondon 2017). The concretization progressed to include the milieu of hundreds of millions of users searching a countless number of queries. Surveillance capitalism is the opportunistic application of the discovery of behavioral surplus—the "extra" data that was unintentionally collected. It puts this excess to profitable use and so is purposeful deception as the means to economic gain. From the perspective of design, user-centeredness is here applied in the most perverse sense. Surveillance capitalism turns user-centered design on its head. Behavioral surplus and context-aware computing have their origins in user-centered design and in effect continue to rely on its expertise to craft mobile applications and services to further exploit, deceive, and freely capture behavioral data.

While the examples given are anti-biographies, they function just like biographies of the designer of things. The M-16/AR-15 and the *Camden Bench*, described in the prologue to chapter 7, have at their origins the human designer as a speaking subject that can, so to speak, tug at the kite string in one way or another—all with the hopes of shaping the future life of the thing or assembly of human-things. I call this intention, or the explicit attempt to shape the outcome for an expressed goal, a *program*. This program at the origin of the designed thing is sometimes successful and can have a lasting effect. In this respect, the agentic capacities of the human designer have the power to shape outcomes, though it is limited and never a guarantee. For example, many of Stoner's other rifle designs like the AR-10 and AR-16 failed to go into production. However, despite the presence of a program, a more typical biography and anti-biography of a designer and thing is taken up by the forces of the designer of things—trajectories and efficacies—in ways not foreseen by the speaking subject. For example, the behavioral surplus created by Google engineers aimed to improve user experiences of their search engine but created the trajectories of data surveillance that assembled to become surveillance capitalism.

At times, the question of which came first, the origins or trajectory, is not all that clear. For example, are tactical attachments the result of the original program of modularity in the design of the M-16/AR-15 or the result of the trajectory or ensuing logic of the modularity of the thing? Regardless, this led to new efficacies in the form of tactical attachments and the rationalization by current speaking subjects of the need for "personalization." And so, whether programs for things are created by speaking subjects at the origins or later, during the life of a thing in which a new program is created to opportunistically incorporate the trajectories, is not really important because the outcome is the same. The *Camden Bench* that I discussed in the prologue to this chapter is quite literally a brute-force attempt to sustain the program or design problem set at its origins. It enforces a dominance over what is public space through the sheer mass and form of almost 1,800 kilograms of concrete. The *Camden Bench* is a prime example of an attempt to design a dominant stability, a sleep-prevention bench or callous object (Rosenberger 2014, 2017).

Some may argue that these examples, with exception of the *Camden Bench*, are merely illustrations of unintended consequences. However, in the case of shared agency across humans and nonhumans, unintended consequences are everywhere and inevitable. If anything, the distributed agentic capacities ensure an abundance of intentions rather than a lack of intentions, and in that sense they are not worth illustrating anything exceptional or irregular. Rather, what makes these examples anti-biographies is the construction of the exclusionary design problem, a severely constricted design world that has literally choked out the very life and politics of the world it is designing within. The design problem excludes the participation of things, the thingpolitics, until after the designers have done their work. Anti-biographies perform what Rosenberger calls a *political occlusion* (Rosenberger 2017). Political occlusion is keeping politics hidden away or occluded by privileging or asserting norms. Latour would describe this as things paraded as *matters of fact* when they are *matters of concerns*—a collection of competing concerns or issues (Latour 2004b). The design problem is radical fiction that eclipses and occludes designers from their own real lifeworlds and biographies. This creates illusions of a world of no waste for the *Bag with handle of weldable plastic material*; a world in which a military-grade weapon like the AR-15 for civilian use is a requirement to protect individual freedoms; a world in which relentless and exploitative surveillance is a worthy price to pay for a good user experience of an app like the Weather Channel app; and a world in which what we call public is an exclusionary space enforced by social amenities like the *Camden Bench*. This separation of designer from lifeworld—in the name of the design problem—is a defiant act of the speaking subject to turn away and renounce the entanglements of designing-with.

Is it possible to maintain a togetherness between designer, thing, and lifeworld throughout a biography from the beginning, when a thing is being designed to the end of the thing, and avoid the fate of anti-biographies? To do this I turn to the question of how a designer of things *becomes* within a gathering, a constituency, that is expansive beyond the design problem.

Constituency

The aim of a constituency is to find ways for nonhumans to actively participate and be represented in their diversity, disagreements, and overlapping concerns to make the matters of concern and care present in the world of design in ways that they cannot so easily be excluded from the designer of things or the designing of things. In this way, engaging in the politics of things will become deeply entangled with the assemblies of designing things.

Developing new approaches for design to better engage in politics, ethics, and values is not unexplored territory for design researchers and theorists. For example, Victor Papanek (1971) aimed to correct the irresponsibilities and missed opportunities for social change in industrial design in the early 1970s. Tony Fry deconstructed values of progress in design through his concept of defuturing (Fry 1999) and aimed to radically rethink design in a post-democratic form that he saw necessary to tackle the existential environmental crisis we face (Fry 2010). Steadily over the years of sociotechnical and critical technical approaches to design—see, for example, Bijker, Hughes, and Pinch (1987) and Agre (1997), discussed in chapter 2—a substantial body of work has arisen around the very question of what we mean by values and ethics in technology design (Shilton 2018). Batya Friedman and her colleagues tackle ethics and design in what is known as *value sensitive design* (Friedman, Kahn, and Borning 2009; Friedman, Hendry, and Borning 2017; Friedman and Hendry 2019). Value sensitive design is a combination of theoretical, empirical, and design methods that work together to apply ethics in design or to centralize human values as the matter being shaped through the actions of designing. The aims of value sensitive design include (1) proactive orientation toward influencing design; (2) carrying critical analyses of human values into the design and engineering process; (3) enlarging the scope of human values; and (4) broadening and deepening methodological approaches (Friedman and Hendry 2019, 4). I share the need to engage design in a way that is not only a theoretically derived awareness of ethics but also a realist view that is materially grounded in the lived experiences, practices, and outcomes of design, and to engage proactively, if not radically reshape, what we call design. However, the concept of constituency that I propose requires a commitment to designing-with. This necessitates engaging the politics and ethics of design in a shared arena of human and nonhuman agencies. This calls for

The Constituency of the Designer 213

more-than-human participation and requires that we reconsider the autonomy of the human designer to instill ethics into design, for an *ethics-with*, in which values are mediated by and co-shaped with nonhumans (Verbeek 2006; Puig de la Bellacasa 2017). In this regard, what I mean by ethics follows Puig de la Bellacasa:

> "Ethics" in an ethics of care cannot be about a realm of normative moral obligations but rather about thick, impure, involvement in a world where the question of how to care needs to be posed. That is, it makes ethics a hands-on, ongoing process of re-creation of "as well as possible" relations. (Puig de la Bellacasa 2017, 6)

In addition to making ethics situated, this hands-on ethics is generative or about creating possibilities of care.

Infrastructuring, Publics, Constituencies

Along intersecting paths with value sensitive design, participatory design (PD) arose with the aim to make design an emancipatory discipline (Ehn 1988; Schuler and Namioka 1993). As I previously discussed in chapter 3 in relation to the nomadic practice of designing artifacts, PD originated from the democratic pursuit of empowering all stakeholders in the decision making behind systems design. I described how design *artifacts* are highly flexible. With PD, a design artifact is temporally fluid in that it includes design process outcomes like "scenarios, prototypes, mock-ups" that are in the present within the design process yet also stretch into the future as a way "of anticipating new or changed computer artifacts and use situations" (Bødker et al. 1988, 384). Two decades from the start of PD, Pelle Ehn (2008) intervened to reconsider participatory design. Borrowing terms from Redström, he described traditional PD as looking to anticipate use or to construct *use-before-use* (Redström 2008; Ehn 2008). Here *use* is seen as the conceptualized or future use that participatory designers develop as prototypes and scenarios that occur before the actual *use* of the product or system that comes after the design process. Ehn argued for a new form of participatory design that in contrast to traditional PD aimed to construct *design-after-design*, meaning the participatory design would lead to new and indeterminate forms of design not by designers but by the participants of PD (Ehn 2008; Binder et al. 2015). Ehn and colleagues aim to shift participatory design from the goal of co-designing future "useful products and services" to co-designing the conditions or environment "to produce a public thing open for controversies from which new objects of design can emerge in use" (Ehn 2008, 96). The new design outcomes are sociomaterial processes intended to sustain and develop communities of participants and future participants that in turn can be configured by the participants to address their own concerns. Ehn and others would go on to call this *infrastructuring* (Ehn 2008; Le Dantec and DiSalvo 2013). Infrastructuring formed what PD infrastructuring called *publics*, after Latour informed by John Dewey via Noortje Marres (2007). Publics are the creation, organization, and sustenance of evolving collectives that are bound by the desire to address an issue (Le Dantec 2016). Examples of publics are common forms of civic engagement including co-designing services to extend social networks of senior citizens, networking libraries and cultural centers for grassroots mobilizations (Olander et al. 2011), open hardware movements (Ehn, Nilsson, and Topgaard 2014), community information services for emergency shelter for single-parent families (Le Dantec 2016), and robotics workshops for local and community interventions (Le Dantec and DiSalvo 2013).

PD infrastructuring deepens and widens the desires of PD for a democratic ideal. The term *infrastructuring* is borrowed from the sociologist Susan Leigh Star, for whom infrastructure is a working relation between local practices and large-scale technologies that shifts from practice to practice and so is not fixed (Star and Ruhleder 1996). This helps to conceptualize PD infrastructuring, especially in thinking through the outcomes of the process. Yet, the more central influence is Latour's idea of matters of concern (Latour 2005a). Others describe PD infrastructuring as an "encounter between codesign and ANT" (Binder et al. 2015, 152), where ANT refers to Latour's theorizing of nonhumans as Actor Network Theory (Latour 2005b). The critical relevance of PD infrastructuring for the idea of constituency is PD's inclusion of nonhumans as actors in designing (Ehn 2008; Binder et al. 2015). Equally important and related is that nonhuman actors, according to Latour, gather together many associations or matters of concern that engage things in the politics of contestations and affinities.

Despite the abdication and exclusion of space for contestation in antibiographies, things rarely go uncontested. Camden Borough skateboarders targeted the *Camden Bench* to subvert its anti-skating design by creating new techniques and tricks adapted to the "anti-crime" features of the bench (Quinn 2014). Plastic bags are increasingly banned at municipal, provincial, and national levels. Gun control measures that include the AR-15 and far simpler weapons have been put in place internationally, even for a time in the United States from 1994 to 2004. The European Union introduced in 2016 the General Data Protection Regulation (GDPR) to control personal data collection and its exchange. Anti-biographies, which unfortunately occur in most design, place these political matters beyond and outside of the design problem and the designer to be dealt with by others—after the harm is done. Thomas Binder and colleagues have paraphrased a keynote address by Latour arguing that design produces "things that are thrown into the world to become contested expressions of matters of concern" (Binder et al. 2015, 153).

Things for Latour have dual interrelated meanings. Firstly, a thing is a nonhuman that gathers or assembles diverse, far-reaching, divisive, and entangled issues or attachments. In other words, a thing can be seen as a gathering of matters of concern. The *Tilting Bowl* study (chapter 5) showed the complex discussion attached to a ceramic bowl that tilts, from shifting bounds of normalcy to self-doubt, surveillance, human migration, and nonanthropocentric empathy as matters of concern (Wakkary et al. 2018). In the aftermath of the September 11, 2001, terrorist attacks, Latour observed the public gatherings, angry and passionate emails, and long-winded newspaper editorials about the different architectural plans from Daniel Libeskind's firm to replace Minoru Yamasaki's Twin Towers in Manhattan (Latour 2004a). In either case, the making visible of the matters of concern is to "detect how many participants are gathered in a thing to make it exist and to maintain its existence" (Latour 2004a, 246). A second related meaning also hinges on the act of gathering. Latour reminds us that etymologically the word *thing* is traceable to an archaic parliament or assembly among the Nords and Saxons, such as the Icelandic *Althing*, an open-air site of the annual parliament dating back to 930 AD. To *thing* can mean to gather to discuss and contest (Latour 2005a). Puig de la Bellacasa sees Latour's thing as a "staging of their lively existence" as well as "a representation of things that gives them a valid voice" in a "democratic assembly" (Puig de la Bellacasa 2017, 38). The dual meanings are to be taken together. Understanding things this way is to rightfully ask who (inclusive of nonhumans) should participate and what matters to all involved. This makes clear that things as nonhumans participate in our lifeworlds and are in need of representation in the gatherings that aim to co-shape lifeworlds through design.

This idea of designing-with matters of concern is a far less radical construction than design problems of anti-biographies. Anti-biographies disavow the things they make as self-evident matters of fact to be thrown into the world (a magical world not cohabited by the designer) to be contested and to divide. Peter Sloterdijk, who Latour referred to as the philosopher for designers (Latour 2008), disparagingly referred to designers as the "hoping class" alongside developers, brokers, and bankers (Sloterdijk and Stiegler 2016). Designing-with matters of concern is to make the gathering of the issues that are attached to things, so they can be contested and discussed, central to design. This in turn keeps designers and things together in the same world. However, Bennett and Latour make obvious the challenges of mute things speaking, especially about complicated, far-reaching, and heterogeneous matters of concern. Both see the need for a polity or a "conceptual institution," as Latour describes it, a place that allows for humans and nonhumans to speak of what things are and what matters and where provisional agreements and disagreements can be made (Latour 2004b, 2005a; Bennett 2010). Such a place does not exist; rather, this place or "this institution is what we have to invent" (Latour 2004b, 68). With respect to design in the nomadic sense, infrastructuring is one invention of this institution, an outward-facing assembly of things whereas constituency is another invention that is an inward-facing assembly of things. This directionality of outward and inward pivots around a shared point, before and after the designer.

PD Infrastructuring is after the designer. For the civic engagements of PD infrastructuring, matters of concern are the objectives of design. The aim is to *design* publics or to design sociomaterial processes so that citizens can engage matters of concern they share (Le Dantec 2016). Infrastructuring and publics require designers and citizens, even though the actions of designing are shared. A constituency is before the designer. Constituencies gather the matters that matter and make them visible and active, in order to foster and develop the designers of things. By this, I don't mean the knowledge, methods, and skills to design, although those are important, but rather what constitutes the designer of things. This includes virtually all that I have been discussing so far that can be boiled down to designing-with—that is, instilling the interconnectedness and relationality of things, the vitality of things, and the exceptional though limited role of the speaking subject in a designer of shared human and nonhuman agencies and intentionalities. It is understanding the conditions in which unintended consequences are

The Constituency of the Designer

inevitably attached to things. And that things are always open to contestation, debate, and negotiation. Constituencies do not design; rather, they gather an arena of matters of concern that makes design expansive, and through this expansiveness and inclusion, designers of things are formed and informed.

As mentioned at the beginning of the chapter, a constituency is the kitchen as gathering, where everything is assembled before the cooking and the meals. If traditional PD is said to be *use-before-use* and PD infrastructuring is *design-after-design*, then constituencies are *things-before-things*.

Constituencies are particular to the nomadic practice of designing things, but they are akin to many current forms of organization across other nomadic practices. And so, in the language of constituencies I refer to these as *proto-constituencies* (incomplete forms of constituencies). Through a posthuman lens, they can be said to be gatherings of humans and nonhumans to be at the ready to design things, artifacts, objects, or products. My own design research studio known as the Everyday Design Studio is a proto-constituency. Up to this point, it has been gathering *matters of academic research*. Aleph Zero, the architectural firm behind *Children Village* (discussed in chapter 6) is a proto-constituency like all other design firms, consultancies, or agencies, although it is focused on gathering *matters of the profession*. Superstudio challenged the proto-constituencies of the design profession by gathering a collective, another form of proto-constituency but one shaped by ideology that engages *matters of anti-consumerism*. It is worth noting in a cautionary way that corporate assemblies like Google and Facebook can also be seen as proto-constituencies. In many respects, technology companies have quickly grasped the entanglements and opportunities of the posthuman that go beyond efficiencies and scale of nonhuman productivity (i.e., automation and robotics). As the scale one design of Facebook, the behavioral surplus discovered by Google, or the complex web of corporate actors in surveillance capitalism reveal, corporations have literally capitalized on, and constantly seek new ways to capitalize on, the shared agencies and participation of nonhumans as *matters of capitalism*. Braidotti makes the point that "advanced capitalism seems to be faster in grasping the creative potential of the posthuman than some of the well-meaning and progressive neo-humanist opponents of the system" (Braidotti 2013, 45).

And so, as a process of conversion from one nomadic practice to another or simply to learn how to develop a constituency based on historical practices, how does the shift from proto-constituency to constituency happen? Through horizontal and relational expansiveness and inclusion. By this I mean adopting the *stubbornly realist attitude*, as Latour (2004a, 231) calls it, in which we need to get closer to nonhumans as matters of fact, not because that is what nonhumans or things really are (as has been a well-repeated point in this chapter) but because it is in proximity to matter that the matters of concern arise. To get closer is to have a position, a perspective, a place from which to know that shares the same horizontal surface, as if to lie down next to the matter to know. This positionality and perspectival knowing is not unlike Haraway's *situated knowledges* that reformulate objectivity to be embodied, partial, and accountable to the knowing subject that organizes what is seen and understood (Haraway 1988). For Puig de la Bellacasa, this is "a new sense of 'empirical philosophy' . . . that would place us in the flow of this moving experience" (Puig de la Bellacasa 2017, 33). This type of realism, in Latour's terms, means following and analyzing the actors one at a time from networked relation to networked relation to the point that a constituency emerges. As Bennett would have it, posthuman empiricism requires getting dirty, immersing oneself to live-with, as Charles Darwin did when spending days following the permeability between worms and soil that helped organize a view of natural evolution (Bennett 2010). This is not a one-time analysis but a constant active reflection as constituencies change and offer different partial views. In all cases, this realism is a middle ground that maintains posthuman relationality without giving in to relativism. And further, constituencies understood in this realist attitude, as a gathering or "a thing, conceived as such, is then both construction and reality" (Puig de la Bellacasa 2017, 33).

For constituencies and design, this is a way to understand matters of concern without getting trapped in the idealist position of maintaining exclusionary and abstract ideas of the "design problem," "academic research," or "the profession," or being trapped within ideological positions of external moralities, be they "anti-consumerism" or "capitalism." Arguably, these are common or shared concerns, and constituencies require affinities, a gathering around shared concerns. However, either position, the idealist or ideologue, are ultimately limited and predetermined. To build a solid collective of humans and nonhumans like a constituency requires a "multifarious inquiry" that is expansive and inclusionary: "A gathering, that is, a thing, an issue, inside a Thing, an arena, can be very sturdy, too, on the condition that the number of its participants, its ingredients, nonhumans as well as humans, not be limited in advance" (Latour 2004a, 246). In other words, the shared matters of concern that bring a constituency together need to be as expansive as possible without losing their affinities.

Assembly of Matters

And so, what is assembled in a constituency? In the prologue, I discussed another proto-constituency in the form of the citizen initiative *Lifepatch*. In following the various retellings of *Lifepatch* from supporting organizations (Hatanaka 2016), art residencies (Air Antwerpen 2017), or ethnographies (Lin and Lindtner 2016; Lin, Lindtner, and Wuschitz 2019), *Lifepatch* as an assembly is a gathering of diverse matters: the rivers of Yogyakarta, *E .coli*, electronic sensors, tools, engineers, biologists, hackers, makers, artists, open-source hardware, open-source PHP software, yeast, wine, art hacker networks, academics, Europeans, workshops, wetware, hackathons, international flights, mothers, *Nenek-nenek*, residents, *buat sendiri*, do-it-yourself (DIY), farmers, yoga masters, kampungs, postcolonialism, transnationalism, maker movement, sovereignties, state-run women organizations, educational workshops, Ars Electronica, ethnographers, curators, Jakarta Biennale, Gadjah Mada University, École Polytechnique Fédérale de Lausanne, Hacketeria Lab, art collectives, and so on. This is an undifferentiated and far from exhausted list of the gathering that constitutes *Lifepatch* in one way or another.

These things, humans, and matters of concern and care are gathered in advance of any projects or makers being formed. It is from this gathering that an assembly of humans and things form to create a designer of things to design, for example, a fermentation workshop requiring the know-how, tools, materials, and methods of fermentation. The fermentation, wine, yeast, *E.coli*, *Saccharomyces cerevisiae*, speaking subjects, and wetware participate and conspire together to instantiate a fermentation workshop. A program for the workshop emerges in which the collective enactments of local river water are either harmful or pleasurable living matter.

What does this tell us about a constituency? It again shows how a constituency is a gathering of things as matters of concern that are "variegated, uncertain, complicated, far reaching, heterogeneous, risky, historical, local, material and networked" (Latour 2005a, 23). And this gathering is neither neutral nor expedient but is convened in ways situated and hands-on, which Puig de la Bellacasa would argue leads to an ethics of care that is generative in that it is about creating possibilities for care. This hands-on ethics emerges from "thick, impure, involvement in a world where the question of how to care needs to be posed" (Puig de la Bellacasa 2017, 6). This ethos, expressed as do-it-with-others (DIWO) or *buat sendiri*, and the assemblies of matter that gather precede the designer of fermentation workshops and river projects or are expressed through them. And care as such in the context of designing things establishes the trajectories or orientations of designing-with, embracing the necessity of the togetherness of designer and thing within a shared biography. This at minimum makes it harder to separate *Lifepatch*, workshops, rivers of Yogyakarta, and residents, and so it is easier to avoid the fate of anti-biographies.

But how is the convening or constituency organized and brought into view? *Lifepatch* comes to the majority of us as overlapping retellings, promoted narratives, and ethnographic analyses, each of which is represented by a speaking subject or speaking subjects, as conveners of partial views of the constituency. The speaking subject of the constituency precedes the speaking subject of the designer and need not be the same. In one telling, *Lifepatch* members together with AIR, an artist residency program in Antwerp (Air Antwerpen 2017), speak of the convening of matters of community, cross-disciplinarity, Indonesian-centric collaboration composed of self-practice, collaboration, and invention. The matter assembled includes the tools, techniques, know-how, and human actors of art, science, and technology that can be reconfigured locally with local resources like humans, soil, water, bacteria, and so on. In another telling that is more of a story within a story, Lin and Lindtner (2016) retell how Sachiko Hirosue, an academic scientist from École Polytechnique Fédérale de Lausanne in Switzerland became an early collaborator with and advocate for *Lifepatch*. Hirosue met *Lifepatch* member Nur Akbar Arofatullah (mentioned in the prologue), at a do-it-yourself biology (DIYbio) workshop while serving as a collaborator on the river projects in Yogyakarta in 2012. Hirosue viewed *Lifepatch* within postcolonial and Global South concerns. In this retelling, the gathering of *Lifepatch* is a unique and credible challenge to the privileging of Global North narratives of the maker movement as the dominant and democratizing mode for hacker or DIY knowledge production. Hirosue speaks of *Lifepatch* as an equal and distinct assembly of knowledge production that gathers tools, humans, know-how, and locale along with deeply held interdisciplinary and collectivist commitments. In Hirosue's telling, this is an assembly of scientific work that her European and international colleagues could learn from.

The ethnographies of Lin and her colleagues similarly hold a postcolonial position from which to understand the making practices of *Lifepatch*. They are necessarily skeptical of the dominant discourses of the innovation of the "global maker movement," yet in pursuing alternative and diverse descriptions, they are well aware that the descriptions represent different politics that are irresolvable and as a whole do not form a complete picture. In a later ethnography with *Lifepatch*, Lin and her colleagues focused on the subaltern perspective of the making within the kampung, a village or neighborhood, in Yogyakarta that was the familial and professional home of *Lifepatch* members:

> Because of their location in the kampung, Lifepatch paid no rent for their DIY laboratory. They turned their own homes and that of their families into their workspaces. Crucially, working within the kampung provided a safety net; it offered not only free space, but also access to a clientele Lifepatch wanted to work with. Neighbors, especially women and children, patronized Lifepatch's in-house workshops and exhibitions and viewed their work as services to the kampung. In exchange, they reciprocated by supporting Lifepatch with security and housekeeping services when its members were out of town for artist residency and events. (Lin, Lindtner, and Wuschitz 2019, 1574)

Kampungs are in many instances politically organized. Dating back to President Suharto's "New Order" regime from 1966 to 1998, federal and political support was given to volunteer women's organizations to deliver healthcare, education, and financial services at the local level. Lin and colleagues augmented their ethnographic work with the scholarship of others (Newberry 2006; Newberry 2014; Newman 2017; N. Sullivan 1995; J. Sullivan 1992) to describe the central role of the Nenek-neneks, the mothers and grandmothers of the kampung, and in the case of *Lifepatch*, the preceding maternal generation or *their* mothers and grandmothers. The labor of the Nenek-nenek through state-run organizations contributed in large measure to explicit nation building, community care, and family care. For example, Lin and colleagues report on the mother of one of *Lifepatch*'s cofounders, Maria, who was a member of the *Pembinaan Kesejahateraan Keluarga* (PKK, the National Housewives Association) and *Dharma Wanita* (DW, the Wives of Civil Servants). These organizations tended to the maintenance and promotion of health, literacy, cooking, family planning, and microfinancing within the kampungs. Nenek-neneks would organize educational workshops and services and microfinancing through an *arisan*, or a rotary association. As a result, the women balanced state initiatives alongside the well-being of their families and the families of the kampung. It is within the kampung and familial structures that Maria's son spoke of his mother as a "DIY genius" through her volunteer and community involvement, making explicit the inheritance of the DIWO ethos of *Lifepatch*. In the telling by Lin and colleagues, Maria says she does not know what "DIY" is, but she does understand *buat sendiri*—to make your own resources as in the stabilizing and trust labor of participation in the kampung. Here arise different tensions and subtle but key differences that are generational as they are postcolonial in notions of DIY and buat sendiri. Yet the relations are intertwined through family and care. Lin and colleagues draw out the convening together of kampungs, political and feminized care labor of the Nenek-neneks, and counterculture claims of makers and hackers: "This paper focuses on the domestic care work and unpaid labor that enabled these Indonesian biohackers to be regarded as legitimate producers of technology in [a] transnational network of electronics art and tech innovation" (Lin, Lindtner, and Wuschitz 2019, 1572). In this telling, *Lifepatch* is the gathering of DIY, buat sendiri, Nenek-neneks, mothers, grandmothers, family planning, arisan, family homes, sons, state organizations, residents, nation building, community service, and national regimes of government.

I focus on *Lifepatch* not to hold up a DIYbio collective as the exemplar of a constituency or to valorize the virtuous Global South over neoliberal maker movement of the West. Rather, *Lifepatch* offers a view of the human and nonhuman matters that are materially arranged within a constituency. But, as was also discussed, it makes visible how these matters are "complex assemblies of contradictory issues" that overlap and intersect within a constituency. Thanks in large part to the knowing positionality of the collective's members who understood they were seen as "golden boys" of a globalized maker movement (referring to their "other" glamour and skin color), and thanks to the ethnographies of Lin and her colleagues who made visible the intergenerational feminine labor and state support behind the emancipatory actions of the collective, we can see the matters that are assembled (Lin, Lindtner, and Wuschitz 2019)—matters that form the discussions, debates, and compromises that make the *progressive composition* of the constituency (Latour 2004b).

The Constituency of the Designer

Perhaps it is in the context and focus of a Global South DIYbio collective that the expansiveness of the things and matter can be, relatively speaking, laid bare and made so visible. What external speaking subjects could make of my own Everyday Design Studio is work yet to be done. Nevertheless, *Lifepatch* shows how constituencies are not only what is gathered but how these matters and things are gathered. This creates overlapping tellings that interact as frictions and affinities. The challenge to realizing constituencies of designers is to make these accounts internal to the constituency. The examples of *Lifepatch* I've retold are in different ways external. The tellings about the art residency in Antwerp are outward facing, directed to an external audience as an often-rehearsed artist statement. Hirosue speaks as a partner but ultimately an external collaborator to the gathering, and the well accounted for ethnographies are by definition external and retrospective analyses. To move these tellings to be internal to a constituency is to make the accounts actively reflective and ongoing on the part of the speaking subjects of the constituency. This makes the matters gathered more visible and allows for proactively engaging the contestations between them as the means to the "construction and reality" of the constituency (Puig de la Bellacasa 2017, 33). In addition, there are other tellings of the gathering to be found in the mute nonhumans that have been gathered and that need to be spoken for more actively and explicitly by the speaking subjects. This all calls for an intensifying of the reports of the speaking subjects who speak for themselves and for others simultaneously. Before addressing this challenge, however, there is a need to elaborate more clearly on the role of the speaking subjects that appear in both designers and constituencies.

Politics of the Speaking Subject

I've invoked the speaking subject as a member of the constituency and, in fact, the convener of the constituency. In chapter 6, I described the speaking subject as the convener, at the origins, of the human and nonhuman assembly of the designer of things. I also described how the speaking subject is accountable for the outcomes created by the designer. This accountability is limited, assigned by default, given the exceptional power to speak among nonspeaking others (i.e., nonhumans). This power is open to contestations and mediations and the ongoing vitalities of efficacies and trajectories of things. The speaking subject or subjects of constituencies hold the same exceptional but limited powers, though as matters of responsibility rather than accountability, and the roles share much even though attention and care are directed differently. The speaking subject of the constituency attends to the reality and construction of the constituency and not to the making of things.

The notion of speaking subject is informed by Latour, whose work began in what is called science studies, or the studying of the practice of science. From these studies he came to see scientists as "spokespersons" of nonhumans. For example, in *Pandora's Hope* (Latour 1999), he gives an ethnographic/philosophical account of his field study of three scientists, a pedologist, botanist, and geographer, in the Amazon forest in the northern part of Brazil known as Boa Vista. The scientists were there to understand the soil interactions at the border between the forest and the savannah and to determine whether soil from the savannah was encroaching on the forest or the forest soil was encroaching on the savannah. Latour details the work of the scientific trio to show science as a series of interactions between humans and nonhumans that translate and mediate the phenomena of study or the reference, in this case the mysterious soil of the Amazon forest. Latour aims to show that the science here is the detailed work of assembling a long chain of references, what he refers to as the *circulating reference*, in which the nonhuman, the soil, is mediated at each link in the chain by humans and nonhumans. And at each link it becomes a different entity yet always refers to the same phenomenon, whether it be the soil in the ground, the collected samples, arrays of analysis by different instruments, charts, color categorizations, biological field notes, and so on that move from field to lab to published journal article, all in reference to the soil of Boa Vista. In these interactions, the scientists collected the soil, crumbled it between their fingers to feel its clayness versus its soilness, spit on it to feel its texture, squinted at it through specially made cards to determine its color, analyzed it with a range of instruments and techniques, wrote about it in field notes, drew it and diagrammed it with charts and illustrations, and converted it into numbers and names. The scientists are the spokespersons for the soil. They ensure it is present and active in the science making and, like a nonhuman whisperer, translate its representations and transformations into language to give it voice on matters to be negotiated, agreed on, or argued over between the trio of scientists and other speaking subjects or, more formally, written conclusively in a scientific article: "We have to acknowledge that the notion of

The Constituency of the Designer 225

spokesperson lends itself admirably to the definition of the work done by scientists in the lab coats" (Latour 2004b, 64).

But what of designers, even the most traditional designer of any one of the nomadic practices I discussed? And by traditional, I mean one that is seen to be exclusively human with all illusions of autonomy intact. Even in these instances, a designer is also a spokesperson for nonhumans. Designers manipulate, experiment with, and analyze materials of all kinds, from yarns to electronics to digital algorithms. Designers also want to know what things do and how they can be translated and shaped for design. Designers invent and modify instruments and techniques to know things better but also to experiment with and transform, often in combination with other things and humans. Designers are translators who translate the benefits, harms, and unexplored potential of nonhumans. Designers also translate policies, standards, guidelines, and new technologies. They create experiments, tools, and methods to divine the mediating effects of nonhumans on user tastes, satisfaction, productivity, sustainability, behaviors, sociality, injustices, postcolonialism, empowerment, and so on. Donald Schon (1992) said all along that *design is a reflective conversation with materials*. That a designer designs-with nonhuman materials means that the designer brings nonhumans in to participate in the design process. And what materials say or do is not fixed but is dynamic in the phenomenological sense. The materials, the designer, and the conversation change depending on how they are situated together—what is referred to as a *design situation* (Schon 1984). And so, in the most traditional of design practices, nonhumans may not be seen as agentic, but they are certainly seen as animate. As such, it is accepted that nonhumans participate in design in at least some weak sense, but more importantly here, the nonhumans are not self-evident, not facts, but require translations, transformations, and mediation by humans to participate in design. There is more than enough in traditional design from which to imagine, in the context of decentered human agency, the role of humans as spokespersons, or what I call speaking subjects, for and with nonhumans in design.

The decentered position of the designer or scientist reveals the "exceptional" though limited power of the speaking subject, whether as a botanist, a designer of things, or a convener of the constituency. In design, it is through the decentering of human agency, the sharing of the center with nonhumans, that the real significance of the speaking subject becomes clear. What I am seeking is an inclusionary and expansive world of design for making things that in every way are the same as the lifeworld of things once designed. The extant and ongoing concretization or designing of things assumes this continuity. And for some reason, it takes extra effort to bring this into design, to expand the notion of the design problem so that the highly restricted design problem is left behind. The speaking subject is pivotal and critical to this effort. The speaking subject makes thingpolitics present and lively in design in multiple ways. Firstly, the speaking subject has the exceptional power to speak on behalf of nonhumans in the constituency and the designer of things. Who else can speak about modularity as freedom or death, allowing it to participate in an open discussion and contestation; or invite digital data as deception and ease-of-use to the debate; or form a bench that one cannot lie flat on so as to police public space? Secondly, the speaking subject speaks-with or thinks-with in ways that keep necessary relationality and all its complications visible. The question is always there to ask: On whose behalf are speaking subjects speaking? Is it always nonhumans or themselves? Who inserted that bit about death when talking for modularity? The speaking subject only speaks in relation to nonhumans and to keep this relationality visible is to take the utterances and the actions of the speaking subject both seriously and with some skepticism. This is what Latour calls the *enigma* of the speaking subject (Latour 2004b, 70). The role of speaking subject is itself political since it is to be taken seriously but remain open to serious doubt:

> In politics, there is a very useful term for designating the whole gamut of intermediaries between someone who speaks and someone who speaks in that person's place, between doubt and uncertainty: "spokesperson." If I speak in the name of another, I am not speaking in my own name. Conversely, if I were to affirm without further ado that another is speaking through me, I would be demonstrating great naiveté, a naiveté that certain epistemological myths manifest ("facts speak for themselves") but political traditions prohibit. To describe intermediary states, we can use the notions of translation, betrayal, falsification, invention, synthesis, or transposition. In short, with the notion of the spokesperson, we are designating not the transparency of speech in question, but the *entire gamut* running the complete doubt (I may be a spokesperson, but I am speaking in my own name and not in the name of those I represent) to total confidence (when I speak, it is really those I represent who speak through my mouth). (Latour 2004b, 64)

And so, the speaking subject is to be taken with the *entire gamut* as an *enigma*, meaning all the representations and mediations between the nonhumans speak for themselves and the speaking subject speaks for themselves. This constructs a necessarily more complicated and less easily resolvable space than the construction of the design problem that holds false illusions of autonomy and solutions. This leads to the third and last way that the speaking subject makes thingpolitics present and lively in design. The speaking subject, despite its limitations and uncertainties, acknowledges the necessity or what Latour calls the right of nonhumans to speak and participate. For Latour, a democracy resides in the "new assembly of humans and nonhumans" in which all have a right to speak (Latour 2004b, 69). For design, I invoke the realist attitude that things will eventually speak and participate in our world, perhaps in muted ways and with all of the ambiguity if not more in the utterances of speaking subjects. By design, the participation of nonhumans is often made to occur after the designers have abandoned their posts and run elsewhere to solve another design problem. This creates anti-biographies. The politics of the speaking subject in design is that while not being able to make nonhumans speak fully or without a human agenda, it makes the *necessity* of nonhumans speaking present and lively in design.

In describing nonhumans as speaking, Bennett asks, "What if we loosened the tie between participation and human language use, encountering the world as a swarm of vibrant materials entering and leaving agentic assemblies?" (Bennett 2010, 107). That is, what if speaking was not through language but through effects? This clearly does happen. Consider the effects of plastics in our oceans or the more complex interactions of climate change on the dropping of the atmosphere over Mount Everest or, as Bennett asks, "Does the typical American diet make Americans more susceptible to militaristic propaganda?" (Bennett 2010, 107). This form of speech as a matter of agential realism (Barad 2007) or vital materialism has been discussed in design (Frauenberger 2019; Devendorf et al. 2016; Andersen et al. 2019). Even in the more traditional sense of design methods, designers aim to realize effects of nonhumans, though in highly constrained ways. In fact, the knowledge, methods, and skills to design that are at the center of most discussions on design are focused on speaking on behalf of nonhumans and their mediations or effects.

Repertoires of a Constituency

To conclude this chapter, I focus on the needs of a constituency of the designer or what is needed to make the most of such a gathering, to bring a proto-constituency closer to becoming a constituency. The speaking subject features prominently in these concluding comments. Fortunately, the reader of this book, who has persistently read the text to this point, is likely a speaking subject. The speaking subject is important in the designer but more so as a member of the constituency. Constituencies are *things-before-things* that can be more fully expressed as *gatherings before designing things*. It is to gather those who are concerned, as well as the matters that cause their concerns, to debate and discuss designing *something*, without assuming or committing to the need for a designer of things, and then to debate and discuss what kind of designer the constituency wants. This expansive and inclusionary gathering is proactive. It gathers the material arrangements of the constituency, human and nonhuman alike, to experiment with and to form the designer with an eye toward the potential biographies that will emerge. To *gather while designing things* is too late and gathers too little, and to *gather after designing things* is catastrophically too late and creates anti-biographies.

The need for constituencies is a pressing matter. Even the most privileged proto-constituencies of our time, technology corporations, endured a spring awakening of discontent in late 2019 and early 2020. During this period, Google fired two employees, Laurence Berland and Rebecca Rivers, for their activism over sexual harassment policies, exploitive labor practices, and contracts with the military, border control, and authoritarian governments[10] (Conger and Scheiber 2020; Conger and Wakabayashi 2019). Tim Bray resigned as a vice president for Amazon to protest the firing of Courtney Bowden, Gerald Bryson, Maren Costa, Emily Cunningham, Bashir Mohammed, and Chris Smalls, who protested against unsafe working conditions in Amazon warehouses during the COVID-19 pandemic (Bray 2020; Sainato 2020). During this same period Facebook employees staged a virtual walkout over the company's refusal to comment, flag, or censure violent and racist messages posted to Facebook by the US president during protests for racial justice (Frenkel et al. 2020)—and like Latour (2018), I cannot utter or put to print his name. There is an innocence to design today, an awakening or shock that the technology sector is in anyway a part of the indecencies of late capitalism. Within these technology corporations, which are indeed a type of assembly or proto-constituency of humans and nonhumans, politics have been muted and things kept silent to whatever degree is possible. That these kinds of proto-constituencies are the mass producers of anti-biographies is

The Constituency of the Designer   229

only logical. Moving past the innocence of design and the narrow mindedness of the design problem, it is critical to refigure or reassemble constituencies of designing things that are expansive and political enough to create biographies. And so, as speaking subjects, constituencies need to be the "center of our attention" (Latour 2005a, 23).

There is the need to intensify the knowledge, methods, and skills needed to transform and mobilize design constituencies through what I call *repertoires*. Repertoires are experimental and reflexive practices or mobilizing actions of the speaking subject. They can include processes that seriously and deliberately engage efficacies and trajectories, constantly flying the kite on endless test runs, so to speak. This helps to realize and make visible the force of the nonhuman and human designer in the designing of things. Latour described the invention of *speech prostheses* by scientists to allow the nonhuman participation of soil, plants, or glaciers to make contributions to the construction of science (Latour 2004b, 67). We can then think about repertoires that involve new techniques and tools as speech prostheses that account for and realize nonhumans in design in forms of speech beyond human language, in ways that make contributions to designing things. As Latour also warns, such inventions are not easy as they proceed with *"all the difficulties* that a human encounters in speaking to humans about nonhumans *with* their participation" (Latour 2004b, 68).

Repertoires as speech prostheses for representing nonhumans can become the building blocks for other needs of constituencies. There is the need for repertoires for convening constituencies that find ways for nonhumans to be more present, more participatory, more cared-with and lively within constituencies. The cultivation and development of repertoires by speaking subjects are critical to the full participation of all assembled in the constituency and making material the expansive matters of concern and care. Specifically, within constituencies, there is the need for repertoires that aid the formation of designers. Repertoires cultivate and foster the arrival of resolutions of what kind of assembly is required to form a designer for the design of particular things that lead to accountable biographies.

Even with the development of repertoire or posthuman design methodologies, nonhumans will remain comparatively silent while still actively participating. The sheer mass and mass of relations of the nonhumans gathered in constituencies silently stabilize like a ballast or conversely capsize, like misplaced cargo, the constituencies they help form. All speaking aside, the matter of constituencies even in mute form holds power, whether the *arisan* of the Nenek-nenek, *Saccharomyces cerevisiae*, or open-source wetware. Between the challenges to make visible and the realities of their invisibility, we don't know how to make the most of nonhuman participation. Like new equipment without manuals or buttons and functions we cannot recognize, there is a need to learn more about how to speak-with, participate-with, and care-with at the level of a constituency. There is a need to invent repertoires to recruit, maintain, and attend to the relations or the mass of things that form the constituency.

Lastly, even with developed repertoires in place, there is the constant need to learn and develop the role of the convener that belongs to the speaking subject. As discussed earlier, there is a need to learn how the speaking subject can be internal to constituencies rather than external or speaking outwardly. The speaking subject as convener need not be the same human as the speaking subject of the designer. In many ways, to convene humans and nonhumans to participate together is its own skill set. To convene is not only to gather but to invoke all to speak and engage in repertoires to engage matters of concern and care. This is not a one-time event but an ongoing effort whose values are multiplicity, expansiveness, and inclusion. Given this, a speaking subject as convener invokes overlapping representations of a constituency that are not there to be flattened or made into a hierarchy but to create a dynamic and more real lifeworld within which designers of things, things, and biographies arise.

Conclusion

Chapter 8: Designing-with

At the outset of the book, I stated that I wanted to "unbuild" design as we typically know it in order to speculate critically and creatively on what posthumanist design might mean. Throughout the book, I rethought design in posthuman terms by de-emphasizing the human role in order to illuminate and assert the role of nonhumans, of which I largely focused on what I called *things*. This decentering of the human in design held for me deep entanglements that raised several questions that I responded to with several answers: How do we know what design is? I answered that we understand design pluralistically and nomadically (chapters 2 and 3). What is the something that is designed? I answered that it is a relational and agentic thing (chapters 4 and 5). Who is the designer? I answered that the designer is an assembly of humans and nonhumans (chapters 6 and 7). It was also important to me to stay close to the paradox that posthumanism, more so than humanism, attends to the specificity of being human in the world and how this impacts design (Wolfe 2010). This allowed me to focus in detail on the human designer not as the privileged force in design but as a unique member of an expanded and agentic human-nonhuman assembly that together designs things. And so, a central story of the book is that human designers (who should be seen as plural, heterogeneous, and differentiated actors) entangled within assemblages of nonhuman designers (also plural, heterogeneous, and differentiated actors) are powerful but limited in their powers. And so, a leitmotif of the book is a desire for *humility* in the human designer—a humility borne out of a posthuman subjectivity that is emergent, fallible, and a matter of differences rather than the universalizing ideal of humanism (Braidotti 2013). This understanding of subjectivity gives cause for humility in design; a cause that I wanted to deepen further by establishing posthumanist *relationality* as the basis for seeing the gatherings of the nomadic practices of design (Haraway 1985; Latour 1993; Verbeek 2005; Barad 2007) in which humans, things, and world can only be understood in relation to each other. An ongoing question in the book is not what does it mean to design, but what does it mean to *design-with*, or as I asked in the introduction, What does it mean to design for more than human-centered worlds? What I have tried to express is that to design-with is humbling in that one is defined in relation to others, acts alongside others, and co-shapes with other humans and nonhumans. To design-with is also expansive in its togetherness with others, co-constitution with others, and cohabiting of worlds with others. To design-with is to rethink design in ways that humans and nonhumans are bound together materially, ethically, and existentially.

In this concluding chapter, I summarize the nomadic practice of designing things, then turn to remaining questions when it comes to designing-with. What is it that I am asking of human designers and the commitments required? How can we design things without fully knowing the consequences of what is designed and the challenges of not having the abilities to fully know or understand nonhumans? And I explore how generosity is a necessary commitment in designing things.

Nomadic Practice of Designing Things

I set out to unbuild design in three parts that led to what I called the nomadic practice of designing things. Part I is the "unbuilding" of *design* as a discipline (chapters 2 and 3). Part II is a description of *things* (chapters 4 and 5). Part III focuses on the *designer* of things (chapters 6 and 7).

In part I, design was unbuilt as a discipline to be seen as *nomadic practices*. Nomadic practices are a way to see design in multiplicity, as any number of distinct and concurrent practices, each directing itself or gathering around a particular *something* to design without a shared foundation or universal knowledge of design. The development of nomadic practices as a theory was guided by posthuman epistemologies in which knowledge of design is plural, relational, situated, and constantly on the move. In this way, each nomadic practice understands what it means to design from its own position(s) with respect to skills, methods, or dynamics of any kind. It can also be said to be making a claim to design without any claim to

Designing-with   235

a singular understanding of design. This is a shift away from humanist underpinnings—namely, disciplinary thinking—and assumes a nomadic fluidity in thinking of design that embraces relationality and expansiveness by accepting that design is plural, a series of concurrent, conflicting, and overlapping alternatives.

I have described three different nomadic practices (there are many others) that each design a different something: *designing artifacts* that contribute to human progress through supporting complex human use and practices; *designing objects* that aspire to higher principles of morality and goodness; and *designing products* for economic gain and well-being as a matter of financial transactions. These multiple framings of design are grounded in the idea of different ways of addressing the world through design or different intentionalities made up of differently constituted subject-objects of design. The specific intentionality or nomadic practice that I have focused on in this book is *designing things*, a posthuman conceptualization of design. At this juncture, it makes sense to take stock of the plurality of nomadic practices of design discussed in this book in the form of a summary table (see table 8.1) that allows for a comparison of the nomadic concepts discussed in chapter 3 with the nomadic practice of designing things.

Table 8.1
Different nomadic practices of design

Designing artifacts	Designing objects	Designing products	Designing things
Artifacts contribute to human progress by supporting productive and complex use and practices. Artifacts are both conceptual and tangible, embodying paths to ideal future uses and human experiences.	Objects represent cultural aspirations governed by transcendental principles of a higher order of morality and goodness. Objects aim to be timeless and of a standard more enduring than social conventions or economic gain.	Products are capitalist means of increased production and economic development in industrial-scale economies. Products aim to serve the human economic goals of fair transactions between profit and consumer satisfaction.	Things transform what it means to be human by being co-constitutive. Things are relational and so are highly interpretive, multistable, and ultimately political. Each thing has unique intentionalities and agentic capacities that are shared with humans.

In part II, I tackled the *thing* designed in the nomadic practice of designing things by addressing the different philosophical concepts, or legs of the stool I used to define things (see figure 1.1). Chapter 4 expanded on the philosophical concept of *mediating technologies* (Ihde 1990; Latour 1992; Verbeek 2005) that describes how things, like technologies, are *interconnected* with who we are as humans such that humans are *prosthetic creatures* (Wolfe 2010). In this interconnectedness, things are commensurate with being human through various descriptions of human-things. I gave examples of how things *transform* what it means to be human so that the relations between humans and things are co-constitutive: Things equally shape humans as humans shape things. Further, I wanted to make clear that the co-constitutive nature of human-things is embodied, as it is to be human. Things can be understood as embodied relations to the world in any given moment with all its particularities and differences across experiences. In this way, things (or the meaning of things) are performative in that they are only meaningful when experienced within an embodied situation. As a result, things also hold different meanings depending on different embodied situations. Lastly, in chapter 4, I showed the expansiveness of the interconnectedness of things that comes from larger assemblages of humans and nonhumans. Within an assemblage, things equally interact with other things, as much if not more than humans, and these active relations are ongoing and parallel. And so, things are not only directed at humans but are also directed at other things. This gives assemblages of things complex dynamics and a precariousness that can play out in many ways simultaneously, making the knowing of things uncertain, partial, and relational.

In chapter 5, I introduced the second philosophical concept supporting the definition of things, *assembly of vital matter*, that refers to the dynamics of how things are relational, as things are seen to have agentic qualities and unique intentionalities. This concept allowed me to build on the work of the previous chapter to further examine how things are not fixed; rather, they are highly interpretive, multistable, and as a consequence, political. Things can now be described as non-neutral: They can contribute to both the construction of normative values and the destabilizing of norms, which together opens things to other interpretations and political realities. This leads to a political ecology understanding of things in which the non-neutrality of things acts in ways that are more intra-action or interrelated than causal yet with the capacity to qualitatively shift normative values one way or another. This widening of the transformative power of things was given a more detailed analysis by borrowing from vital materialism concepts of distributed agencies between humans and nonhumans. Here I especially drew on the idea of *agentic capacities* (Coole 2005), in which things direct themselves uniquely at the world and have sufficient qualities of agency to have the effects of an agent. In particular, I focused on two qualities, *efficacy* and *trajectory*, drawing on Bennett (2010, 31). Trajectory is the direction of the force, a movement or progression without suggesting "purposiveness." This describes the mobilizing of actions and events across an assemblage. Efficacy is the creative aspect of the force; it can be said to mark points along trajectories in which changes or new things are created. It is important to see agentic capacities as distributed; then, not having a subject as its root cause, efficacy is seen more as effects than actions. Additionally, the nonhuman qualities of vitality or agency open things to nonhuman temporalities and scale that can have ongoing effects beyond a human lifetime.

In part III, I explored what a *designer* is, based on the ideas of interconnectedness, transformation, relationality, and vitality of things. Given the assumptions of designing things developed in the earlier chapters, it should be unsurprising that there was no way to conceive of the designer of things as exclusively human. Between the relationality of humans and the vitality of things, the designer is described as an assembly of humans and nonhumans. The creative dimension of the vitality of things is given full measure in its role in designing and creating new things. I called this expanded agency of the designer—that is, nonhumans contribute as creative actors in the design of things, as designers as *force*. In describing the force of the designer, the agentic capacities of trajectory and efficacy (from chapter 5) are reprised but in a more explicitly creative function or having the qualities of a designer.

In chapter 6, I situated the human designer in various ways. Firstly, I described a unique human role in the assembly as the *speaking subject* of the designer, drawing on Latour's idea of spokesperson for nonhumans (Latour 2004b). The speaking subject has a dual role: One is to give purpose or reason to the assembly—in other words, to speak to what is being designed and why. The second role is to speak on behalf of nonhumans in the assembly and those the assembly interacts with. This role does not control or lead the assembly; rather, as Latour describes his notion of the spokesperson, a speaking subject is to be taken seriously while listened to with great suspicion. The point is that while it is clear who is *doing* the speaking, it is not entirely clear who *is* speaking, the human or nonhuman, and with what authority (Latour 2004a). The role of the speaking subject puts the human designer in the heart of the political ecology of things, which is explored again in chapter 7. To further understand the assembly of the designer I argued that the configuration of the designer as speaking subject and forces would ebb and flow over the life of things and assemblages arising in moments of *intensity* in which the designer is clearly present and affecting change such as a redesign, a hybridization, or a morphing into a new thing altogether. One other such event is *origins*, again drawing on Bennett (2010), in which humans as speaking subjects are intensively present among the designer assembly at the beginning of a design of a thing. But being intensively present at the beginning—that is, having providence of origins—rarely leads to causal significance in the eventual outcome.

Across chapters 6 and 7, I focused on the specificity of the human role in the designer and its entanglements within the political ecology of things. In these chapters, I expanded on the third philosophical concept that defines things (see figure 1.1), *matters of concern and care*, which draw on ideas of thingpolitics (Latour 2004a, 2005a) and more than human care (Puig de la Bellacasa 2017). Latour's matters of concern is the bringing together of the multiplicity of associations and attachments related to things that are open to discussion and contestations. Matters of care extends Latour's idea to draw out the "affective and ethical connotations" of concerns more precisely. As a way to emphasize and make matters of concern and care both persistent and significant, I argued for a binding together of the human designer and the thing designed in what I called the *biography* of the designer. A biography views the designer and the things it designs as inscribing themselves into the same lifeworld they cohabit. The purpose is to define a way to make the designer of things accountable for what it designs into the world and what it leaves behind. In other words, the value of the designer of things cannot be separated from the lifeworld it contributed to through designing things. Biographies tie together the interdependencies of the assembly and lifeworld of a designer into one entity that may live on well beyond the human lives of the designer of things. This is critical to getting beyond the willful exclusion of matters of concern and care that attach to the things that are designed. Further, this exclusion is endemic to what I call *anti-biographies*, in which concerns are restricted to the *design problem* to avoid the vitality and politics of things.

In chapter 7, I argued for a political structure for designing things that convenes humans and nonhumans together to continually ask who participates and who is represented among speaking subjects and the mute things that go on to assemble into designers. I call this convening a *constituency*, and it is a structure that gathers to engage matters of concern and care within the commitment (or not) to assemble a designer and to design things. In this way, a constituency is what Karen Barad describes as the "open-ended and dynamic material-discursive practices, through which specific 'concepts' and 'things' are articulated" (Barad 2007, 334). This means to engage in the material arrangements of humans and nonhumans as descriptions or tellings while also desiring specific possibilities that emerge from such descriptions. The human role in a constituency is as the convener that assembles and maintains the collective and, in an extension of the speaking subject role, speaks on behalf of and ensures the participation of nonhumans. Constituencies are a reaching back to the earliest concerns of acting through design, before designers and before things, in what I called *things-before-things*. Constituencies infuse the origins of designing things to become an expanded and rich problematic of matters of concern and care from which to decide who and what becomes the assembly of the designer and what the thing is to be designed. The constituency assembles to discuss, debate, contest, and enact design such that the designer of things is immanent expansively and politically.

Lastly, in chapter 7, I gave many examples of what I called *anti-biographies*. As the name suggests, anti-biographies are the opposite design response to a posthuman understanding of design. As such, they served as a foil to designing things. Central to anti-biographies is the *design problem*, which I argued is a radical reduction of design concerns that privilege the human designer and exclude every aspect of designing things, including the participation of nonhumans, the interconnectedness and agentic role of things and matter, and the matters of concern or thingpolitics. Anti-biographies dramatically reduce the concerns of design whereas their counterpart, biographies, dramatically expand the concerns of design. Anti-biographies find accountability in the illusion of solving a problem, but in doing so, they separate the designer, thing, and lifeworld from each other such that no serious accountability can be had.

Ways We Could Design-with

With the look-back at the earlier chapters complete, I now turn to looking forward and reflect on what I am asking of human designers: where to start with methods to design while not-knowing things, and thoughts on the generosity of designing things.

The "Ask" of the Designer

Constituencies are one of the inventions of this book, alongside biographies and nomadic practices. The idea of constituencies arose from a critical imagining of a political structure for designing things that drew on previous ideas, such as *parliament of things* (Latour 2005a) and *publics* (Binder et al. 2015; Ehn 2008; Le Dantec 2016), and on my experiences of designing and the things of the prologues of the book. As such, constituencies emerged from what I have called a critical (analytical) and creative (inventive) speculation—a form of speculation that I also described as both "construction and reality" after Puig de la Bellacasa (2017, 33). Throughout the book, I have tried to adopt the *stubbornly realist attitude* of scrutinizing the relations of the things and assemblages I brought forward (Latour 2004a). There is of course my positionality from which this realist approach is taken. It is a position that is bound in my privileges, limitations, and background, though also informed by what I can barely hide as my desire to refigure my understanding of my design experiences into a construction of how I want to see things made in the world. What I want from designing things can be seen as a moralizing position—though a position that I see as largely immanent, lying somewhere between emerging from and bringing forward the thicket of entanglements, relationality, multistability, agentic forces, and nonhuman vitalities of posthuman design. And so while cognizant of the certain pitfalls of making posthuman thinking in and of itself virtuous, I see the moralizing position, the ask of the human designers, as produced by a way of thinking that Didier Debaise and Isabelle Stengers view as speculation that *maximizes* its "friction with experience" (Debaise and Stengers 2017, 16) or that was arrived at by placing myself in the "flow of this moving experience" (Puig de la Bellacasa 2017, 33). Nevertheless, I have asked human designers (myself included!) to act with and on behalf of nonhumans in ways that are accountable for how we quite literally live-together—even after our human life is over. The ask is to design-with as expressed in the values of humility, togetherness, cohabitation, and caring over diverse concerns.

In a practical sense, what am I asking of designers? And by designers, in this case, I mean differentiated human designers but also those practicing within their own nomadic practice of design. What are the commitments being asked of a commercial designer, a designer of products or services that works for hire or for clients? What are the commitments required from a designer of artifacts, typically a researcher whether academic or industrial? And what am I asking of the designer of objects that straddles the economic domains of products and research as the means to find a secure space from which to design objects? A clear challenge to any commitments is the matter of economics, which might include financial dependency on and accountability to clients and employers, or the need to maintain the business of a consultancy or a technology company. And then there are the substantial investments in social, political, and economic infrastructures and the incentives they create to direct research on ideological grounds of national and industrial policies (i.e., grants, publications, tenure, and peer recognition). Such structures are the colossal massing of material arrangements that stabilize and enforce a "common sense" that mostly makes arguments like mine, in the near term, remote or nice places to visit but near impossible to cohabit permanently. Ironically, these politico-economic matters are the very "missing masses" or nonhuman arrangements that have sedimented into practices and assumptions, making them appear partly invisible or immovable. However, there are clear fissures in the firmaments that are not difficult to see, such as the rarified few who exercise undue influence through venture capitalism and stock market purchases to fuel the design of unneeded and even deceptive technologies for profit; the rise of monopolistic and predatory practices to control the market for such technologies; the ongoing concerns of government-funded research that serves private good over public good; and the ongoing debates about what even is meant by *public good*. The political economy of design and technologies is work that needs to be done and is being carried out by others (Nardi 2015; Ekbia and Nardi 2017; Light, Powell, and Shklovski 2017; Zuboff 2019). It is undoubtedly a critical project unto itself and a project that would inform what is required of economic and political structures to support designing things. And the further necessity to bring together these political economy concerns with political ecology concerns that unsparingly shed light on the current ecological crisis. This work is yet to be done and would be part of larger transformations that go well beyond the discussion at hand. And so, this is why I am focusing now on what I call a *moral ask*. It is an appeal to the strength of the argument that to *design-with* is a *good* needed to be pursued. In response to the challenges of now, a moral ask operates on a longer temporal curve, aiming for the blessings of time.

With this in mind, it is important to consider effects at the level of practices from one nomadic practice to another, which is at the intersections, affiliations, appropriations, and persuasions across the terrain in which nomadic practices influence each other like overlapping gravitational forces—shifting the nomadism, the directions, and shapes of each other's practices. In this way, the very idea and construction of the nomadic practice of designing things can also be seen as a way to influence and move other nomadic practices toward ideas of biography, constituencies, and the mediating, vital, and political ecology of things—and to influence other nomadic practices like products or artifacts into forming new or adapted modes of accountability that consider designing-with. In this respect, the analytical work offered here provides a framework for new ways to consider the role of nonhumans in the designing of products, objects, or artifacts. For example, a designer's intuitive responses and conversations with materials and technologies can be seen as leading to unexpected but valued outcomes as the role of distributed agency is shared with nonhumans. Or, for example, consider the inevitability of unintended consequences as the result of multiple agencies beyond human, and in response, develop new techniques to work with the multiple agencies when designing with materials or artificial intelligence. This could mean designing outcomes for limited durations to allow time to experience the consequences and stop them if necessary, or making stakeholders in a design collective owners to empower their ability to respond to unintended consequences that affect them, or viewing functionality ecologically such that design outcomes become missing pieces rather than proprietary wholes on a take-it-or-leave-it basis.

This is a piecemeal offering for the taking by any designer of any other nomadic practice that comes with no explicit commitments. In this practical adoption, the moral ask is latent; it is a slow shifting of the ground toward designing-with, while showing a wariness toward contributing to anti-biographies and deceptive corporate practices. This is an incrementalism in which, as stated earlier, even a humbler positioning of designers, with respect to the cohabitants of nonhumans, would be a remarkable step in the right direction.

My real desire is that given the strength of the arguments laid out in this book, the explicit moral ask to design-with in its fullest is seen as persuasive and worthy of new commitments. Design as nomadic practices is premised on the idea of creating gatherings around particular *somethings* to design, and so my ultimate goal is to attract you, advocates and practitioners of other variants of design, to gather to design things and to join and form constituencies for designing things. So, yes, I ask you to abandon your current positions to consider this unbuilt variant of posthuman design—and in doing so, to commit to the need for repertoires, speech prostheses, and the training and development of speaking subjects with a thorough understanding of the becoming and criticality of biographies through the things we design.

The commitments from a human designer of things are to put these possibilities into action. Yet how is one to act when the same arrangements I have argued for diminish the human designer's autonomy to act? In other words, in the posthumanism of designing things, how is the human designer to act responsibly or ethically when the very autonomy to do so is questioned? Early on, I described the responsibility as shared across the assemblage rather than individual humans in the examples of the electrical power grid failure (Bennett 2010) or the speed bump (Latour 1992). But this is not the whole picture. In discussing morality and technological mediation, Verbeek, influenced by the work of Steven Dorrestijn, argues that ethical action lies in our relations to the mediation by technologies, arguing further for a moral *mediated* subject that is responsible without autonomy (Dorrestijn 2004, 2012; Verbeek 2011). Both are indebted to Michel Foucault's work on the self-formation of the ethical self whose relation to autonomy is mediated by power (Foucault 1978). Verbeek sees a similar self-formation of a moral subject in relation to mediations of technology. In short, he sees the capacity to act responsibly as a mediated subject by beginning with the question: "What kind of mediated subjects do we want to be?" (Verbeek 2011, 83). That is, he argues for a *self-practice* in which technology use is deliberate and resolute by anticipating and shaping the mediation of technology with the full realization that this will also shape our subjectivity. In other words, seriously and reflexively engaging technological mediation is the means to shaping our own mediated subject or becoming the mediated subject we desire. This does not mean adhering to a moral code of being good but rather a constant ongoing forming of the self that requires "experimentation"—attempts to both distance oneself from technological mediation while also deliberately experiencing mediation to see what co-shaping possibilities emerge and what capacity there is to realize these possibilities.

This can readily be applied to acting within constituencies and biographies. It starts by asking the question, What kind of designer (that is both human and nonhuman) do we want to be? In fact, this is the explicit question or the very rationale of the constituency: What kind of designer do we want to emerge from the constituency? The aim of the constituency is to decide to form a designer and to decide what kind of designer that ought to be, and so it is a more collective understanding of self-formation as the designer emerges from those who are convened. The activities of the constituencies are to engage in forms of *self-practice* and *experimentation* that I described at the end of chapter 7 as repertoires. The explicit demand on the speaking subject is to engage and investigate the matters of concern and care seriously and deliberately to foster the kind of designer the constituency sees as needed, given the particularities of the thing to be designed. The speaking subject convenes to determine the assembly of the designer that transforms being deliberate into deliberations and being resolute into resolutions. In the process, the speaking subject and the constituency engage in a process of self-formation or what Verbeek, after Foucault, referred to as *autopoeisis*, the ability to self-produce as in the self-formation of the mediated subject (Verbeek 2011).

This way to act for the speaking subject can be added to or be arrived at from another more expansive perspective such as Haraway's notion of *response-ability*. This refers to the capacity to affect others and be affected by others and so accountable by becoming-with and making each other capable in the process (Haraway 2016). For Haraway, response-ability is well illustrated by the game of cat's cradle in which string figures, patterns of looped and knotted string, are created by passing a loop of string back and forth between the hands and fingers of multiple players. The game creates the string figure by maintaining the pattern while simultaneously experimenting with new possibilities and doing so collectively. Haraway sees in this collectivity the need for action and response, detachment and attachment, in the way one acts to invent while others remain steady to conserve the pattern. This combination of risk and trust, talking and listening, thinking and observing, goes beyond the metaphor of the game to cultivate the capacity for responses more complexly, in ways that are together and so without autonomy. Expanding the collective capacity to act responsibly relies on accepting the "risk of relentless contingency" and the risk of not-knowing what to expect "from unexpected worlds" (Haraway 2016, 34). Response-ability is the cultivating of abilities to do and think. In this way, the implied morality is to not only act when one does not fully know but to also try to think what one does not know.

Response-ability is thinking-with that aligns well with constituencies and adds to how the speaking subjects, which are invariably differentiated with particular privileges and limitations, can act ethically. It expands the mediations and desires necessary to form the designer we want and does so collectively and expansively. Whereas self-formation of the mediated subject is described by Verbeek after Foucault as *autopoeisis*, Haraway refers to response-ability as *sympoiesis*. *Sympoiesis* is the collective self-formation or collectively producing entity; as a result, it is unlike *autopoeisis* and does not self-limit its boundaries like with a subject but rather through its collectivity it is multiple, distributed, and relational in ways that help answer the question of how to act on behalf of a constituency as a speaking subject.

Not-Knowing Things

The humanist illusion of human autonomy and the ability to objectively know a world separate from us makes the ability to *fully* know paramount. Earlier, in the discussion of anti-biographies in chapter 7, I argued against the *design problem*, since it allowed designers to radically reduce and exclude the political and uncontrollable aspects of designing a thing, product, artifact, or object. The reduction of the "space" in the design problem is a way to maintain an illusion of more fully knowing what concerns the design at hand and the autonomy to act with that knowledge. In the process, the design problem creates a space of fuller knowing within the design problem and a space outside the design problem that is unknowable and replete with unintended consequences. However, a close look at design problems, specifically through the lens of Donald Schon's *frame reflection*, shows a more porous boundary between inside and outside the design problem or the spaces of knowing and not-knowing (Schon and Rein 1994). The circumscribing of the design problem becomes liminal. Schon sees the design problem as dually complex, vague, and indeterminate but in need of a solution. *Framing* the design problem is to arrange and rearrange the problem as an experiment of alternatives, reflecting on and changing the assumptions to find ways to make the problem intelligible—that is, to select or even create what to know, in order to act.

In chapter 2, I briefly described these ideas as Schon's *naming and framing*, along with *generative metaphors* as adapted by Philip Agre (1997). In both instances, framing is positioned within the agenda of the one doing the framing. The practitioner "reflects on the meaning" of the problem "from a position within it" (Schon and Rein 1994, 105). This declaration of positionality, though still limited and within a humanist perspective, resonates with the earlier discussions of the need for positionality in the designing of things. It is a partial but positioned knowing. Schon's frame reflection is a deeply pragmatist argument that also sees the necessity for tacit beliefs, judgments, and intuitions to allow for radical and relational moves in reconstituting the design problem, and in ways that are more suitably normative for the ones doing the framing (i.e., solvable for them). Despite the drive to solve the problem (which is ultimately about constructing a place where the subject knows the most), frame reflection relates to the previous discussion of ethical acting of the speaking subject and shows the familiarity in current design practices for action when knowing is uncertain, partial, and relational. The need is to dramatically push this understanding to be expansive, to go beyond design matters of concern as they are narrowly construed—and, more challengingly, to push to give up on the illusion of solving the problem, to focus on developing ways of not-knowing in design that stay with the problem (or the trouble) through strategies of mediation and care of the things designed. And so, there are starting points to foster a practice that acts from a position of not-knowing or partial knowing. This means that we can look to ideas of the mediated subject, response-ability, and an expanded frame reflection to begin developing the material-discursive practice or methods to act on the ethos of humility, togetherness, cohabitation, and caring over diverse concerns.

The not-knowing in designing things extends to the things themselves. I have been discussing up until now the not-knowing of speaking subjects with regards to their doings, but there is also the not-knowing of the speaking subjects of the things they speak on behalf of. That is, how can we speak on behalf of nonhumans and participate together if on many levels they are unknowable to us for the simple fact that they are not human? Where do we start in cultivating Latour's speech prostheses as the repertoires I discussed at the end of chapter 7? There is a need to create posthuman methodologies or repertoires for designing things so that we can design together with things while also not fully knowing things.

A starting point for these repertoires can be found in the string figures of techniques from the critical posthumanist philosophies I've allied with to help my cause. There are important examples in works less present in the book, such as Anna Tsing's *noticing* of the happenings and interplay in what she refers to as *polyphonic assemblages* of nonhumans and humans (Tsing 2015), and Vinciane Despret's generous undoing of the language and theories of science that are too frugal and de-animating to see animal agencies (Despret 2016). Haraway (2003) gives a lesson in accounting for multispecies kinship and companionship in her *Companion Species Manifesto*. Relatedly, in this book I retold various "soil stories" that exemplify the realist approach to nonhuman relations and the crossing over toward seeing and hearing of nonhumans. For example, I described Latour's analysis of the soil in the Amazon forest in Boa Vista by soil scientists (Latour 1999). Latour scrutinized not only an ethnographic account of the scientists but their ongoing actions and relations to the soil and, in particular, the ways they presented and represented the soil to themselves, colleagues, and their academic community. The details of the representations of the soil are repertoires to make nonhumans present and active in the making of the science. There is the example that Bennett (2010) provides that she refers to after the fact as a posthuman empiricism of getting dirty, immersing oneself to live with soil, as did Charles Darwin, empathizing to the boundaries of anthropomorphism to *see* the permeability and the intra-action between worms and soil. It was Puig de la Bellacasa (2017) who first noted the prevalence of "soil stories" among nonhumanist thinkers, and this is particularly noteworthy given her concept of *permaculture ethics* as a way toward nonhuman care. The permaculture movement, though difficult to sum up, cultivates practices of sustaining and fostering life through its natureculture interdependencies such as those between biology and farming in agriculture. For Puig de la Bellacasa, the journey toward theories of nonhuman care involved participation in permaculture collectives, allowing her to get up close to the soil and its relations to her. (Latour suggested getting close to what are seen as facts in order to understand the matters of concern—see Latour 2004a.) Puig de la Bellacasa's approach to knowing is to radically situate oneself within and with soil with the aim to "thicken the meanings" of what we take for granted or think is inaccessible (Puig de la Bellacasa 2017, 145). These repertoires to not-know things almost require a transmogrification—that is, a surprisingly if not a seemingly magical change of who we are, in relation to things and nonhumans. Darwin, according to Bennett, became nonhuman, a worm-soil in his observations; Latour observed scientists who tasted soils as if they were preparing for a gourmet dinner of Amazonian clay; and Haraway (2016) in emphasizing kinship with other species and nonhumans refigures *humans* to become *humus* or soil, compostable and lifegiving.

We can also look to the string figures of techniques from the designed things that populate this book as nonhuman witnesses. *Lifepatch* showed the tentacular nature of a designer that is collective but also gathers the speech prostheses of biological science with those of hacking and design. In the river project of Yogyakarta, the "hacker" assumed the roles necessary to enliven and enlist humans, soil, water, and bacteria (Lin and Lindtner 2016). Designing things does not require interdisciplinary thinking as much as porous knowing, such as *Lifepatch* assembling biologists, hackers, and residents to be speaking subjects in the assembly and specialists in their own right that can speak to and on behalf of things. In chapter 6, I devoted substantial discussion to autobiographical design (Neustaedter and Sengers 2012; Desjardins and Ball 2018). The autoethnographic techniques that focus on relations to things are a critical starting point in not-knowing things. However, autobiographical design also shows the subtle transmogrification of the designer from an outsider to an insider that is active within the designer's own living world. The designer is transformed into a cohabitant that designs. This human designer is bound to the world it acts in, within its limits as well as bound in material detail and real time to the world she is affecting. This was the kernel for the concept of *biography*, but it can also be seen as the necessary transformation of the speaking subject in order to not-know, and to not only execute repertoires but to embody the repertoires.[1]

The critical and creative speculations of this book extend to many of the things discussed that I often, and loosely, called speculative design. The examples though are of a particular kind of speculative design that fits the overall critical and creative speculation approach. The speculations through design featured here are material and empirical, speaking to a notion of speculation that *maximizes* its "friction with experience" (Debaise and Stengers 2017, 16). For example, Bellini's *Kar-a-sutra* is a thing to *know* things (Bellini 1972). That is, in refiguring cars and mobility, the not-knowing act is to materialize a "car" that can then be arranged in the world to ask what it does not know. My speculative design work, like the *Tilting Bowl* and *Morse Things*, are designed as things to be lived-with and that cohabit in order to inquire about what we do not know of relations with things through a materialist and temporal inquiry (Wakkary et al. 2018, 2017). As discussed earlier, these works use an approach called *material speculation* that combines the speculative technique of designing a *counterfactual artifact* (which by most standards and norms should not exist) and asking what-if research questions with empirical approaches of long field studies and analyses of lived-with experiences (Wakkary et al. 2015). In addition, my colleagues and I, and others, have augmented material speculation with *co-speculative* approaches in which we work closely with participants with either philosophical or artistic backgrounds to co-speculate with us on things we have designed—acting as speaking subjects for things (Wakkary et al. 2017, 2018; Desjardins et al. 2019). These are but a few starting points for repertoires to not-know nonhumans. In addition, the many things described in the prologues not only helped me elaborate on concepts but also offer methodological approaches to not-knowing things. For example, *Olly* and the *Obscura 1C Digital Camera* query data to see if it is co-constitutive of the human-things of music-listener-music-player or photographer-camera (Odom et al. 2019; Pierce and Paulos 2015); the wearables of *New Faces, New Identities* reverse the interrogation to trick and test facial recognition software (Baeza Argüello et al. 2021); *Green Screen Dress* fosters digital kinships with augmented reality and social media to express itself (Mackey et al., "Blending Clothing and Digital Expression," 2017); and *Being the Machine* literally unpacks 3D printers to become cyborgs of craft and additive fabrication (Devendorf and Ryokai 2015).

Relatedly, there are other approaches that were not discussed in this book that could also be kernels of not-knowing repertoires, like Kristina Andersen's *Magic Machine Workshops* that enlist magical thinking to explore the machines we desire materially over the teleological explorations of technologies (Andersen and Wakkary 2019); Lenneke Kuijer extends theories of social practice to ask of the potential agency of the material actors in social practices in what she sees as technologies *co-performing* with humans (Kuijer and Giaccardi 2018); Rachel Clarke's participatory performances under the fictional collective of the *Ministry of Multispecies Communications* create imaginaries for multispecies urban spaces (Clarke 2020); Cyn Liu's nonanthropocentric design strategy of *decomposition* explores techniques of fragmentation and tracing among others (Liu, Bardzell, and Bardzell 2019); and Doenja Oogjes's thing-centered approaches for making thing-perspectives and presences more felt are early forays into speech prostheses for things (Oogjes and Wakkary 2017; Oogjes et al. 2020). This is also an appropriate time to bring back the fellow travelers from the introductory chapter of Daniela Rosner's critical fabulations, Arturo Escobar's pluriverses, and Lars Spueybroek's sympathy of things. This list could go on. What is clear is that the terrain of not-knowing things is rich with deeply critical and serious speculations of making that can readily become repertoires to not-know things. And further, these can and should be brought together in a joining of the string figures with speculations of critical posthumanism.

Generosity

A paired phrasing that appears and reappears throughout the book is *relationality and expansiveness*. This phrasing was a constant point of return. Each new concept began with the question, How it can be relational and expansive? I started by refiguring design to be relational, seeing it as multiple intersecting nomadic practices that are fluid and constantly on the move, changing form to match the terrain each travels along. Design becomes expansive, without a singular claim and without foundations or boundaries. I described things as relational and multistable and so without fixed meaning. Things are interconnected with humans and assemblages. Things were described as expansive as they include agentic capacities, concretizations, and nonhuman relations equal to if not more than human relations. I aimed to refigure the designer into a relational and expansive figure that is an assembly of humans and nonhumans to be integrated into larger forms such as biographies and constituencies. At this point, I realize I could have reduced this pair of words to a single word: *generosity*. What I was actually trying to articulate is a generous understanding of what we call design. And so, I want to conclude the book with an argument for generosity as a way to understand design from a posthuman subjective position like my own.

Designing-with

I recognize that some (or many!) readers were never able to get past the idea of letting go of human-centeredness or the privileging of human values despite getting to this point in the book. In the introductory chapter, I framed the issue in existential terms in which I asked, What if human-centered thinking (and its underlying humanism) is not the answer to these problems (e.g., extinction of other species, climate change, exploitation, Anthropocene), but rather, in its dominant role, may be part of the problem? Attached to my moral ask of designing-with was the urgency of existential consequences. I argued with other enlisted theorists that human survival was dependent on nonhuman survival. Yet for some readers, this may not be sufficiently convincing to question the ideal of human progress or the goal of the perfection of humanity and design's supporting role in this enterprise. For those, I argued for at least a shift in considering that human values and goals entangle the fate of others. This would be a small move toward a more generous way of thinking *human* as a designer: a step toward humility.

For others, the argument may have been intellectually convincing, yet the all-too-human in you makes it a challenge to *think-with* or *design-with*. Aside from our deep and lifelong training in humanism, as a matter of survival, as Bennett argues, it is unavoidable to not identify with one's own species (Bennett 2010). Nevertheless, what are the acts, the embodied acts, that can move one toward a generous view of design that is to design-with. For ways to educate, practice and tackle the matters of concern of designing things, I offer a metaphor for embodied generosity: *horizontality*. In many respects the dominant human orientation toward space has been verticality, whether seen as the separator of our species from all others by standing vertical on the savannah, or the transcendental orientations toward divinities from above, or the triumphant phallic verticality of power and secular mastery, verticality has been the orientational metaphor for humans (Lakoff and Johnson 2003). To assume horizontality embodies all the resistance to the loss of human privilege, a fall to the ground. It is a reminder of what needs to be left behind and where we need to go. That is, horizontality embodies the relationality and expansiveness as action required for designing-with. This speaks to positioning oneself alongside other humans and nonhumans to literally expand the points of contact and increase the multiplicity of relations through greater proximity, like Darwin in the soil with the worms. This metaphorical position, in the context of designing things, is to design-with the greatest amount of contact and alongside nonhumans as humanly possible.

Generosity is risky. To assume horizontality is to risk humility by giving up the distant and all-seeing position of verticality. To be generous can lead to embracing too much that runs the risk of discerning too little. The embrace of everything can become an embrace of nothing. But I did not adopt generosity as the solution but as the cautious way forward in rethinking or unbuilding design. Most starting points for what design ought to be begin by seeking out a majoritarian position that I referred to earlier in the book as a discipline's aspiration to be a major science (Deleuze and Guattari 1987; DeLanda 2016; Braidotti 2013). For majoritarian ambitions, generosity is a vulnerability. It potentially allows contradictory assumptions and critical positions to form. Peter Sloterdijk characterizes this vulnerability through his concept of *immunology* in which he argues that humans continually seek to surround themselves in protective spheres—symbolically or physically, whether bubbles of interpersonal relationships, biological immunity, soothing architecture, or thought (Sloterdijk 2013). Open your sphere too generously and you open yourself to risk. And so, it may seem to make sense to construct ways of thinking about design that seek protections in bubbles that, by necessity, are frugal and paucal. But, I argue, it makes much more sense to take the risk and accept the vulnerabilities in order to foster a more generous design.

Notes

Chapter 1

1. Some may note that ideas of Object-Oriented-Ontology (OOO) and Speculative Realism (Bryant, Srnicek, and Harman 2011; Harman 2018; Morton 2013) are absent from much of the discussion in this book. This may seem like an omission given that these philosophies focus on objects and assemblages in ways that are not distant to the ideas of critical posthumanism, especially the vital and feminist materialisms that will feature in this book (e.g., Bennett 2010; Braidotti 2002). OOO and Speculative Realism are also quite indebted to Latour's Actor Network Theory and draw heavily on his work as I do. The main reason for the absence is that the space that critical posthumanism opens for design is suitably materialist. A critical posthumanist critique of OOO and Speculative Realism is that it is overly metaphysical and disembodied in its thinking (Braidotti and Vermeulen 2014). OOO and Speculative Realism explicitly argue against the materialist position of critical posthumanism, labeling it pejoratively as *overmining* in OOO language. To overmine is to focus on the effects of things, what they do rather than what they are ontologically (the goal of OOO and Speculative Realism). As a result, the arguments of multiplicity, dynamism, immanence, contingency, and so on that occupy much of this book have little place in OOO and Speculative Realism (e.g., Harman 2016).

2. For example, the discussion includes agential realism (Frauenberger 2019), Anthropocene (Light, Powell, and Shklovski 2017), human-machine configurations (Andersen et al. 2019; Devendorf and Rosner 2017; Devendorf and Ryokai 2015; Leahu 2016), material aesthetics (Van Dongen 2019), natureculture (Liu, Bardzell, and Bardzell 2018; Smith, Bardzell, and Bardzell 2017), object ontologies (Encinas et al. 2020; Lindley, Coulton, and Cooper 2017), postanthropocentricism (Devendorf et al. 2016; DiSalvo and Lukens 2011), technological mediation (Hauser 2018; Hauser, Oogjes, et al. 2018; Pierce and Paulos 2013; Wakkary et al. 2018; Wiltse and Stolterman 2010), and thing-centeredness (Giaccardi et al. 2016; Oogjes and Wakkary 2017; Wakkary et al. 2017).

3. One hundred and seventy-four climbers have summited Mount Everest without supplemental oxygen as of 2017 (Himalayan Database 2019).

Chapter 3

1. For a debate on the role of ethnography within design disciplines see Paul Dourish's 2006 article, *Implications for Design* (Dourish 2006).

Chapter 4 Prologue

1. "The Great Pacific Garbage Patch," *The Ocean Cleanup*, accessed November 15, 2020, https://www.theoceancleanup.com/great-pacific-garbage-patch/.

Chapter 4

1. Bruno Latour more pointedly states that "we would die on the spot" without the nonhumans that together make up our "humanness" (Latour 2011, 5).

2. Rich Site Summary or RSS is a subscription to digital content that allows users and applications to access updates to online content in a standardized, computer-readable format.

3. See "What Is the Great Pacific Garbage Patch?," *The Ocean Cleanup*, accessed November 15, 2020, https://www.theoceancleanup.com/great-pacific-garbage-patch/#what-is-the-great-pacific-garbage-patch.

Chapter 5

1. Rosenberger notes that an ANT interpretation of the "sleep-prevention bench" could be seen as the delegation of human enforcement—for example, increased police presence relegated to nonhuman protrusions or barriers added to the benches. Additionally, the sleep-prevention adjustments can be interpreted as "anti-programs" or nonhuman adjustments to shift human behavior (Latour 1992). While Rosenberger values the network relations at play, he argues that postphenomenology brings to an ANT interpretation a more nuanced and better understanding of the intersection of humans and technologies or things that reveals a different structuring of relations.

2. I owe this visit to my colleague Russell Taylor, who made all the arrangements as the director of the Dutch Field School at Simon Fraser University.

3. In conversation with Claudy Jongstra on May 10, 2019, Spannum, Netherlands.

Chapter 6 Prologue

1. The same exhibition included Bellini's *Kar-a-Sutra* (see chapter 3).

Chapter 6

1. Latour refers to the biosphere as the *critical zone* or the *sub-lunar* terrain that is the bios of the Anthropocene, starting with the relatively shallow geological surface of the soil and geological layers to the atmosphere and in between. The critical zone as conceived in James Lovelock's *Gaia* and evidenced in the Anthropocene both shapes the inhabitants and is shaped by the inhabitants; to cohabit is to mutually constitute both inhabitant and habitat (Latour 2017).

2. This constant change and integral relation of dweller and things challenges the vision of the Internet of Things (IoT) and smart computing in the home, which in *Living in a Prototype*, we argued leaves little space for ongoing reconfigurations or the mutual constitution of dweller and thing (Desjardins and Wakkary 2016).

3. In the second fiscal quarter of 2020, Facebook reported 2.7 billion monthly users.

4. Value sensitive design of Batya Friedman and colleagues also considers design beyond a single human lifespan in what they refer to as *multi-lifespan design* (Friedman and Nathan 2010; Friedman and Hendry 2019)

5. Equity in the context of nonhumans is not equality, although, as Braidotti's biological egalitarianism suggests, it is more a matter of de-privileging rather than a flat equality across nonhumans and humans (Braidotti 2013). Haraway (2003) more explicitly states that in the context of companion species, her companion dog Cayenne would not survive a full equality of species and that equity is an issue with all its differences and troubles intact.

6. See, for example, the analysis by Lee, Williams, and Frame (2019) of forty years of wind shear data that they report has increased in response to global warming and how these changes have had an effect on the North Atlantic polar jet stream.

Chapter 7

1. World Watch Institute estimates, https://www.worldwatch.org/node/5565.

2. See Plastic Oceans, https://plasticoceans.org/the-facts/, for facts on the proliferation of plastics products.

3. See Simon Reddy, "Plastic Pollution Affects Sea Life throughout the Ocean," *Pew*, September 24, 2018, https://www.pewtrusts.org/en/research-and-analysis/articles/2018/09/24/plastic-pollution-affects-sea-life-throughout-the-ocean.

4. See "Plastic Statistics," *Ocean Crusaders*, accessed November 18, 2020, http://oceancrusaders.org/plastic-crusades/plastic-statistics/.

5. "Inventor: Sten Gustaf Thulin," *Disposable America* (blog), accessed November 18, 2020, https://disposableamerica.org/the-plastic-bag/inventor-sten-gustaf-thulin/.

6. This failure is hardly due to American politics alone. In Canada, where I live, a wide assault rifle ban, which includes the AR-15, was proposed by the Federal Cabinet in response to the worst mass killing in Canada of twenty-two victims on Portapique and Shubenacadie Nova Scotia, which occurred in April 2020 as I was writing this chapter. Even worse, the government had only just announced the intent to ban the Ruger Mini-14 that was used in Canada's second worst shooting of fourteen women victims at the Polytechnique Montréal in Montreal, which occurred some thirty years ago in 1989 (Tasker 2020).

7. See my own early research on location tracking for museum visits (Wakkary and Hatala 2006).

8. According to the *New York Times*, in 2018 there were almost 1,200 apps with location-sharing code for Google's Android system and 200 such apps for Apple iOS. One of the largest data aggregators, Reveal Mobile, had embedded location-sharing code in more than 500 apps. Ground Truth, another company that also owns a weather app for Apple iOS known as WeatherBug, shared location data with forty other companies (Valentino-DeVries et al. 2018).

9. Relatedly, see Hamid Ekbia and Bonnie Nardi's analysis of "participation" in digital life that they call *heteromation*, the extraction of low- to no-cost labor in computer-mediated networks (Ekbia and Nardi 2017).

10. This was at a time when US federal government policy was to separate from their families and imprison child migrants and refugees, while the Chinese were surveilling and imprisoning millions of Uighurs in Xinjiang.

Chapter 8

1. This humility and urgency in the forming of a biography is akin to Latour's ideas of *earthbound*, a term used for humans to better situate ourselves within the critical-zone or sub-lunar terrain of soil and atmosphere that is our world, to thrive in together or die together rather than casting the eyes of a *human* at fatal imaginary horizons of other planets or abstract conceptions like global economies that are unsustainable (Latour 2017).

References

Abowd, Gregory D., Christopher G. Atkeson, Jason Hong, Sue Long, Rob Kooper, and Mike Pinkerton. 1997. "Cyberguide: A Mobile Context-Aware Tour Guide." *Wireless Networks* 3 (5): 421–433. https://doi.org/10.1023/A:1019194325861.

Ackerman, Mark S., Christine A. Halverson, Thomas Erickson, and Wendy A. Kellogg, eds. 2007. *Resources, Co-Evolution, and Artifacts: Theory in CSCW*. Computer Supported Cooperative Work. Berlin: Springer-Verlag.

Agre, Philip E. 1997. *Computation and Human Experience*. Cambridge: Cambridge University Press.

Air Antwerpen. 2017. "Lifepatch," August–October. http://www.airantwerpen.be/en/residents/lifepatch.

Akemu, Ona, Gail Whiteman, and Steve Kennedy. 2016. "Social Enterprise Emergence from Social Movement Activism: The Fairphone Case." *Journal of Management Studies* 53 (5): 846–877. https://doi.org/10.1111/joms.12208.

Akrich, Madeleine. 1992. "The De-Scription of Technical Objects." In *Shaping Technology/Building Society: Studies in Sociotechnical Change*. Cambridge, MA: MIT Press.

Alcoff, Linda Martin. 2006. *Visible Identities: Race, Gender, and the Self*. Oxford: Oxford University Press.

Aldea, Eva. 2014. "Nomads and Migrants: Deleuze, Braidotti, and the European Union in 2014." *OpenDemocracy*, September 10. http://www.opendemocracy.net/can-europe-make-it/eva-aldea/nomads-and-migrants-deleuze-braidotti-and-european-union-in-2014.

"Aleph Zero." 2018. Aleph Zero. Accessed December 5, 2018. http://www.alephzero.arq.br/english/.

Ambasz, Emilio, ed. 1972. *Italy: The New Domestic Landscape*. 1st ed. New York: Museum of Modern Art.

Andersen, Kristina, and Ron Wakkary. 2019. "The Magic Machine Workshops: Making Personal Design Knowledge." In *Proceedings of the 2019 CHI Conference on*

Human Factors in Computing Systems (CHI '19), 1–13. Glasgow, UK: Association for Computing Machinery. https://doi.org/10.1145/3290605.3300342.

Andersen, Kristina, Ron Wakkary, Laura Devendorf, and Alex McLean. 2019. "Digital Crafts-Machine-Ship: Creative Collaborations with Machines." *Interactions* 27 (1): 30–35. https://doi.org/10.1145/3373644.

Andrade, F. A., H. A. Al-Qureshi, and D. Hotza. 2011. "Measuring the Plasticity of Clays: A Review." *Applied Clay Science* 51 (1): 1–7. https://doi.org/10.1016/j.clay.2010.10.028.

Apparatus for separating and sealing bags. 1967. UK patent GB1075713A, filed June 8, 1965; issued July 12, 1967. https://patents.google.com/patent/GB1075713A/en?assignee=Celloplast+AB.

Apparatus for stacking bags. 1968. UK patent GB1136703A, filed May 4, 1967; issued December 18. https://patents.google.com/patent/GB1136703A/en?assignee=Celloplast+AB.

Archizoom and Superstudio. 1966. "Superarchitettura Manifesto." Superarchitettura Exhibition: Galleria Jolly 2.

Baeza Argüello, Saúl, Ron Wakkary, Kristina Andersen, and Oscar Tomico. 2021. "Exploring the Potential of Apple Face ID as a Drag, Queer and Trans Technology Design Tool." In *Proceedings of the 2021 ACM Designing Interactive Systems Conference*. In press. ACM Press.

Barad, Karen. 2007. *Meeting the Universe Halfway: Quantum Physics and the Entanglement of Matter and Meaning*. Durham, NC: Duke University Press.

Becvar, Amaya, James Hollan, and Edwin Hutchins. 2008. "Representational Gestures as Cognitive Artifacts for Developing Theories in a Scientific Laboratory." In *Resources, Co-evolution, and Artifacts*, 117–143. Computer-Supported Cooperative Work. London: Springer. https://doi.org/10.1007/978-1-84628-901-9_5.

Bellini, Mario. 1972. "Kar-a-Sutra." In *Italy: The New Domestic Landscape*, edited by Emilio Ambasz, 200–210. New York: Museum of Modern Art.

Benjamin, Ruha. 2019. *Race after Technology: Abolitionist Tools for the New Jim Code*. Medford, MA: Polity.

Bennett, Jane. 2010. *Vibrant Matter: A Political Ecology of Things*. Durham, NC: Duke University Press.

Berg, Marc, and Geoffrey Bowker. 1997. "The Multiple Bodies of the Medical Record: Toward a Sociology of an Artifact." *The Sociological Quarterly* 38 (3): 513–537.

Bijker, Wiebe E., Thomas Parke Hughes, and Trevor Pinch. 1987. *The Social Construction of Technological Systems: New Directions in the Sociology and History of Technology*. Cambridge, MA: MIT Press.

References

Binder, Thomas. 1999. "Setting the Stage for Improvised Video Scenarios." In *CHI '99 Extended Abstracts on Human Factors in Computing Systems (CHI EA '99)*, 230–231. New York: Association for Computing Machinery. https://doi.org/10.1145/632716.632859.

Binder, Thomas, Eva Brandt, Pelle Ehn, and Joachim Halse. 2015. "Democratic Design Experiments: Between Parliament and Laboratory." *CoDesign* 11 (3–4): 152–165. https://doi.org/10.1080/15710882.2015.1081248.

Binder, Thomas, Giorgio De Michelis, Pelle Ehn, Giulio Jacucci, Per Linde, and Ina Wagner. 2011. *Design Things*. Cambridge, MA: MIT Press.

Bødker, Susanne. 2006. "When Second Wave HCI Meets Third Wave Challenges." In *Proceedings of the 4th Nordic Conference on Human-Computer Interaction: Changing Roles*, 1–8. New York: Association for Computing Machinery.

Bødker, Susanne, Pelle Ehn, Joergen Knudsen, Morten Kyng, and Kim Madsen. 1988. "Computer Support for Cooperative Design (Invited Paper)." In *Proceedings of the 1988 ACM Conference on Computer-Supported Cooperative Work (CSCW '88)*, 377–394. New York: Association for Computing Machinery. https://doi.org/10.1145/62266.62296.

Borgmann, Albert. 1987. *Technology and the Character of Contemporary Life: A Philosophical Inquiry*. Chicago: University of Chicago Press.

Bostrom, Nick. 2005. "A History of Transhumanist Thought." *Journal of Evolution and Technology* 14 (1): 1–25.

Bowden, Sean. 2012. "Gilles Deleuze, a Reader of Gilbert Simondon." In *Gilbert Simondon: Being and Technology*, edited by Arne De Boever, Alex Murray, and Jon Roffe, 135–153. Edinburgh, UK: Edinburgh University Press.

Braidotti, Rosi. 2002. *Metamorphoses: Towards a Materialist Theory of Becoming*. Cambridge: Polity.

Braidotti, Rosi. 2012. *Nomadic Theory: The Portable Rosi Braidotti*. New York: Columbia University Press.

Braidotti, Rosi. 2013. *The Posthuman*. Cambridge: Polity.

Braidotti, Rosi. 2016. "The Critical Posthumanities; Or, Is Medianatures to Naturecultures as Zoe Is to Bios?" *Cultural Politics* 12 (3): 380–390. https://doi.org/10.1215/17432197-3648930.

Braidotti, Rosi, and Timotheus Vermeulen. 2014. "Borrowed Energy." *Frieze*, December 8. https://frieze.com/article/borrowed-energy.

Branzi, Andrea. 1984. *The Hot House: Italian New Wave Design*. Cambridge, MA: MIT Press.

Bray, Tim. 2020. "Bye, Amazon." *Ongoing* (blog), May 5. https://www.tbray.org/ongoing/When/202x/2020/04/29/Leaving-Amazon#p-3.

Brignull, Harry. 2011. "Dark Patterns: Deception vs. Honesty in UI Design." *A List Apart* (blog), November 1. https://alistapart.com/article/dark-patterns-deception-vs-honesty-in-ui-design/.

Brookman, Justin, Phoebe Rouge, Aaron Alva, and Christina Yeung. 2017. "Cross-Device Tracking: Measurement and Disclosures." *Proceedings on Privacy Enhancing Technologies* 2017 (2): 133–148. https://doi.org/10.1515/popets-2017-0020.

Bryant, Levi, Nick Srnicek, and Graham Harman, eds. 2011. *The Speculative Turn: Continental Materialism and Realism*. Melbourne: re.press.

Burgen, Stephen. 2018. "'For Me, This Is Paradise': Life in the Spanish City That Banned Cars." *The Guardian*, September 18, Cities. https://www.theguardian.com/cities/2018/sep/18/paradise-life-spanish-city-banned-cars-pontevedra.

Carroll, John M., and Caroline Carrithers. 1984. "Training Wheels in a User Interface." *Communications of the ACM* 27 (8): 800–806. https://doi.org/10.1145/358198.358218.

Carroll, J. M., and W. A. Kellogg. 1989. "Artifact as Theory-Nexus: Hermeneutics Meets Theory-Based Design." In *Proceedings of the SIGCHI Conference on Human Factors in Computing Systems (CHI '89)*, 7–14. New York: Association for Computing Machinery. https://doi.org/10.1145/67449.67452.

Carroll, John M., and Mary Beth Rosson. 1992. "Getting around the Task-Artifact Cycle: How to Make Claims and Design by Scenario." *ACM Transactions on Information Systems* 10 (2): 181–212. https://doi.org/10.1145/146802.146834.

Carroll, Lewis. 1889. *Sylvie and Bruno*. London: Macmillan.

Clarke, Rachel E. 2020. "Ministry of Multispecies Communications." In *Companion Publication of the 2020 ACM Designing Interactive Systems Conference (DIS '20)*, 441–444. Eindhoven, Netherlands: Association for Computing Machinery. https://doi.org/10.1145/3393914.3395845.

Conger, Kate, and Noam Scheiber. 2020. "The Great Google Revolt." *New York Times*, February 19. https://www.nytimes.com/interactive/2020/02/18/magazine/google-revolt.html.

Conger, Kate, and Daisuke Wakabayashi. 2019. "Google Fires 4 Workers Active in Labor Organizing." *New York Times*, November 25. https://www.nytimes.com/2019/11/25/technology/google-fires-workers.html.

Coole, Diana. 2005. "Rethinking Agency: A Phenomenological Approach to Embodiment and Agentic Capacities." *Political Studies* 53 (1): 124–142. https://doi.org/10.1111/j.1467-9248.2005.00520.x.

Coole, Diana, ed. 2010. *New Materialisms: Ontology, Agency, and Politics*. Durham, NC: Duke University Press.

Coole, Diana. 2013. "Agentic Capacities and Capacious Historical Materialism: Thinking with New Materialisms in the Political Sciences." *Millennium* 41 (3): 451–469. https://doi.org/10.1177/0305829813481006.

Crabtree, Andrew, Tom Rodden, Peter Tolmie, and Graham Button. 2009. "Ethnography Considered Harmful." In *Proceedings of the SIGCHI Conference on Human Factors in Computing Systems (CHI '09)*, 879–888. New York: Association for Computing Machinery. https://doi.org/10.1145/1518701.1518835.

Crary, Jonathan. 1992. *Techniques of the Observer: On Vision and Modernity in the 19th Century*. Reprint ed. Cambridge, MA: MIT Press.

Cross, Nigel. 2006. *Designerly Ways of Knowing*. Berlin: Springer.

Davies, Robert J., and Paul J. Rankin. 2007. Localised audio data delivery. US patent US7197277B2, filed June 7, 2001; issued March 27, 2007. https://patents.google.com/patent/US7197277B2/en.

Debaise, Didier, and Isabelle Stengers. 2017. "The Insistence of the Possible." *Parse* 6 (Autumn): 12–19.

DeLanda, Manuel. 2016. *Assemblage Theory*. Edinburgh, UK: Edinburgh University Press.

Deleuze, Gilles. 1995. *Difference and Repetition*. Translated by Paul Patton. Rev. ed. New York: Columbia University Press.

Deleuze, Gilles, and Felix Guattari. 1987. *Thousand Plateaus: Capitalism and Schizophrenia*. 2nd ed. Minneapolis: University of Minnesota Press.

Deleuze, Gilles, and Claire Parnet. 2002. *Dialogues II*. New York: Columbia University Press.

Deming, W. Edwards. 1993. *The New Economics for Industry, Government, Education*. Cambridge, MA: MIT Center for Advanced Engineering Study.

De Preester, Helena. 2011. "Technology and the Body: The (Im)Possibilities of Re-Embodiment." *Foundations of Science* 16 (2): 119–137. https://doi.org/10.1007/s10699-010-9188-5.

Desjardins, Audrey. 2016. "Design-in-Living." Doctoral thesis, Simon Fraser University, Burnaby, British Columbia.

Desjardins, Audrey, and Aubree Ball. 2018. "Revealing Tensions in Autobiographical Design in HCI." In *Proceedings of the 2018 Designing Interactive Systems Conference (DIS '18)*, 753–764. New York: Association for Computing Machinery. https://doi.org/10.1145/3196709.3196781.

Desjardins, Audrey, Cayla Key, Heidi R. Biggs, and Kelsey Aschenbeck. 2019. "Bespoke Booklets: A Method for Situated Co-speculation." In *Proceedings of the 2019 on Designing Interactive Systems Conference (DIS '19)*, 697–709. San Diego, CA: Association for Computing Machinery. https://doi.org/10.1145/3322276.3322311.

Desjardins, Audrey, and Ron Wakkary. 2016. "Living in a Prototype: A Reconfigured Space." In *Proceedings of the 2016 CHI Conference on Human Factors in Computing Systems (CHI '16)*, 5274–5285. New York: Association for Computing Machinery. https://doi.org/10.1145/2858036.2858261.

Despret, Vinciane. 2016. *What Would Animals Say If We Asked the Right Questions?* Minneapolis: University of Minnesota Press.

Devendorf, Laura, Abigail De Kosnik, Kate Mattingly, and Kimiko Ryokai. 2016. "Probing the Potential of Post-anthropocentric 3D Printing." In *Proceedings of the 2016 ACM Conference on Designing Interactive Systems (DIS '16)*, 170–181. San Diego, CA: Association for Computing Machinery. https://doi.org/10.1145/2901790.2901879.

Devendorf, Laura, and Daniela K. Rosner. 2017. "Beyond Hybrids: Metaphors and Margins in Design." In *Proceedings of the 2017 Conference on Designing Interactive Systems (DIS '17)*, 995–1000. Edinburgh, UK: Association for Computing Machinery. https://doi.org/10.1145/3064663.3064705.

Devendorf, Laura, and Kimiko Ryokai. 2015. "Being the Machine: Reconfiguring Agency and Control in Hybrid Fabrication." In *Proceedings of the 33rd Annual ACM Conference on Human Factors in Computing Systems (CHI '15)*, 2477–2486. New York: Association for Computing Machinery. https://doi.org/10.1145/2702123.2702547.

Dew, Kristin N., and Daniela K. Rosner. 2018. "Lessons from the Woodshop: Cultivating Design with Living Materials." In *Proceedings of the 2018 CHI Conference on Human Factors in Computing Systems (CHI '18)*, 1–12. New York: Association for Computing Machinery. https://doi.org/10.1145/3173574.3174159.

Didero, Maria Cristina, Evan Snyderman, Deyan Sudjic, and Catharine Rossi. 2017. *SuperDesign: Italian Radical Design 1965–75*. New York: Monacelli.

DiSalvo, Carl, and Jonathan Lukens. 2011. "Nonanthropocentrism and the Nonhuman in Design: Possibilities for Designing New Forms of Engagement with and through Technology." In *From Social Butterfly to Engaged Citizen: Urban Informatics, Social Media, Ubiquitous Computing, and Mobile Technology to Support Citizen Engagement*, edited by Laura Forlana, Marcus Foth, Christine Satchell, and Martin Gibbs, 440–460. Cambridge, MA: MIT Press.

Dorrestijn, Steven. 2004. "Bestaanskunst in de Technologische Cultuur: Over de Ethiek van Door Techniek Beïnvloed Gedrag." Master's thesis, Enschede, University of Twente, Netherlands.

Dorrestijn, Steven. 2012. "Technical Mediation and Subjectivation: Tracing and Extending Foucault's Philosophy of Technology." *Philosophy & Technology* 25 (2): 221–241. https://doi.org/10.1007/s13347-011-0057-0.

Doucette, Kit. 2011. "The Plastic Bag Wars." *Rolling Stone*, July 25. https://www.rollingstone.com/politics/politics-news/the-plastic-bag-wars-243547/.

Dourish, Paul. 2001. *Where the Action Is: The Foundations of Embodied Interaction.* Cambridge, MA: MIT Press.

Dourish, Paul. 2006. "Implications for Design." In *Proceedings of the SIGCHI Conference on Human Factors in Computing Systems (CHI '06)*, 541–550. New York: Association for Computing Machinery. https://doi.org/10.1145/1124772.1124855.

Dourish, Paul. 2017. *The Stuff of Bits: An Essay on the Materialities of Information.* Cambridge, MA: MIT Press.

Dunayer, Joan. 2004. *Speciesism.* Derwood, MD: Ryce.

Dunne, Anthony. 2008. *Hertzian Tales: Electronic Products, Aesthetic Experience, and Critical Design.* Cambridge, MA: MIT Press.

Ehn, Pelle. 1988. *Work-Oriented Design of Computer Artifacts.* Stockholm: Lawrence Erlbaum.

Ehn, Pelle. 2008. "Participation in Design Things." In *Proceedings of the Tenth Anniversary Conference on Participatory Design 2008 (PDC '08)*, 92–101. Indianapolis: Indiana University. http://dl.acm.org/citation.cfm?id=1795234.1795248.

Ehn, Pelle, Elisabet M. Nilsson, and Richard Topgaard, eds. 2014. *Making Futures: Marginal Notes on Innovation, Design, and Democracy.* Cambridge, MA: MIT Press.

Ekbia, Hamid R., and Bonnie A. Nardi. 2017. *Heteromation, and Other Stories of Computing and Capitalism.* Cambridge, MA: MIT Press.

Elfline, Ross K. 2016. "Superstudio and the 'Refusal to Work.'" *Design and Culture* 8 (1): 55–77. https://doi.org/10.1080/17547075.2016.1142343.

Encinas, Enrique, Abigail C. Durrant, Robb Mitchell, and Mark Blythe. 2020. "Metaprobes, Metaphysical Workshops and Sketchy Philosophy." In *Proceedings of the 2020 CHI Conference on Human Factors in Computing Systems (CHI '20)*, 1–13. Honolulu, HI: Association for Computing Machinery. https://doi.org/10.1145/3313831.3376453.

Énon, David. 2019. "Mineral Accretion Factory: An Underwater Production Process with a Positive Impact on the Environment." In *Proceedings of the 4th Biennial Research through Design Conference (RTD 2019)*, March 19–22, Rotterdam, Netherlands, article 8:1–14. figshare. https://doi.org/10.6084/m9.figshare.7855775.v2.

Erichsen, Paula Hohti. 2019. "Exploring Historical Blacks: The Burgundian Black Collaboratory." *Refashioning the Renaissance*, February 21, 2019. http://refashioningrenaissance.eu/exploring-historical-blacks-the-burgundian-black-collaboratory/.

Escobar, Arturo. 2018. *Designs for the Pluriverse: Radical Interdependence, Autonomy, and the Making of Worlds.* Durham, NC: Duke University Press.

Fallman, Daniel. 2010. "A Different Way of Seeing: Albert Borgmann's Philosophy of Technology and Human–Computer Interaction." *AI & Society* 25 (1): 53–60. https://doi.org/10.1007/s00146-009-0234-1.

Feenberg, Andrew. 2017. *Technosystem: The Social Life of Reason*. Cambridge, MA: Harvard University Press.

Fischer, Gerhard, and Eric Scharff. 2000. "Meta-Design: Design for Designers." In *Proceedings of the 3rd Conference on Designing Interactive Systems: Processes, Practices, Methods, and Techniques (DIS '00)*, 396–405. New York: Association for Computing Machinery. https://doi.org/10.1145/347642.347798.

Fitzpatrick, Jen, and Karen DeSalvo. 2020. "Helping Public Health Officials Combat COVID-19." Google, April 3. https://blog.google/technology/health/covid-19-community-mobility-reports/.

Forlano, Laura. 2017. "Posthumanism and Design." *She Ji: The Journal of Design, Economics, and Innovation* 3 (1): 16–29. https://doi.org/10.1016/j.sheji.2017.08.001.

Foucault, Michel. 1978. *The History of Sexuality, Volume 1: An Introduction*. Translated by Robert Hurley. New York: Pantheon Books.

Frassinelli, Piero, Alessandro Magris, Roberto Magris, Adolfo Natalani, Alessandro Poli, and Cristiano Toraldo di Francia. 1972. "Superstudio." In *Italy: The New Domestic Landscape*, edited by Emilio Ambasz, 240–250. New York: Museum of Modern Art.

Frauenberger, Christopher. 2019. "Entanglement HCI: The Next Wave?" *ACM Transactions on Computer-Human Interaction* 27 (1): 2:1–2:27. https://doi.org/10.1145/3364998.

Frenkel, Sheera, Mike Isaac, Cecilia Kang, and Gabriel J. X. Dance. 2020. "Facebook Employees Stage Virtual Walkout to Protest Trump Posts." *New York Times*, June 1. https://www.nytimes.com/2020/06/01/technology/facebook-employee-protest-trump.html.

Friedman, Batya, and David G. Hendry. 2019. *Value Sensitive Design: Shaping Technology with Moral Imagination*. Cambridge, MA: MIT Press.

Friedman, Batya, David G. Hendry, and Alan Borning. 2017. "A Survey of Value Sensitive Design Methods." *Foundations and Trends in Human-Computer Interaction* 11 (2): 63–125. https://doi.org/10.1561/1100000015.

Friedman, Batya, Peter H. Kahn, and Alan Borning. 2009. "Value Sensitive Design and Information Systems." In *The Handbook of Information and Computer Ethics*, 69–101. New York: John Wiley.

Friedman, Batya, and Lisa P. Nathan. 2010. "Multi-lifespan Information System Design: A Research Initiative for the HCI Community." In *Proceedings of the SIGCHI Conference on Human Factors in Computing Systems (CHI '10)*, 2243–2246. New York: Association for Computing Machinery. https://doi.org/10.1145/1753326.1753665.

Fry, Tony. 1999. *New Design Philosophy: An Introduction to Defuturing*. 1st ed. Sydney: University of New South Wales Press.

Fry, Tony. 2010. *Design as Politics*. New York: Berg.

References

Fry, Tony. 2012. *Becoming Human by Design*. London: Berg.

Gatens, Moira, and Genevieve Lloyd. 1999. *Collective Imaginings: Spinoza, Past and Present*. London: Routledge.

Gaver, William, Mark Blythe, Andy Boucher, Nadine Jarvis, John Bowers, and Peter Wright. 2010. "The Prayer Companion: Openness and Specificity, Materiality and Spirituality." In *Proceedings of the SIGCHI Conference on Human Factors in Computing Systems (CHI'10)*, 2055–2064. New York: Association for Computing Machinery. https://doi.org/10.1145/1753326.1753640.

Gaver, William W., John Bowers, Andrew Boucher, Hans Gellerson, Sarah Pennington, Albrecht Schmidt, Anthony Steed, Nicholas Villars, and Brendan Walker. 2004. "The Drift Table: Designing for Ludic Engagement." In *CHI '04 Extended Abstracts on Human Factors in Computing Systems (CHI EA '04)*, 885–900. New York: Association for Computing Machinery. https://doi.org/10.1145/985921.985947.

Giaccardi, Elisa, Nazli Cila, Chris Speed, and Melissa Caldwell. 2016. "Thing Ethnography: Doing Design Research with Non-humans." In *Proceedings of the 2016 ACM Conference on Designing Interactive Systems (DIS '16)*, 377–387. Association for Computing Machinery. https://doi.org/10.1145/2901790.2901905.

Gilroy, Paul. 2005. *Postcolonial Melancholia*. New York: Columbia University Press.

"Great Queen Street, Camden." n.d. *Factory Furniture* (blog). Accessed November 18, 2020. https://www.factoryfurniture.co.uk/projects/great-queen-street-camden/.

Gustaf Thulin, Sten. 1965. Bag with handle of weldable plastic material. US patent 3180557A, filed July 10, 1962; issued April 27, 1965. https://patents.google.com/patent/US3180557/en.

Halbert, Helen, and Lisa P. Nathan. 2015. "Designing for Discomfort: Supporting Critical Reflection through Interactive Tools." In *Proceedings of the 18th ACM Conference on Computer-Supported Cooperative Work and Social Computing (CSCW '15)*, 349–360. New York: Association for Computing Machinery. https://doi.org/10.1145/2675133.2675162.

Halbfinger, David M., Isabel Kershner, and Ronen Bergman. 2020. "To Track Coronavirus, Israel Moves to Tap Secret Trove of Cellphone Data." *New York Times*, March 16. https://www.nytimes.com/2020/03/16/world/middleeast/israel-coronavirus-cellphone-tracking.html.

Hallnäs, Lars, and Johan Redström. 2001. "Slow Technology: Designing for Reflection." *Personal Ubiquitous Computing* 5 (3): 201–212. https://doi.org/10.1007/PL00000019.

Halverson, Christine A., and Mark S. Ackerman. 2008. "The Birth of an Organizational Resource: The Surprising Life of a Cheat Sheet." In *Resources, Co-evolution, and Artifacts*, 9–35. Computer-Supported Cooperative Work. London: Springer. https://doi.org/10.1007/978-1-84628-901-9_1.

Hara, Kenya. 2018. *Designing Design*. 4th ed. Baden: Lars Müller.

Haraway, Donna. 1985. "A Manifesto for Cyborgs: Science, Technology, and Social Feminism in the 1980s." *Socialist Review* 5 (2): 65–107.

Haraway, Donna. 1988. "Situated Knowledges: The Science Question in Feminism and the Privilege of Partial Perspective." *Feminist Studies* 14 (3): 575–599. https://doi.org/10.2307/3178066.

Haraway, Donna. 2003. *The Companion Species Manifesto: Dogs, People, and Significant Otherness*. 1st ed. Chicago: Prickly Paradigm.

Haraway, Donna. 2016. *Staying with the Trouble: Making Kin in the Chthulucene*. 1st ed. Durham, NC: Duke University Press.

Harman, Graham. 2016. *Immaterialism: Objects and Social Theory*. Malden, MA: Polity.

Harman, Graham. 2018. *Object-Oriented Ontology: A New Theory of Everything*. London: Pelican.

Harrison, Steve, Deborah Tatar, and Phoebe Sengers. 2007. "The Three Paradigms of HCI." *Alt. Chi (CHI '07)*, April 28–May 3, San Jose, California. http://people.cs.vt.edu/~srh/Downloads/HCIJournalTheThreeParadigmsofHCI.pdf.

Hartman, Saidiya. 2008. "Venus in Two Acts." *Small Axe* 12 (2): 1–14.

Hatanaka, Minoru. 2016. "Lifepatch: The Natural Affinity between Indonesian Culture and Global Peer-to-Peer Culture." Japan Foundation Asia Center, November 17. https://jfac.jp/en/culture/features/asiahundreds014/.

Hauser, Sabrina. 2018. "Design-Oriented HCI through Postphenomenology." Doctoral thesis, Communication, Art, and Technology, School of Interactive Arts and Technology, Simon Fraser University, Burnaby, British Columbia. http://summit.sfu.ca/item/18556.

Hauser, Sabrina, Doenja Oogjes, Ron Wakkary, and Peter-Paul Verbeek. 2018. "An Annotated Portfolio on Doing Postphenomenology through Research Products." In *Proceedings of the 2018 Designing Interactive Systems Conference (DIS '18)*, 459–471. New York: Association for Computing Machinery. https://doi.org/10.1145/3196709.3196745.

Hauser, Sabrina, Ron Wakkary, William Odom, Peter-Paul Verbeek, Audrey Desjardins, Henry Lin, Matthew Dalton, Markus Schilling, and Gijs de Boer. 2018. "Deployments of the Table-Non-Table: A Reflection on the Relation between Theory and Things in the Practice of Design Research." In *Proceedings of the 2018 CHI Conference on Human Factors in Computing Systems (CHI '18)*, paper 201:1–13. New York: Association for Computing Machinery. https://doi.org/10.1145/3173574.3173775.

Hayles, N. Katherine. 1999. *How We Became Posthuman: Virtual Bodies in Cybernetics, Literature, and Informatics*. 1st ed. Chicago: University of Chicago Press.

References

Heidegger, Martin. 1962. *Being and Time.* New York: Harper Perennial Modern Classics.

Heidegger, Martin. 1976. *The Question Concerning Technology, and Other Essays.* Translated by William Lovitt. New York: Harper Torchbooks.

Himalayan Database. 2019. "The Expedition Archives of Elizabeth Hawley." https://www.himalayandatabase.com/downloads.html.

Höök, Kristina, and Jonas Löwgren. 2012. "Strong Concepts: Intermediate-Level Knowledge in Interaction Design Research." *ACM Transactions on Computer-Human Interaction (TOCHI)* 19 (3): 23.

Hustwit, Gary. 2018. *Rams.* Vimeo, December 13. Video documentary. https://vimeo.com/ondemand/ramsfilm.

Hutchins, Edwin. 1996. *Cognition in the Wild.* Rev. ed. Cambridge, MA: MIT Press.

Ihde, Don. 1990. *Technology and the Lifeworld: From Garden to Earth.* Bloomington: Indiana University Press.

Iliadis, Andrew. 2015. "Two Examples of Concretization." *Platform: Journal of Media and Communication* 6:85–95.

Ingold, T. 2010. "The Textility of Making." *Cambridge Journal of Economics* 34 (1): 91–102. https://doi.org/10.1093/cje/bep042.

Ingold, Tim. 2011. *Being Alive: Essays on Movement, Knowledge, and Description.* London: Routledge.

Irani, Lilly, Janet Vertesi, Paul Dourish, Kavita Philip, and Rebecca E. Grinter. 2010. "Postcolonial Computing: A Lens on Design and Development." In *Proceedings of the SIGCHI Conference on Human Factors in Computing Systems (CHI '10)*, 1311–1320. New York: Association for Computing Machinery. https://doi.org/10.1145/1753326.1753522.

Jelbert, S. A., R. J. Hosking, A. H. Taylor, and R. D. Gray. 2018. "Mental Template Matching Is a Potential Cultural Transmission Mechanism for New Caledonian Crow Tool Manufacturing Traditions." *Scientific Reports* 8 (1): 8956. https://doi.org/10.1038/s41598-018-27405-1.

Jones, Sam. 2018. "'It's the Only Way Forward': Madrid Bans Polluting Vehicles from City Centre." *The Guardian*, November 30, Cities. https://www.theguardian.com/cities/2018/nov/30/its-the-only-way-forward-madrid-bans-polluting-vehicles-from-city-centre.

Koenig, Andrew. 1998. "Patterns and Antipatterns." In *The Patterns Handbooks: Techniques, Strategies, and Applications*, 383–389. New York: Cambridge University Press.

Kohlstedt, Kurt. 2018. "Hostile Architecture: 'Design Crimes' Campaign Gets Bars Removed from Benches." *99% Invisible* (blog), February 9. https://99percentinvisible.org/article/design-crimes-artist-launches-campaign-highlight-hostile-architecture/.

Krakauer, Jon, Daniel Rembert, Caroline Cunningham, and Anita Karl. 1999. *Into Thin Air: A Personal Account of the Mt. Everest Disaster*. Reprint ed. New York: Anchor.

Krippendorff, Klaus. 2006. *The Semantic Turn: A New Foundation for Design*. Boca Raton, FL: CRC.

Krippendorff, Klaus. 2016. "Design, an Undisciplinable Profession." In *Design as Research. Positions, Arguments, Perspectives*. Basel, Switzerland: Birkäuser Verlag/De Gruyter.

Kuhn, Thomas S. 1962. *The Structure of Scientific Revolutions*. Chicago: University of Chicago Press.

Kuijer, Lenneke, and Elisa Giaccardi. 2018. "Co-performance: Conceptualizing the Role of Artificial Agency in the Design of Everyday Life." In *Proceedings of the 2018 CHI Conference on Human Factors in Computing Systems (CHI '18)*, 1–13. Montreal: Association for Computing Machinery. https://doi.org/10.1145/3173574.3173699.

Kurzweil, Ray. 2000. *The Age of Spiritual Machines: When Computers Exceed Human Intelligence*. New York: Penguin Books.

Lakatos, Imre. 1976. "Falsification and the Methodology of Scientific Research Programmes." In *Can Theories Be Refuted? Essays on the Duhem-Quine Thesis*, edited by Sandra G. Harding, 205–259. Synthese Library. Dordrecht: Springer Netherlands.

Lakoff, George, and Mark Johnson. 2003. *Metaphors We Live By*. Chicago: University of Chicago Press.

Lang, Peter, and William Menking. 2003. *Superstudio: Life without Objects*. Milano, Italy: Skira.

Laskow, Sarah. 2014. "How the Plastic Bag Became So Popular." *The Atlantic*, October 10. https://www.theatlantic.com/technology/archive/2014/10/how-the-plastic-bag-became-so-popular/381065/.

Latour, Bruno. 1990. "Technology Is Society Made Durable." *Sociological Review* 38 (supp1): 103–131. https://doi.org/10.1111/j.1467-954X.1990.tb03350.x.

Latour, Bruno. 1992. "Where Are the Missing Masses? The Sociology of a Few Mundane Artifacts." In *Shaping Technology/Building Society: Studies in Sociotechnical Change*, edited by Wiebe E. Bijker and John Law, 225–258. Cambridge, MA: MIT Press.

Latour, Bruno. 1993. *We Have Never Been Modern*. Cambridge, MA: Harvard University Press.

Latour, Bruno. 1999. *Pandora's Hope: Essays on the Reality of Science Studies*. 1st ed. Cambridge, MA: Harvard University Press.

Latour, Bruno. 2004a. "Why Has Critique Run Out of Steam? From Matters of Fact to Matters of Concern." *Critical Inquiry* 30 (2): 225–248. https://doi.org/10.1086/421123.

References

Latour, Bruno. 2004b. *Politics of Nature: How to Bring the Sciences into Democracy.* Translated by Catherine Porter. Cambridge, MA: Harvard University Press.

Latour, Bruno. 2005a. "From Realpolitik to Dingpolitik." In *Making Things Public*, edited by Bruno Latour and Peter Weibel, 14–44. Cambridge, MA: MIT Press.

Latour, Bruno. 2005b. *Reassembling the Social: An Introduction to Actor-Network-Theory.* Clarendon Lectures in Management Studies. Oxford: Oxford University Press.

Latour, Bruno. 2008. "A Cautious Prometheus? A Few Steps toward a Philosophy of Design (with Special Attention to Peter Sloterdijk)." In *Networks of Design: Proceedings of the 2008 Annual International Conference of the Design History Society*, 2–10. Boca Raton, FL: Universal Publishers.

Latour, Bruno. 2011. "From Multiculturalism to Multinaturalism: What Rules of Method for the New Socio-scientific Experiments?" *Nature and Culture* 6 (1): 1–17. https://doi.org/10.3167/nc.2011.060101.

Latour, Bruno. 2014. "Agency at the Time of the Anthropocene." *New Literary History* 45 (1): 1–18. https://doi.org/10.1353/nlh.2014.0003.

Latour, Bruno. 2017. *Facing Gaia: Eight Lectures on the New Climatic Regime.* Translated by Catherine Porter. 1st ed. Cambridge: Polity.

Latour, Bruno. 2018. *Anthropocene Lecture: Bruno Latour.* Haus der Kulturen der Welt, Berlin, June 18. YouTube video, 43:20. https://www.youtube.com/watch?v=UtaEJo-jo8Q.

Lawrie, Eleanor. 2020. "Why Millions Will Soon Be Using Coronavirus Apps." *BBC News*, April 30, Explainers. https://www.bbc.com/news/explainers-52442754.

Leahu, Lucian. 2016. "Ontological Surprises: A Relational Perspective on Machine Learning." In *Proceedings of the 2016 ACM Conference on Designing Interactive Systems (DIS '16)*, 182–186. Brisbane, QLD, Australia: Association for Computing Machinery. https://doi.org/10.1145/2901790.2901840.

Le Dantec, Christopher A. 2016. *Designing Publics*. Cambridge, MA: MIT Press.

Le Dantec, Christopher A., and Carl DiSalvo. 2013. "Infrastructuring and the Formation of Publics in Participatory Design." *Social Studies of Science* 43 (2): 241–264.

Lee, Simon H., Paul D. Williams, and Thomas H. A. Frame. 2019. "Increased Shear in the North Atlantic Upper-Level Jet Stream over the Past Four Decades." *Nature*, August 1–4. https://doi.org/10.1038/s41586-019-1465-z.

Light, Ann, Alison Powell, and Irina Shklovski. 2017. "Design for Existential Crisis in the Anthropocene Age." In *Proceedings of the 8th International Conference on Communities and Technologies (C&T '17)*, 270–279. Troyes, France: Association for Computing Machinery. https://doi.org/10.1145/3083671.3083688.

Lin, Cindy, and Silvia Lindtner. 2016. "Legitimacy, Boundary Objects, and Participation in Transnational DIY Biology." In *Proceedings of the 14th Participatory Design Conference: Full Papers—Volume 1 (PDC '16)*, 171–180. Aarhus, Denmark: Association for Computing Machinery. https://doi.org/10.1145/2940299.2940307.

Lin, Cindy, Silvia Lindtner, and Stefanie Wuschitz. 2019. "Hacking Difference in Indonesia: The Ambivalences of Designing for Alternative Futures." In *Proceedings of the 2019 Designing Interactive Systems Conference (DIS '19)*, 1571–1582. San Diego, CA: Association for Computing Machinery. https://doi.org/10.1145/3322276.3322339.

Lindley, Joseph, Paul Coulton, and Rachel Cooper. 2017. "Why the Internet of Things Needs Object Orientated Ontology." *Design Journal* 20 (supp1): S2846–2857. https://doi.org/10.1080/14606925.2017.1352796.

Liu, Szu-Yu (Cyn), Jeffrey Bardzell, and Shaowen Bardzell. 2018. "Photography as a Design Research Tool into Natureculture." In *Proceedings of the 2018 Designing Interactive Systems Conference (DIS '18)*, 777–789. Hong Kong: Association for Computing Machinery. https://doi.org/10.1145/3196709.3196819.

Liu, Szu-Yu (Cyn), Jeffrey Bardzell, and Shaowen Bardzell. 2019. "Decomposition as Design: Co-creating (with) Natureculture." In *Proceedings of the Thirteenth International Conference on Tangible, Embedded, and Embodied Interaction (TEI '19)*, 605–614. Tempe, AZ: Association for Computing Machinery. https://doi.org/10.1145/3294109.3295653.

Lovell, Sophie, Klaus Kemp, and Jonathan Ive. 2011. *Dieter Rams: As Little Design as Possible*. London: Phaidon.

Mackey, A. M., R. L. Wakkary, S. a. G. Wensveen, and O. Tomico Plasencia. 2017. "'Can I Wear This?' Blending Clothing and Digital Expression by Wearing Dynamic Fabric." *International Journal of Design* 11 (3): 51–65.

Mackey, Angella, Ron Wakkary, Stephan Wensveen, Oscar Tomico, and Bart Hengeveld. 2017. "Day-to-Day Speculation: Designing and Wearing Dynamic Fabric." In *Proceedings of the 3rd Biennial Research through Design Conference (RTD 2017)*, March 22–24, Edinburgh, UK, article 28:438–454. figshare. https://doi.org/10.6084/m9.figshare.4747018.v1.

Mackey, Angella, Ron Wakkary, Stephan Wensveen, Annika Hupfeld, and Oscar Tomico. 2020. "Alternative Presents for Dynamic Fabric." In *DIS 2020—Proceedings of the 2020 ACM Designing Interactive Systems Conference*, 351–364. New York: Association for Computing Machinery. https://dl.acm.org/doi/abs/10.1145/3357236.3395447.

Malpass, Matt. 2017. *Critical Design in Context: History, Theory, and Practices*. London: Bloomsbury Academic.

Mancini, Clara. 2011. "Animal-Computer Interaction: A Manifesto." *Interactions* 18 (4): 69–73. https://doi.org/10.1145/1978822.1978836.

Mancini, Clara, and Jussi Lehtonen. 2018. "The Emerging Nature of Participation in Multispecies Interaction Design." In *Proceedings of the 2018 Designing Interactive Systems Conference (DIS '18)*, 907–918. New York: Association for Computing Machinery. https://doi.org/10.1145/3196709.3196785.

Marres, Noortje. 2007. "The Issues Deserve More Credit: Pragmatist Contributions to the Study of Public Involvement in Controversy." *Social Studies of Science* 37 (5): 759–780. https://doi.org/10.1177/0306312706077367.

Merleau-Ponty, Maurice. 1962. *Phenomenology of Perception*. Translated by Colin Smith. London: Routledge/Kegan Paul.

Moore, G. W. K., and John L. Semple. 2004. "High Himalayan Meteorology: Weather at the South Col of Mount Everest." *Geophysical Research Letters* 31 (18). https://doi.org/10.1029/2004GL020621.

Moravec, Hans P. 1999. *Robot: Mere Machine to Transcendent Mind/Hans Moravec*. Oxford: Oxford University Press.

Morton, Timothy. 2013. *Hyperobjects: Philosophy and Ecology after the End of the World*. Minneapolis: University of Minnesota Press.

Nardi, Bonnie. 2015. "Inequality and Limits." *First Monday* 20 (8). https://firstmonday.org/article/view/6126/4845.

Nelson, Harold G., and Erik Stolterman. 2012. *The Design Way: Intentional Change in an Unpredictable World*. 2nd ed. Cambridge, MA: MIT Press.

Neustaedter, Carman, and Phoebe Sengers. 2012. "Autobiographical Design in HCI Research: Designing and Learning through Use-It-Yourself." In *Proceedings of the Designing Interactive Systems Conference (DIS '12)*, 514–523. New York: Association for Computing Machinery. https://doi.org/10.1145/2317956.2318034.

Newberry, Janice C. 2006. *Back Door Java: State Formation and the Domestic in Working Class Java*. Toronto: University of Toronto Press.

Newberry, Jan. 2014. "Women against Children: Early Childhood Education and the Domestic Community in Post-Suharto Indonesia." *TRaNS: Trans-Regional and -National Studies of Southeast Asia* 2 (2): 271–291. https://doi.org/10.1017/trn.2014.7.

Newman, Karen. 2017. "Reflections from Indonesia—Female Empowerment through Tech." *British Council Creative Economy* (blog), April 10. https://creativeconomy.britishcouncil.org/blog/17/04/10/reflections-indonesia/.

Niera, Juliana. 2017. "Mario Bellini Talks about His 1972 'Kar-a-Sutra' Concept Car." *Designboom | Architecture & Design Magazine*, January 20. https://www.designboom.com/design/mario-bellini-kar-a-sutra-concept-car-01-20-2017/.

Norman, Donald. 2010. "Why Design Education Must Change." *Core77*, November 26. https://www.core77.com/posts/17993/why-design-education-must-change-17993.

Odom, William T., Abigail J. Sellen, Richard Banks, David S. Kirk, Tim Regan, Mark Selby, Jodi L. Forlizzi, and John Zimmerman. 2014. "Designing for Slowness, Anticipation, and Re-visitation: A Long Term Field Study of the Photobox." In *Proceedings of the 32nd Annual ACM Conference on Human Factors in Computing Systems (CHI '14)*, 1961–1970. New York: Association for Computing Machinery. https://doi.org/10.1145/2556288.2557178.

Odom, William, and Ron Wakkary. 2015. "Intersecting with Unaware Objects." In *Proceedings of the 2015 ACM SIGCHI Conference on Creativity and Cognition (C & C '15)*, 33–42. New York: Association for Computing Machinery. https://doi.org/10.1145/2757226.2757240.

Odom, William, Ron Wakkary, Jeroen Hol, Bram Naus, Pepijn Verburg, Tal Amram, and Amy Yo Sue Chen. 2019. "Investigating Slowness as a Frame to Design Longer-Term Experiences with Personal Data: A Field Study of Olly." In *Proceedings of the 2019 Conference on Human Factors in Computing Systems (CHI'19)*, paper 34:1–16. New York: Association for Computing Machinery.

Olander, Sissel, Tau Ulv Lenskjold, Signe Louise Yndigegn, and Maria Foverskov. 2011. "Mobilizing for Community Building and Everyday Innovation." *Interactions* 18 (4): 28–32. https://doi.org/10.1145/1978822.1978829.

Oogjes, Doenja, and Ron Wakkary. 2017. "Videos of Things: Speculating on, Anticipating and Synthesizing Technological Mediations." In *Proceedings of the 2017 CHI Conference on Human Factors in Computing Systems*, 4489–4500. New York: Association for Computing Machinery. http://dl.acm.org/citation.cfm?id=3025748.

Oogjes, Doenja, Ron Wakkary, Henry Lin, and Omid Alemi. 2020. "Fragile! Handle with Care: The Morse Things." In *Proceedings of the 2020 ACM Designing Interactive Systems Conference (DIS '20)*, 2149–2162. Eindhoven, Netherlands: Association for Computing Machinery. https://doi.org/10.1145/3357236.3395584.

Orlikowski, Wanda J. 2000. "Using Technology and Constituting Structures: A Practice Lens for Studying Technology in Organizations." *Organization Science* 11 (4): 404–428. https://doi.org/10.1287/orsc.11.4.404.14600.

Papanek, Victor. 1971. *Design for the Real World: Human Ecology and Social Change*. 2nd ed. Chicago: Chicago Review Press.

Pierce, James, and Eric Paulos. 2013. "Electric Materialities and Interactive Technology." In *Proceedings of the SIGCHI Conference on Human Factors in Computing Systems (CHI '13)*, 119–128. New York: Association for Computing Machinery. https://doi.org/10.1145/2470654.2470672.

Pierce, James, and Eric Paulos. 2015. "Making Multiple Uses of the Obscura 1C Digital Camera: Reflecting on the Design, Production, Packaging and Distribution of a Counterfunctional Device." In *Proceedings of the 33rd Annual ACM Conference on*

Human Factors in Computing Systems, 2103–2112. New York: Association for Computing Machinery. http://dl.acm.org/citation.cfm?id=2702405.

Pilsch, Andrew. 2017. *Transhumanism: Evolutionary Futurism and the Human Technologies of Utopia*. Minneapolis: University of Minnesota Press.

Popper, Karl. 1959. *The Logic of Scientific Discovery*. 2nd ed. Abingdon, UK: Routledge.

Pschetz, Larissa, and Richard Banks. 2013. "Long Living Chair." In *CHI '13 Extended Abstracts on Human Factors in Computing Systems (CHI EA '13)*, 2983–2986. New York: Association for Computing Machinery. https://doi.org/10.1145/2468356.2479590.

Puig de la Bellacasa, María. 2012. "'Nothing Comes without Its World': Thinking with Care." *Sociological Review* 60 (2): 197–216. https://doi.org/10.1111/j.1467-954X.2012.02070.x.

Puig de la Bellacasa, María. 2017. *Matters of Care: Speculative Ethics in More than Human Worlds*. 3rd ed. Minneapolis: University of Minnesota Press.

Quinn, Ben. 2014. "Anti-Homeless Spikes Are Part of a Wider Phenomenon of 'Hostile Architecture.'" *The Guardian*, June 13, Art and Design. https://www.theguardian.com/artanddesign/2014/jun/13/anti-homeless-spikes-hostile-architecture.

Rams, Dieter. 1995. *Less but Better*. Bilingual ed. Hamburg: Gestalten.

Redström, Johan. 2008. "RE: Definitions of Use." *Design Studies* 29 (4): 410–423. https://doi.org/10.1016/j.destud.2008.05.001.

Redström, Johan. 2017. *Making Design Theory*. Cambridge, MA: MIT Press.

Redström, Johan, and Heather Wiltse. 2020. *Changing Things: The Future of Objects in a Digital World*. London: Bloomsbury Visual Arts.

Ricker, Thomas. 2017. "Lightlines Are Humanity's Latest Attempt to Protect Smartphone Zombies." *The Verge*, February 15. https://www.theverge.com/2017/2/15/14621968/lightlines-protect-distracted-smartphone-users.

Rosenberger, Robert. 2014. "Multistability and the Agency of Mundane Artifacts: From Speed Bumps to Subway Benches." *Human Studies* 37 (3): 369–392. https://doi.org/10.1007/s10746-014-9317-1.

Rosenberger, Robert. 2017. *Callous Objects: Designs against the Homeless*. 3rd ed. Minneapolis: University of Minnesota Press.

Rosenberger, Robert, and Peter-Paul Verbeek. 2015. "A Field Guide to Postphenomenology." In *Postphenomenological Investigations: Essays on Human-Technology Relations*, edited by Robert Rosenberger and Peter-Paul Verbeek, 9–41. Lanham, MD: Lexington Books.

Rosner, Daniela K. 2018. *Critical Fabulations: Reworking the Methods and Margins of Design*. Cambridge, MA: MIT Press.

Ruskin, John. 1885. *The Elements of Drawing in Three Lessons to Beginners.* New York: John Wiley.

Sainato, Michael. 2020. "Amazon Is Cracking Down on Protesters and Organizing, Workers Say." *The Guardian*, May 5, Technology. https://www.theguardian.com/technology/2020/may/05/amazon-protests-union-organizing-cracking-down-workers.

Savičić, Gordan, and Selena Savić. 2013. *Unpleasant Design.* Belgrade: G.L.O.R.I.A.

Schon, Donald A. 1984. *The Reflective Practitioner: How Professionals Think in Action.* 1st ed. New York: Basic Books.

Schon, Donald A. 1992. "Designing as Reflective Conversation with the Materials of a Design Situation." *Research in Engineering Design* 3 (3): 131–147. https://doi.org/10.1007/BF01580516.

Schon (Schön), Donald A. 1993. "Generative Metaphor: A Perspective on Problem-Setting in Social Policy." In *Metaphor and Thought*, edited by Andrew Ortony, 137–163. 2nd ed. Cambridge: Cambridge University Press. https://doi.org/10.1017/CBO9781139173865.011.

Schon, Donald A., and Martin Rein. 1994. *Frame Reflection: Toward the Resolution of Intractable Policy Controversies.* New York: Basic Books.

Schuler, Douglas, and Aki Namioka, eds. 1993. *Participatory Design: Principles and Practices.* Hillsdale, NJ: CRC/Lawrence Erlbaum.

Scully, Kiri. 2017. "Special Traffic Lights in Bodegraven to Alert Smartphone Addicts." *I Am Expat*, February 16. https://www.iamexpat.nl/read-and-discuss/expat-page/news/bodegraven-special-traffic-lights-to-alert-smartphone-addicts.

Seok, Jin-min, Jong-bum Woo, and Youn-kyung Lim. 2014. "Non-Finito Products: A New Design Space of User Creativity for Personal User Experience." In *Proceedings of the SIGCHI Conference on Human Factors in Computing Systems (CHI '14)*, 693–702. New York: Association for Computing Machinery. https://doi.org/10.1145/2556288.2557222.

Shaw, Elizabeth. 1972. "Italy, the New Domestic Landscape." Press Release, Museum of Modern Art, May 26.

Shilton, Katie. 2018. "Values and Ethics in Human-Computer Interaction." *Foundations and Trends in Human-Computer Interaction* 12 (2): 107–171. https://doi.org/10.1561/1100000073.

Simon, Herbert. 1981. *The Sciences of the Artificial.* 2nd ed. Cambridge, MA: MIT Press.

Simondon, Gilbert. 2017. *On the Mode of Existence of Technical Objects.* Translated by Cecile Malaspina and John Rogove. Minnesota: University of Minnesota Press.

Sloterdijk, Peter. 2011. *Bubbles: Spheres Volume I: Microspherology.* Translated by Wieland Hoban. Los Angeles: Semiotext.

References

Sloterdijk, Peter. 2013. *You Must Change Your Life*. 1st ed. Cambridge: Polity.

Sloterdijk, Peter, and Bernard Stiegler. 2016. "Welcome to the Anthropocene: Debate with Peter Sloterdijk and Bernard Stiegler." Presented at Radboud Reflects, Radboud Universiteit, Nijmegen, Netherlands, June 27. YouTube video, 1:32:12. https://www.youtube.com/watch?v=ETHOqqKluC4.

Smith, Karl. 2016. "Concept Car of the Week: The Kar-A-Sutra (1972)." *Car Design News*, October 21. Accessed August 17, 2018. https://cardesignnews.com/articles/concept-car-of-the-week/2016/10/kar-a-sutra.

Smith, Nancy, Shaowen Bardzell, and Jeffrey Bardzell. 2017. "Designing for Cohabitation: Naturecultures, Hybrids, and Decentering the Human in Design." In *Proceedings of the 2017 CHI Conference on Human Factors in Computing Systems (CHI '17)*, 1714–1725. New York: Association for Computing Machinery. https://doi.org/10.1145/3025453.3025948.

Spuybroek, Lars. 2012. *The Sympathy of Things: Ruskin and the Ecology of Design*. Rotterdam: nai010.

Spuybroek, Lars. 2017. "Gothic Ontology and Sympathy: Moving Away from the Fold." In *Speculative Art Histories*, edited by Sjoerd Van Tuinen. Edinburgh, UK: Edinburgh University Press. Edinburgh Scholarship Online, 2018. https://doi.org/10.3366/edinburgh/9781474421041.003.0009.

Star, Susan Leigh, and Karen Ruhleder. 1996. "Steps toward an Ecology of Infrastructure: Design and Access for Large Information Spaces." *Information Systems Research* 7 (1): 111–134. https://doi.org/10.1287/isre.7.1.111.

Stevens, E. S. 2001. *Green Plastics: An Introduction to the New Science of Biodegradable Plastics*. 1st ed. Princeton, NJ: Princeton University Press.

Stiegler, Bernard. 1998. *Technics and Time, 1: The Fault of Epimetheus*. Translated by Richard Beardsworth and George Collins. Stanford, CA: Stanford University Press.

Stolterman, Erik, and Mikael Wiberg. 2010. "Concept-Driven Interaction Design Research." *Human-Computer Interaction* 25 (2): 95–118. https://doi.org/10.1080/07370020903586696.

Suchman, Lucy A. 1987. *Plans and Situated Actions: The Problem of Human-Machine Communication*. Cambridge: Cambridge University Press.

Sullivan, John. 1992. *Local Government and Community in Java: An Urban Case-Study*. Singapore: Oxford University Press.

Sullivan, Norma. 1995. *Masters and Managers: The Study of Gender Relations in Urban Java*. Reissue ed. St. Leonards, Australia: Allen & Unwin.

Tankersley, Jim. 2018. "A Winter-Coat Heavyweight Gives Trump's Trade War the Cold Shoulder." *New York Times*, November 23, Business. https://www.nytimes.com/2018/11/23/business/economy/columbia-sportswear-trump-trade-war.html.

Tasker, John Paul. 2020. "Liberals Hope to Ban Firearms Used in Polytechnique, Dawson College Shootings: Sources." *CBC News*, April 29. https://www.cbc.ca/news/politics/liberal-government-gun-control-friday-1.5549969.

Toussaint, Lianne. 2018. "Wearing Technology: When Fashion and Technology Entwine." Doctoral thesis, Radbout University, Nijmegen, Netherlands.

Troscianko, Jolyon, and Christian Rutz. 2015. "Activity Profiles and Hook-Tool Use of New Caledonian Crows Recorded by Bird-Borne Video Cameras." *Biology Letters* 11 (12): 20150777. https://doi.org/10.1098/rsbl.2015.0777.

Tsing, Anna Lowenhaupt. 2015. *The Mushroom at the End of the World: On the Possibility of Life in Capitalist Ruins*. Princeton, NJ: Princeton University Press.

Tuana, Nancy. 2008. "Viscous Porosity: Witnessing Katrina." In *Material Feminisms*, 188–213. Bloomington: Indiana University Press.

Utrecht University. 2019. "Burgundian Black." ARTECHNE—Technique in the Arts, 1500–1950. https://artechne.wp.hum.uu.nl/workshops/burgundian-black/.

Valentino-DeVries, Jennifer, Natasha Singer, Michael H. Keller, and Aaron Krolik. 2018. "Your Apps Know Where You Were Last Night, and They're Not Keeping It Secret." *New York Times*, December 10. https://www.nytimes.com/interactive/2018/12/10/business/location-data-privacy-apps.html.

Van der Welden, Maja. 2014. "Re-politicising Participatory Design: What Can We Learn from Fairphone." Presented at the *Ninth International Conference on Culture and Technology and Communication (CaTaC)*, Oslo, Norway, June 19–20. https://www.duo.uio.no/bitstream/handle/10852/42038/CATaC+2014+Proceedings.pdf?sequence=1#page=143.

Van der Zee, Renee. 2015. "How Amsterdam Became the Bicycle Capital of the World." *The Guardian*, May 5. https://www.theguardian.com/cities/2015/may/05/amsterdam-bicycle-capital-world-transport-cycling-kindermoord.

Van Dongen, Pauline. 2019. *A Designer's Material-Aesthetics Reflections on Fashion and Technology*. Eindhoven, Netherlands: Artez.

Van Doren, Harold Livingston. 1954. *Industrial Design: A Practical Guide to Product Design and Development*. New York: McGraw-Hill.

Verbeek, Peter-Paul. 2001. "Don Ihde: The Technological Lifeworld." In *American Philosophy of Technology: The Empirical Turn*, 119–146. Bloomington: Indiana University Press.

Verbeek, Peter-Paul. 2005. *What Things Do: Philosophical Reflections on Technology, Agency, and Design*. University Park: Pennsylvania State University Press.

Verbeek, Peter-Paul. 2006. "Materializing Morality Design Ethics and Technological Mediation." *Science, Technology & Human Values* 31 (3): 361–380. https://doi.org/10.1177/0162243905285847.

Verbeek, Peter-Paul. 2008. "Cyborg Intentionality: Rethinking the Phenomenology of Human Technology Relations." *Phenomenology and the Cognitive Sciences* 7 (3): 387–395.

Verbeek, Peter-Paul. 2011. *Moralizing Technology: Understanding and Designing the Morality of Things*. Chicago: University of Chicago Press.

Verbeek, Peter-Paul. 2016. "Toward a Theory of Technological Mediation: A Program for Postphenomenological Research." In *Technoscience and Postphenomenology: The Manhattan Papers*, 189–204. London: Lexington Books.

Wainwright, Oliver. 2018. "The World's Best Building? A Remote Brazilian School Made out of Wood." *The Guardian*, November 21, Art and Design. https://www.theguardian.com/artanddesign/2018/nov/21/children-village-brazilian-school-riba-international-prize-best-building-in-the-world.

Wakkary, Ron, Audrey Desjardins, and Sabrina Hauser. 2016. "Unselfconscious Interaction: A Conceptual Construct." *Interacting with Computers* 28 (4): 501–520.

Wakkary, Ron, and Marek Hatala. 2006. "Ec(h)o: Situated Play in a Tangible and Audio Museum Guide." In *Proceedings of the 6th Conference on Designing Interactive Systems (DIS '06)*, 281–290. New York: Association for Computing Machinery. https://doi.org/10.1145/1142405.1142448.

Wakkary, Ron, William Odom, Sabrina Hauser, Garnet Hertz, and Henry Lin. 2015. "Material Speculation: Actual Artifacts for Critical Inquiry." In *Proceedings of the Fifth Decennial Aarhus Conference on Critical Alternatives (AA '15)*, 97–108. Aarhus, Denmark: Aarhus University Press. http://dx.doi.org/10.7146/aahcc.v1i1.21299.

Wakkary, Ron, Doenja Oogjes, Sabrina Hauser, Henry Lin, Cheng Cao, Leo Ma, and Tijs Duel. 2017. "Morse Things: A Design Inquiry into the Gap between Things and Us." In *Proceedings of the 2017 Conference on Designing Interactive Systems (DIS '17)*, 503–514. New York: Association for Computing Machinery. https://doi.org/10.1145/3064663.3064734.

Wakkary, Ron, Doenja Oogjes, Henry W. J. Lin, and Sabrina Hauser. 2018. "Philosophers Living with the Tilting Bowl." In *Proceedings of the 2018 CHI Conference on Human Factors in Computing Systems (CHI '18)* 94:1–12. New York: Association for Computing Machinery. https://doi.org/10.1145/3173574.3173668.

"Weather: Forecast & Radar Maps—Apps on Google Play." n.d. Accessed June 11, 2020. https://play.google.com/store/apps/details?id=com.weather.Weather&hl=en_CA.

"Weather—The Weather Channel." n.d. App Store. Accessed June 11, 2020. https://apps.apple.com/us/app/weather-the-weather-channel/id295646461.

White, Jeremy. 2019. "When Lawmakers Try to Ban Assault Weapons, Gunmakers Adapt." *New York Times*, July 31, US. https://www.nytimes.com/interactive/2019/07/31/us/assault-weapons-ban.html.

Willis, Anne-Marie. 2006. "Ontological Designing." *Design Philosophy Papers* 4 (2): 69–92. https://doi.org/10.2752/144871306X13966268131514.

Wilson, Mark. 2018. "Dieter Rams Wants Silicon Valley to Stop." *Fast Company*, August 10. https://www.fastcompany.com/90246965/dieter-rams-wants-silicon-valley-to-stop.

Wiltse, Heather, and Erik Stolterman. 2010. "Architectures of Interaction: An Architectural Perspective on Digital Experience." In *Proceedings of the 6th Nordic Conference on Human-Computer Interaction: Extending Boundaries (NordiCHI '10)*, 821–824. New York: Association for Computing Machinery. https://doi.org/10.1145/1868914.1869038.

Wingrove, Elizabeth. 2016. "Materialisms." In *The Oxford Handbook of Feminist Theory*, 454–671. New York: Oxford University Press.

Winner, Langdon. 1980. "Do Artifacts Have Politics?" *Daedalus* 109 (1): 121–136.

Winograd, Terry, and Fernando Flores. 1987. *Understanding Computers and Cognition: A New Foundation for Design*. Boston: Addison-Wesley.

Wolfe, Cary. 2010. *What Is Posthumanism?* Minneapolis: University of Minnesota Press.

Wolfe, Cary. 2012. *Before the Law: Humans and Other Animals in a Biopolitical Frame*. Chicago: University of Chicago Press.

Zhang, Sarah. 2016. "Throwing This Out Here: Plastic Bags Are Amazing and You Should Appreciate Them More." *Wired*, January 25. https://www.wired.com/2016/01/plastic-bags/.

Zuboff, Shoshana. 2019. *The Age of Surveillance Capitalism: The Fight for a Human Future at the New Frontier of Power*. New York: Public Affairs.

Index

Page numbers followed by *f* refer to figures.

Academic research, matters of, 217–218
Acceptance, problematizing of, 140–141
Accountability
  anti-biographies and, 239
  of nomadic practices, 54, 242
  response-ability, 244–246
  situated knowledges and, 48–49
  of speaking subjects, 223–224
Action, situated, 67
Actor Network Theory (ANT), 111–112, 144–145, 214, 253n1
Adolph, Sven, 107
Affirmative design, 78
Afterbodies, 4
Afterhuman ideas of posthumanism, 4
Agency and agentic capacities, 12, 47.
  See also Vitality of things
  agential realism, 253n2
  causality, 157–158
  concept of, 3, 21, 151–156
  designer as force, 179–185
  distributed, 160
  efficacy, 156, 160, 179, 184, 237
  shared, 4, 23
  trajectory, 157, 160, 179, 184, 237
Agre, Philip E., 41–45, 212
Aldea, Eva, 49
Aleph Zero, 24, 163, 169, 184, 217.
  See also *Children Village*

Aliveness. *See* Vitality of things
Alpha-Mobile, 58
Alterity relations, 104–106, 118
Althing, 215
Ambasz, Emily, 62
Andersen, Kristina, 249
Animal-computer interaction (ACI), 99–100
Animal-things, 107
ANT. *See* Actor Network Theory (ANT)
Anthropocene, 253n2
  critical zone in, 255n1
  human-thing relations in, 3–4, 117
Anthropocentric thinking, 9, 45, 176
Anti-biographies, 24–25, 205–211, 239
  Bag with handle of weldable plastic material, 193–195, 194f, 205–206
  Camden Bench, 197–198, 197f, 210–211, 214
  concept of, 193, 204–205, 239
  contestation of, 214–215
  context-aware computing, 196–197, 207–210, 256n8
  Lifepatch collective, 25, 198–200, 199f, 219–223, 248
  M-16/AR-15 rifle, 25, 196, 206–207, 210, 256n6

Anti-biographies (cont.)
  political occlusion by, 211
  Weather Channel Weather App, 196–197
Anti-consumerism, 175, 217–218
Anti-design movements, 78
Anti-patterns, 193
Anti-programs, 254n1
Apple, 74. *See also* Ive, Jonathan
  FaceID system, 89
  location-based technologies for, 196–197, 256n8
  Rams' criticism of, 78
Appropriation of artifacts, 72–73
AR-15 rifle, 25, 196, 206–207, 210, 256n6
Architectural Association (London), 168
Architectural design
  Children Village, 24, 169–172, 171f, 172f, 184, 217
  intensities and origins in, 190
  Supersurface installation, 24, 78, 168–169, 169f, 170f, 183–184, 190
Archizoom Associati
  Radical Design movement and, 78
  Superarchitettura exhibition, 80, 81f
Arendt, Hannah, 157, 189
Aristotle, 142
Armalite, 25, 196
Arofatullah, Nur Akbar, 198
ARTECHNE (Utrecht University and University of Amsterdam), 129. *See also Burgundian Black Collaboratory*
Artifact-in-itself, 67
Artifact-in-use, 67
Artifacts, 15, 235. *See also* Human-computer interaction (HCI)
  appropriation of, 72–73
  cognitive, 69
  concepts and theories embodied in, 68–70
  counterfactual, 26, 121–122
  embedding or situating of use in, 67

ethnomethodologist approaches to, 71–72
Fairphone campaign, 15, 57–58, 59f, 73
flexibility of, 67–68, 108, 213
intentionality of, 70–73, 116–117
Long-Living Chair, 15, 32–33, 33f, 40
meta-design, 72
motivation for, 65–66
Olly, 15, 33–34, 34f, 40
participatory design, 8, 65–68, 70–71, 213–217
Photobox, 15, 31–32, 32f, 34–35, 40, 157
situated knowledges in, 82–83
slow technology, 15
as somethings, 66
technological, 106–107
temporal plasticity of, 67–68, 118
things compared to, 108–109
user co-design of, 65, 70, 72–73
Artificial intelligence (AI), 41–42, 180, 242
"Artillery" Bow with Thumb Ring (Ihde), 107
Assemblages
  biographical aspects of, 178
  concept of, 17–19, 236
  fluid, 8, 209
  +Lichtlijn project, 18, 87, 90, 91f, 110–113, 111f, 118–119, 179, 188–189
  Object-Oriented-Ontology and, 253n1
  Prayer Companion, 18, 87, 90–91, 92f, 113–116, 118–119
  Speculative Realism and, 253n1
Assemblies of vital matter, 12, 16, 136f, 203f, 236–237. *See also* Agency and agentic capacities; Multistability; Vitality of things
Autobiographical design
  definition of, 164, 176–177
  Greenscreen Dress, 164, 166–167, 166f, 167f, 177, 182, 190

Index

Living in a Prototype, 163–164, 165f, 176–178, 182, 186, 190
   maker/user in, 164
   tinkering in, 164
Autopoeisis, 244–245

Baeza, Saúl, 89
Bag with handle of weldable plastic material (Gustaf Thulin)
   design of, 25, 193–195, 194f
   environmental impact of, 205–206
Barad, Karen, 239
Bauhaus, 60
Becoming-minor, 140
Becoming-minoritarian, 140
Behavioral surplus, 209–210, 217
Being, revealing/concealing, 6–7
Being and Time (Heidegger), 102
Being the Machine (Devendorf and Ryokai), 22, 121
   causality in, 157–158
   description of, 123–124, 124f, 125f
   multiplicity of human-thing alternatives in, 159
   non-hylomorphism in, 142
Bellini, Mario, 15, 62–64, 78–79. See also *Kar-a-Sutra* (Bellini)
Benches, public, 160–161
   ANT interpretation of, 254n1
   as callous objects, 143–145, 144f
   Camden Bench, 25, 197–198, 197f, 210–211, 214
   multiplicity of, 151, 159–160
   multistability of, 143–145, 144f
   political dimension of, 160–161
Bennett, Jane, 251
   on agentic capacities, 179, 184, 186, 237
   on politics of things, 192
   on posthuman empiricism, 218
   on relationality of things, 19
   on vitality of things, 8, 20–21, 25, 148, 151–152, 174, 186–187, 227

Bergson, Henri, 8
Berland, Laurence, 228
Beta-Mobile, 58
Bijker, Wiebe E., 212
Binder, Thomas, 8, 215
Biographies. See also Anti-biographies; Autobiographical design
   designers as, 22–24, 164, 174–179, 238–239
   limitations of, 192
   radically situated, 167, 175–176
Bios, 176
Bios egalitarianism, 176
Biosphere, cohabitation of, 177, 255n1
Bodegraven traffic system. See *+Lichtlijn* (HIG Traffic Systems)
Bødker, Susanne, 38–39, 43
Borgmann, Albert, 8
Boulboullè, Jenny, 22, 121. See also *Burgundian Black Collaboratory*
Bowden, Courtney, 228
Braidotti, Rosi
   on biological egalitarianism, 99, 176, 255n5
   on defamiliarization, 138–140
   on human subjectivity, 185–186, 188
   on matters of capitalism, 217
   on posthumanism, 2, 4
   on shared desire for transformations, 146
   on *zoe*/vitality, 156, 176
Braun MPZ 2 Citromatic, 74–75, 75f, 175
Braun Pocket Receivers
   description of, 15, 58, 60–62, 60f
   design principles governing, 76–77, 175
   intersection with products, 82
Bray, Tim, 228
Brignull, Henry, 193
Bryson, Gerald, 228
Buat sendiri. See Do-it-with-others (DIWO) ethos
Budiarto, Agus Tri, 198

Burgundian Black Collaboratory, 22, 121, 129–131, 131f, 154–156, 155f
By-wire.net, 87

Callous objects, 143–145, 151, 198. *See also* Sleep-prevention bench
Camden Bench, 25, 197–198, 197f, 210–211, 214
Camera project. See *Obscura 1C Digital Camera* (Pierce and Paulos)
Camper van project. See *Living in a Prototype* (Desjardins)
Canuana school housing. See *Children Village*
Capitalism, matters of, 1, 5–6, 217
Car Design News, 79
Care, matters of, 12, 22, 24, 203–204, 238. *See also* Constituencies; Politics of things
Carroll, John, 68–72
Carroll, Lewis, 183
Cartesian rationalism, shift away from, 41
Causality, 157–158, 160, 189–190
Celloplast, 193–195, 205–206. See also *Bag with handle of weldable plastic material* (Gustaf Thulin)
Cézanne, Paul, 76
Changing Things (Redström and Wiltse), 8
Chess, sedentary order represented in, 50–52, 51f
Children Village
  description of, 24, 169–172, 171f, 172f
  designer as force in, 184
  as proto-constituency, 217
Chthulucene, 3–4
Circulating reference, 224–225
Clarke, Rachel, 250
Climate change, 1–2, 182, 227, 251
Co-constituting force, matter as, 152, 188
Co-designers, users as, 65, 70, 72–73

Cognition, distributed, 69
Cognitive artifacts, 69
Cognitive psychology, artifacts in, 68–70
Colt Manufacturing, 196, 207. *See also* M-16/AR-15 rifle
Columbia sportswear, tariff engineering at, 80
Composite intentionality, 20, 101, 149–151
Computer modeling, critical technical practices in, 41–42
Computer-supported cooperative work (CSCW), 66, 72–73
Concept car project. See *Kar-a-Sutra* (Bellini)
Conceptual constructs, 54
Concern, matters of, 12, 22, 24, 202–203, 238. *See also* Constituencies; Politics of things
Concrete tailoring, 145
Concretization, 181–185, 188–190, 209
Condensing of technical objects, 181
Conflict-free smartphone. See *Fairphone*
Constituencies, 22, 213–217. *See also* Anti-biographies
  assembly of matters in, 219–223
  concept of, 24, 201–205, 212–213, 239
  infrastructuring and publics in, 213–217
  progressive composition of, 204, 222
  proto-constituencies, 217–218, 228–229
  purpose of, 202–203, 212, 244
  repertoires of, 227–230
  stubbornly realist attitude toward, 218–219, 240
Consumerism, 1, 78. *See also* Anti-consumerism
Context-aware computing, 207–210, 256n8
Coole, Diana, 8, 21, 47, 151–152, 156

Index

Co-performing technologies, 250
Coproduction, 123
Co-speculation, 122. See also *Tilting Bowl* (Wakkary et al.)
Costa, Maren, 228
Counterfactual artifacts, 26, 121–122, 140, 147. See also *Morse Things* (Wakkary et al.); *Tilting Bowl* (Wakkary et al.)
Counterfunctional artifacts, 22, 125–126, 145. See also *Obscura 1C Digital Camera* (Pierce and Paulos)
COVID-19 pandemic, 113, 228
Crabtree, Andrew, 68
Crary, Jonathan, 76
Critical analysis, 72
Critical and creative speculations, 5–9
Critical design, 62, 78–80
Critical fabulations, 7, 250
Critical Fabulations (Rosner), 7
Critical posthumanism, 4–5, 250, 253n1
Critical technical practices, 41–42
Critical utopias, 22, 168. See also *Supersurface* (Superstudio)
Critical zone, 255n1
Crows, technology use by, 97–98, 98f, 99f, 187
CSCW. *See* Computer-supported cooperative work (CSCW)
Cultural cumulative evolution, 98
Cultural Heritage Agency of the Netherlands (RCE), 130. See also *Burgundian Black Collaboratory*
Cultural variances, 137
Cunningham, Emily, 228
Cyborg concept, 16, 100
Cyborg intentionality, 100, 105

Dark patterns, 193
Darwin, Charles, 218, 247–248, 251
Debaise, Didier, 240
Decomposition, 250

Defamiliarization, 79, 121, 138–139, 145, 149, 182. See also *Being the Machine* (Devendorf and Ryokai); *Obscura 1C Digital Camera* (Pierce and Paulos); *Tilting Bowl* (Wakkary et al.)
Defuturing, 6, 212
DeLanda, Manuel, 52, 178, 188
Delegation, 17–18
Deleuze, Gilles, 8, 14, 46, 49–50, 139–140, 153, 178, 180–181
Democratization of workplace, 70–71
Derrida, Jacques, 157
Design-after-design, 213, 217
Design designs, 6
Designed-in-use, 72
Designer. *See also* Anti-biographies; Autobiographical design; Constituencies
  as biography, 22–24, 164, 174–179, 238–239
  embodied nature of, 13–14
  as force, 179–185, 237
  as intensities and origins, 188–192, 238
  moral ask of, 240–245
  as moralist, 77, 80
  response-ability of, 244–245
  as speaking subject, 23, 25–26, 185–188, 210, 223–227, 237–238
Designing artifacts. *See* Artifacts
Designing objects. *See* Objects
Designing products, 15, 235
  intentionality, 79–80
  situated knowledges, 82–83
  tariff engineering, 80
Designing things. *See* Nomadic practices; Things
Designing-with, 5, 191. *See also* Constituencies
  constituencies and, 24, 211, 220
  generosity of, 250–252
  matters of concern, 216

Designing-with (cont.)
  not-knowing in, 245–250
  renunciation of, 205, 211
  shifting toward, 173, 240–245
Design problem, 23, 204, 211, 239, 245
Design situations, 225
Design Things (Binder et al.), 8
Desjardins, Audrey, 163–164, 176, 178, 186, 190. See also *Living in a Prototype* (Desjardins)
D'Este, Franceso, 131f
Deterritorialization, 139
Devendorf, Laura, 22, 121, 123–124, 142. See also *Being the Machine* (Devendorf and Ryokai)
Dewey, John, 214
Dharma Wanita (DW), 221
Dieter Rams (Ive), 74
Di Francia, Cristiano Toraldo, 168. See also *Supersurface* (Superstudio)
Digital camera. See *Obscura 1C Digital Camera* (Pierce and Paulos)
Digital matter
  concretization of, 181–185, 188–190, 209
  intentionality of, 180
  trajectory and efficacy of, 179–180
Digital photos, engagement with. See *Photobox* (Odom et al.)
Disciplinary approaches, 235. *See also* Nomadic practices
  generative metaphors, 41–44, 54
  movement away from, 35–37
  nomadic practices as alternative to, 35–37
  paradigms, 37–39
  programs, 39–41
Discipline of design, movement away from, 35–37. *See also* Nomadic practices
Discursive domains, 42
Disidentification, 138–140, 145
Disposable America, 206

Distributed agency, 160, 237
  causality, 157–158
  efficacy, 156, 179, 184
  trajectory, 157, 179, 184
Distributed cognition, 69
Do-it-with-others (DIWO) ethos, 198–200, 219–220. See also *Lifepatch* collective
Do-it-yourself (DIY) ethos, 164, 198–200, 219–220. *See also* Autobiographical design; *Lifepatch* collective
Dominant stability, 143
Dorrestijn, Steven, 243
Double movements, 6
Dourish, Paul, 72–73, 108
Droplifting, 125
Dunne, Anthony, 78
Dyes and dyeing processes. See *Burgundian Black Collaboratory*
Dynamic fabric. See *Greenscreen Dress* (Mackey et al.)

Eames, Charles, 15, 32–33. See also *Long-Living Chair* (Eames and Eames)
Eames, Ray, 15, 32–33. See also *Long-Living Chair* (Eames and Eames)
Earthbound, 256, 256n1
Efficacy, 156, 160, 179, 184, 237
Egalitarianism between human/nonhuman animals, 99–100
Ehn, Pelle, 70–71, 213
Eindhoven University of Technology, 33
Ekbia, Hamid, 256n9
Electrical power grid failure, 20, 148, 188, 243
Electromagnetic waves, 38
Emancipatory politics, ideal of, 70–71
Embodied relations, 105–106, 118, 148
Embodiment of things, 118, 236
  hammer analogy, 102–103, 118, 174
  human-thing relations resulting from, 106–108

Index

New Faces, New Identities, 89, 90f, 104–105, 108
Phototrope, 18, 87–89, 88f, 89f, 102–110, 118
 ready-to-hand versus present-at-hand, 102–104
 virtual computing and digital networks, 108–109
Empiricism, posthuman, 72, 218, 247
Énon, David, 132. *See also* Mineral Accretion Factory
Epistemology, 35. *See also* Nomadic practices
Equity and equality, 255n5
Escobar, Arturo, 6, 250
Ethical use, *Fairphone* campaign for, 15, 57–58, 59f, 73
Ethics, design, 212–213, 219–220, 243–244
Ethnography
 in human-computer interaction (HCI), 68, 70–72, 254n1
 in *Lifepatch* collective, 221–222
Ethnomethodologies, 70, 72
Evasion design, 168
Everest climbing expeditions, 20–22, 188, 253n3
Everyday Design Studio, 26, 33, 121, 126, 136, 217, 223. See also *Morse Things* (Wakkary et al.); *Tilting Bowl* (Wakkary et al.)
Expansiveness, 45, 192, 217–218, 223, 230, 235–236, 251. *See also* Interconnectedness of humans/things; Relationality of things
Experimentation, 130, 244
ExxonMobil, 195

Facebook, 180–182, 207, 217, 228, 255n3
FaceID system (Apple), 89
Facial prosthetics. See *New Faces, New Identities* (Baeza)

Fact, matters of, 202–203
Factory Furniture, *Camden Bench*, 25, 197–198, 197f, 210–211, 214
Fairphone, 15, 57–58, 59f, 73
Fallman, Daniel, 8
Falsifiability, 38, 40
Feminist objectivity, 37, 48–49
Fischer, Gerhard, 72
Flexibility of artifacts, 67–68, 108, 213
Flickr archive, *Photobox* project for, 15, 31–32, 32f, 34–35, 40, 157
Flores, Fernando, 103
Fluid assemblages, 8, 209
Force, designer as, 179–185, 237
Forlano, Laura, 8
Foucault, Michel, 243, 244–245
Foundational knowledge
 practices without, 44–45
 programs, 39–41
 situated knowledges versus, 36–37
Found tools, nonhuman animal use of, 97–99, 98f, 99f
Fragmentation, 250
Friedman, Batya, 212, 255n4
Fry, Tony, 6, 212

Gaia (Lovelock), 255n1
Gatens, Moira, 146
Gaver, Bill, 90–91, 113–116. See also *Prayer Companion* (Interaction Research Studio)
G-Code, 123, 124f
General Data Protection Regulation (GDPR), 215
Generative metaphors, 37, 41–44, 54
Generosity, 250–252
Globalization, 5
Global North/South designs, 6, 220
Go (game), nomadic order in, 50–52, 51f
Goodall, Jane, 97
Google, 207–208, 217, 228
Goreau, Thomas J., 132

Gothic ontology, 7–8
Great Pacific Garbage Patch, 18, 87, 93, 93f, 116–118, 205–206
Greenscreen Dress (Mackey et al.), 23–24
  description of, 164, 166–167, 166f, 167f
  role of designer in, 177, 182, 190
Greubel, Jurgen, 74–75
Ground Truth, 256n8
Gruppo Strum, 78
Guattari, Felix, 8, 14, 49–50, 140, 153, 178
Guimbal hydropower turbine, 181–182, 184
Gustaf Thulin, Sten, 25, 193–195, 205–206. See also *Bag with handle of weldable plastic material* (Gustaf Thulin)

Hallnäs, Lars, 40
Haraway, Donna
  on Anthropocene, 3–4
  cyborg concept, 16, 100
  on equity versus equality, 255n5
  feminist perspectives, 7, 46–49
  on natureculture, 97, 188
  response-ability concept, 244–245
  on situated knowledges, 218
Harrison, Steve, 43–44
Hartman, Saidiya, 7
Hayles, Katherine, 4
HCI. See Human-computer interaction (HCI)
Heidegger, Martin, 5, 6–7, 102–103, 118, 174, 190
Hermeneutics, 72, 103, 105–106, 118
Heteromation, 256n9
HIG Traffic Systems, 90, 110. See also *+Lichtlijn* (HIG Traffic Systems)
Hilbertz, Wolf, 132
Hirosue, Sachiko, 220
Historical processes, 178
Hof van Busleyden museum, 129. See also *Burgundian Black Collaboratory*

Hol, Jeroen, 33. See also *Olly* (Hol, Naus, and Verburg)
Hook (Everyday Design Studio), 26–28, 27f
Horizontality, 251–252
Hostile architecture, 143
How We Became Posthuman (Hayles), 4
Hughes, Thomas Parke, 212
Human-centered design, 37
  humanist precepts underlying, 1–6, 35
  shortcomings of, 1–2
Human-computer interaction (HCI), 36
  computer-supported cooperative work, 66, 72–73
  embodiment of concepts and theories in, 68–70
  ethnographic-related, 68, 71–72, 245n1
  generative metaphors of, 43–44
  paradigm shifts in, 38–39
  posthumanist philosophies in, 8–9
  purpose of, 65
Humanism, 1–6, 35
Human-machine configurations, 253n2
Human-things, 107. See also Interconnectedness of humans/things
  assemblage of, 110–113
  designers as, 174
  embodied and immanent nature of, 118, 236
  irreducibility of, 107, 118
  in *+Lichtlijn* project, 110, 111f, 112–113, 116–119, 143, 179
  multiplicity of, 159
Husserl, Edmond, 46
Hutchins, Edwin, 69
Hybrid fabrication, 123. See also *Being the Machine* (Devendorf and Ryokai)
Hybrid intentionality, 101, 105, 148
Hylomorphism, 142

Index

Idealism, 1, 77, 80
Identities, facial prosthetics for. See *New Faces, New Identities* (Baeza)
Ihde, Don
  "Artillery" Bow with Thumb Ring, 107
  on intentionality, 47
  on mediating technologies, 17, 95–97, 101, 103–104
  on multistability, 18–19, 141
  on relationality, 135
  on relationality of things, 148
  on technological artifacts, 106–107
  on technologically textured ecosystem, 16
Ill-disciplined history, 7
Illuminated running shirt. See *Phototrope* (van Dongen)
Immunology, 252
Indigo, 155–156, 155f, 160
Individuation, 178, 180–181
Indonesian *Lifepatch* collective.
  See *Lifepatch* collective
Industrial design rules, 60–61, 79–80
Infrastructuring, 213–217
Ingold, Tim, 142, 152, 190–191, 201
Innocence of things, 143, 159–160
"Innocent eye," 75–76
Instructables, 164
Instrumentalism, 5–6
Intensities, designer as, 188–192, 238
Intentionality, 46–47. See also *Morse Things* (Wakkary et al.)
  of artifacts, 70–73, 116–117
  composite, 20, 101, 149–151
  concept of, 13, 19–20, 37, 46–47, 173
  cyborg, 100, 105
  of digital material, 180
  hybrid, 101, 105, 148
  mediated, 100–102, 149–150
  multiplicity of, 13, 36, 53
  of products, 79–80
  technological mediation as, 101
Interactionism, 43

Interaction Research Studio, 18, 87, 90–91, 113–114. See also *Prayer Companion* (Interaction Research Studio)
Interconnectedness of humans/things. See also Assemblages; Mediating technologies
  animal-computer interaction, 99–100
  generosity of, 250–252
  Great Pacific Garbage Patch, 87, 93, 93f, 116–118, 205–206
  +*Lichtlijn* project, 18, 87, 90, 91f, 110–113, 111f, 179, 188–189
  New Faces, New Identities project, 89, 90f, 104–105, 108
  Phototrope project, 18, 87–89, 88f, 89f, 102–110, 118
  Prayer Companion project, 18, 87, 90–91, 92f, 113–116
  ready-to-hand versus present-at-hand experiences, 102–104
  shared technicity and, 97–100
  summary of, 236
  thought experiment for, 95–97
Inter-faciality, 27
Internet as thing, 108–109
Internet of Things (IoT), 23, 127–128, 149, 163, 255n2. See also *Living in a Prototype* (Desjardins)
Italian Radical Design movement, 168
Italy: *The New Domestic Landscape* exhibition, 62, 78, 168, 183. See also *Supersurface* (Superstudio)
Ive, Jonathan, 74, 77–78

Jelbert, Sarah, 97–98
Jongstra, Claudy, 22, 121, 130–131, 154–156. See also *Burgundian Black Collaboratory*

Kali Code, 200
Kar-a-Sutra (Bellini), 15, 62–64, 63f, 78–79, 82, 254n1

Kellogg, Wendy, 68–72
Knowledge, situated, 14, 36–37, 53–54, 82–83, 218
Kodak camera, 195
Koenig, Andrew, 193
Krakauer, Jon, 20
Kuhn, Thomas, 38–39, 41–42
Kuijer, Lenneke, 249

Lakatos, Imre, 40
Language, balancing with things, 25–28
Language-games, 72
Latour, Bruno
  Actor Network Theory, 111–112, 144–145, 214, 253n1
  agency of objects, 152
  concept of things, 7–8
  critical zone, 255n1
  delegation, 17
  dual meaning of things, 215
  earthbound concept, 256, 256n1
  on humanness, 254n1
  matters of concern, 24, 202–203, 215–216
  matters of fact, 211
  progressive composition of the common world, 204
  "scale one," 182–183, 185
  spokeperson concept, 224–227, 229–230, 237–238
  stubbornly realist attitude, 218–219, 240
Lee, Simon H., 255n6
"Less but better" maxim, 60
Libeskind, Daniel, 215
+Lichtlijn (HIG Traffic Systems), 18, 87
  assemblage of, 110–113, 111f, 188
  description of, 90, 91f
  designer as force in, 179
  intensities and origins in, 188–189
Lifepatch collective, 25, 198–200, 199f, 219–223, 248
Lin, Cindy, 198, 200, 220–221

Lindtner, Silvia, 198, 200, 220
Liu, Cyn, 250
Liveliness. *See* Vitality of things
Living in a Prototype (Desjardins)
  description of, 23, 163–164, 165f
  role of designer in, 176–178, 182, 186, 190
Lloyd, Genevieve, 146
Location-based technologies, 207–210, 256n8
Longevity, 60–61, 63, 76–78
Long-Living Chair (Eames and Eames), 15, 32–33, 33f, 40
Lovelock, James, 255n1

M-16/AR-15 rifle, 25, 196, 206–207, 210, 256n6
Machine learning, vitality in, 154
Mackey, Angella, 166, 177, 186, 190. *See also Greenscreen Dress* (Mackey et al.)
Madder plant root, 155, 160
Magic Machine Workshops (Andersen), 249
Magrin, Lisa, 208
Majoritarian position, 37, 252
Major science, sedentary nature of, 52–53, 252
Makers and Maker movement, 164, 200, 220–222. *See also* Autobiographical design; *Lifepatch* collective
Making Design Theory (Redstrom), 39
Making of practices, 44
Marres, Noortje, 214
Material aesthetics, 253n2
Material inscriptions, 145
Materialism, vital. *See* Vital materialism
Material practices, 35
Material speculation, 166. *See also Morse Things* (Wakkary et al.); *Tilting Bowl* (Wakkary et al.)
  definition of, 121, 137, 249

Index

in *Greenscreen Dress*, 177
probing relationality with, 146–147
Matters of academic research, 217–218
Matters of anti-consumerism, 175, 217
Matters of capitalism, 1, 5–6, 217
Matters of concern and care, 12, 22, 24, 202–204, 238. *See also* Constituencies; Politics of things
Matters of fact, 202–203
Matters of the profession, 217
Maxwell, James Clerk, 38
Mediated intentionality, 100–102, 149–150
Mediating technologies, 16–17. *See also* Embodiment of things; Things
   alterity relations in, 104, 118
   animal-computer interaction, 99–100
   characteristics of, 11–12, 117–118, 236
   co-performing technologies, 250
   description of, 11–12
   hammer analogy, 102–103, 118, 174
   hermeneutic relations in, 103, 118
   +*Lichtlijn* project, 18, 87, 90, 91f, 110–113, 111f, 179, 188–189
   mediated intentionality, 100–102, 149–150
   morality and, 243–244
   natureculture, 16–17
   New Faces, New Identities project, 89, 90f, 104–105, 108
   Phototrope project, 18, 87–89, 88f, 89f, 102–110, 118
   Prayer Companion, 18, 87, 90–91, 92f, 113–116
   proto-technologies, 97–99
   ready-to-hand versus present-at-hand, 102–104
   technicity in, 11, 16–17, 95, 97–100, 182
   thought experiment for, 95–97
   transformative nature of, 100–106
   transparency of, 104–105, 109, 145
Mentalist metaphor, 42–43

Merleau-Ponty, Maurice, 46, 151
Meta-design, 72
Metaphors, generative, 37, 41–44, 54
Milieu, object, 181–182
Mineral Accretion Factory, 121, 132–133, 132f, 158
Ministry of Multispecies Communications (Clarke), 250
Minoritarian positions, 35–36
Minor science, nomadic nature of, 52–53
Mobile phones, *Fairphone* campaign, 15, 57–58, 59f, 73
Mock-ups, as design artifacts, 67–68, 213
Mohammed, Bashir, 228
Moral ask to design-with, 240–245
Moralist, designer as, 77, 80
Morse Things (Wakkary et al.)
   agency in, 156, 160
   description of, 22, 121, 126–129, 128f, 129f, 130f
   intentionality in, 149–151
   vitality in, 149–151, 153–154
Moss, Richard, 60
Mount Everest climbing expeditions, 20–22, 188, 253n3
MPZ 2 Citromatic (Braun), 74–75, 75f
Multi-instabilities, 208–209
Multi-lifespan design, 255n4
Multiplicity of intentionalities, 13, 36, 53
Multiplicity of things, 159–160
Multistability, 12, 18, 135, 141–146, 141f, 144f
Museum of Modern Art (New York). See *Italy: The New Domestic Landscape* exhibition
Music player. See *Olly* (Hol, Naus, and Verburg)

Nardi, Bonnie, 256n9
Natalini, Adolfo, 168. See also *Supersurface* (Superstudio)

Natureculture, 11, 16–17, 95, 97–100, 182, 188, 253n2
Naus, Bram, 33. See also *Olly* (Hol, Naus, and Verburg)
Necker Cube, 141f
Netherlands *+Lichtlijn* system. See *+Lichtlijn* (HIG Traffic Systems)
Neustaedter, Carman, 164, 176
New Caledonian crows, technology use by, 97–98, 98f, 99f, 187
New Eden thought experiment, 96–98
New Faces, New Identities (Baeza), 89, 90f, 104–105, 108
Newton, Isaac, 38
9999 studio, 78
Nomadic practices. *See also* Artifacts; Objects; Products; Slow technology
 accountability and credibility of, 14–15, 36, 54
 aims of, 35, 54–55
 autonomy of, 82–83
 concept of, 5, 13–15, 35–37, 44, 234
 as epistemological theory, 35–36
 generative metaphors, 37, 41–44, 54
 intentionality of (*see* Intentionality)
 making of practices, 44
 nomadism in, 14, 37, 49–53
 paradigms and, 38–39
 power of, 15
 practices as transversals, 45
 practices without foundations, 44–45
 programs, 39–41
 sedentary design compared to, 14, 49–52
 situated knowledge, 14, 36–37, 47–49, 53–54, 82–83, 218
 summary of, 234–239
Nomadism, 14, 37, 49–53
Non-finito products, 180
Non-hylomorphism, 142
Non-neutrality of things, 17, 104–105, 107, 109, 126, 141–142, 236–237
Non-speciesist design, 99

"Normal" science, 38, 41
Not-knowing, 245–250

Objectivist positions, 35
Objectivity, 101–102, 107. *See also* Mediating technologies
 ethnomethodological commitments to, 70
 feminist, 48–49
 situated knowledge, 14, 36–37, 47–49, 53–54, 82–83, 218
Object-Oriented-Ontology (OOO), 253n1
Objects, 15, 74–80, 235
 affirmative approach to, 78
 Braun MPZ 2 Citromatic, 74–75, 75f
 Braun Pocket Receivers, 15, 58, 60–62, 60f, 76–77, 82
 critical approach to, 78, 80
 designer as moralist, 77, 80
 Kar-a-Sutra, 15, 62–64, 63f, 78–79, 82, 254n1
 principle of longevity in, 60, 63, 76–78
 Radical Design movement, 78–79
 self-referential nature of, 74–76
 situated knowledges in, 82–83
Obscura 1C Digital Camera (Pierce and Paulos)
 causality in, 157–158
 concrete tailoring in, 145
 description of, 22, 121, 124–126, 126f, 127f
 trajectory of, 157, 179
Ocean Cleanup, The, 93
Odom, William, 31, 32, 33. See also *Photobox* (Odom et al.)
Offloading of functionality, 181
Olly (Hol, Naus, and Verburg), 15, 33–34, 34f, 40
Ontological design, 5–8, 37, 103
Oogjes, Doenja, 250
Origins, designer as, 188–192

Index

Orlikowski, Wanda, 67, 70
Overmining, 253n1

P1 record player, 61
Pacific Trash Vortex. See *Great Pacific Garbage Patch*
Pandora's Hope (Latour), 224–225
Papanek, Victor, 212
Paradigms
  applicability to design practice, 37–39
  incommensurability of, 39
Parliament of things, 240
Participatory design (PD), 8, 213–217
  flexibility of artifacts in, 67–68, 213
  infrastructuring and publics, 213–217
  intentionality of, 70–71
  origins of, 65–66
  temporal plasticity of artifacts in, 67–68, 118
Paulos, Eric, 22, 121, 124, 145. See also *Obscura 1C Digital Camera* (Pierce and Paulos)
Pembinaan Kesejahateraan Keluarga (PKK), 221
Perspectivism, 48–49
Philosophies of technology, 6–8
Photobox (Odom et al.)
  description of, 15, 31–32, 32f
  slow technology in, 40
  trajectory in, 157
  unawareness of, 34–35
Phototrope (van Dongen), 18
  alterity relations in, 103–104
  description of, 87–89, 88f, 89f
  embodied human-thing relationship in, 108–110, 118
  mediated intentionality in, 107
  ready-to-hand versus present-at-hand experiences, 102–103
  transformative aspects of, 104, 109–110, 118

Pierce, James, 22, 121, 124–125, 145. See also *Obscura 1C Digital Camera* (Pierce and Paulos)
Pinch, Trevor, 212
Plastic Oceans, 255n2
Plastic shopping bag. See *Bag with handle of weldable plastic material* (Gustaf Thulin)
Plichto by Rosetti, 130
Pluralism, 45
Pluriverses, 204, 250
Pocket Receivers (Braun). See *Braun Pocket Receivers*
"Poke" feature, Facebook, 180–182
Politics of things. *See also* Constituencies
  concept of, 204, 238–239
  political ecology, 241–242
  political economy, 241–242
  political occlusion, 211
  relationality and, 135, 138, 141, 143, 146–147
  role of designer in, 191–192
  speaking subjects, 223–227
  thingpolitics, 12, 24, 202, 205, 239
  in *Tilting Bowl* project, 137–141
Polyethylene plastic, 195
Poor Clare sisters
  lives and background, 113–114
  Prayer Companion for, 18, 87, 90–91, 92f, 113–116
Popper, Karl, 38, 40
Portable radio. See *Braun Pocket Receivers*
Positioned rationality, 49
Postanthropocentrism, 253n2
Posthumanist design. *See also* Nomadic practices
  afterhuman ideas of, 4
  characteristics of, 2–3
  critical posthumanism, 4–5, 250, 253n1
  definition of, 4–5
  epistemological concepts in, 35–36

Posthumanist design (cont.)
  epistemology for, 44–45
  materialist understanding in, 35
  ontological design compared to, 5–8
  posthumanist philosophies in, 8–9
  relational ontologies in, 4, 135–136
  thinking-with, 4, 13, 176, 245
Posthuman subject, designer as, 185
Postphenomenology, 17, 111–112
Practices. *See also* Nomadic practices
  definition of, 44
  foundationless, 44–45
  making of, 44
  material, 35
  technical, 41–44
  as transversaks, 45, 49
Prayer Companion (Interaction Research Studio)
  description of, 18, 87, 90–91, 92f
  transformative nature of, 113–116
Present-at-hand, 102–104
Present-to-hand, 103
Products, 15
  definition of, 235
  intentionality of, 79–80
  situated knowledges in, 82–83
  tariff engineering, 80
Profession, matters of, 217
Programmes, 40
Programs, 37, 39–41, 210
Progressive composition, 204, 222
Prosthetic creatures, humans as, 9, 12, 96, 107, 236
Prosthetics, facial. See *New Faces, New Identities* (Baeza)
Proto-constituencies. *See also* Anti-biographies
  concept of, 217–218
  Lifepatch collective, 25, 198–200, 199f, 219–223
  technology corporations, 228–229

Proto-technologies, nonhuman animal use of, 97–99, 98f, 99f
Prototypes, as design artifacts, 67–68
Ptolemy, Claudius, 38
Public benches. *See* Sleep-prevention bench
Public good, 241
Publics, 8, 213–217, 240
Puig de la Bellacasa, Maria, 240
  dual meaning of things, 215
  ethics of care, 213, 219–223
  matters of care, 24, 203–204
  realism, 218
  thinking-with, 4, 13, 176, 245
  vital materialism, 8

Raby, Fiona, 78
Radical Design movement, 78–79
"Radical multiplicity" of knowledge, 48, 54
Radically situated, 167, 175–176. *See also* Biographies
Radio design. See *Braun Pocket Receivers*
Rams, Dieter
  affirmative approach of, 78, 80
  Braun MPZ 2 Citromatic, 74–75, 75f
  Braun Pocket Receivers, 15, 58, 60–62, 60f, 76, 82, 175
  "ten principles for good design," 60, 76, 109
Rationalism, 5–6, 41
Rationality, positioned, 49
Ready-to-hand technologies, 102–104
Realism
  agential, 253n2
  constituencies and, 218–219, 240
  speculative, 253n1
  stubbornly realist attitude, 218–219, 240
Reciprocal shaping, 43, 176, 178
Redström, Johan, 8, 39–41, 44–45, 208
Reflective practice, shift to, 36–37
Reflexivity, 42, 72

Index

Relationality of things, 18–19, 135–147, 236–237. See also *Being the Machine* (Devendorf and Ryokai); *Obscura 1C Digital Camera* (Pierce and Paulos); *Tilting Bowl* (Wakkary et al.)
  defamiliarization/disidentification strategies in, 79, 121, 138–139, 145, 149, 182
  generosity of, 250–252
  interpretation and, 135–141
  multistability, 12, 18, 135, 141–146, 141f, 144f
  political dimension of, 135, 138, 141, 143, 146–147
  relational ontologies, 4, 135–136
  Tilting Bowl project, 121–123, 122f, 136–141, 139f, 146–147, 157, 215
Religion, technology and, 18, 87, 90–91, 92f, 113–116
Repertoires of constituencies, 227–230
Response-ability, 244–245
Revolutionary phase of science, 38
Rich Site Summary (RSS), 254n1
Rivers, Rebecca, 228
Rocking chair project. See *Long-Living Chair* (Eames and Eames)
Rosenbaum, Marcelo, 169, 184. See also *Children Village*
Rosenberger, Robert, 101, 141, 143, 145, 211, 254n1
Rosner, Daniela, 7, 250
Ruger Mini-14, 256n6
Running shirt, illuminated. See *Phototrope* (van Dongen)
Ruskin, John, 7, 75–76
Ryokai, Kimiko, 123–124, 142. See also *Being the Machine* (Devendorf and Ryokai)

"Scale one," 182–183, 185, 188
Scenarios, as design artifacts, 67–68, 213
Schon, Donald, 41–42, 44, 152, 225
School of Art of La Réunion, 22, 121. See also Mineral Accretion Factory
Science, reconceptualizations of
  generative metaphors, 41–44
  major versus minor sciences, 52–53
  paradigm shifts, 37–39
  programs, 39–41
Sedentary order, 14, 49–53
Sedimentation, 143, 145–146, 149
Selby, Mark, 31. See also *Photobox* (Odom et al.)
Self-practice, 243–244
Sengers, Phoebe, 43–44, 164, 177
Seok, Jin-min, 180
Siagian, Andreas, 198
Simon, Herbert, 13
Simondon, Gilbert, 181, 184, 188–189
Situated action, 67
Situated interactions, 43
Situated knowledge, 14, 36–37, 47–49, 53–54, 82–83, 218
Situated perspectives, 43
Sleep-prevention bench, 160–161
  ANT interpretation of, 254n1
  as callous object, 143–145, 144f
  Camden Bench, 25, 197–198, 210–211, 214, on vitality of things
  multiplicity of, 151, 159–160
  multistability of, 143–145, 144f
  political dimension of, 160–161
Sloterdijk, Peter, 27, 216, 252
Slow technology
  definition of, 31
  Long-Living Chair project, 15, 32–33, 33f, 40
  Mineral Accretion Factory, 121, 132–133, 132f, 158
  Olly project, 15, 33–34, 34f, 40
  Photobox project, 15, 31–32, 32f, 34–35, 40
  unawareness of, 33–34
Smalls, Chris, 228

Social reality, generative metaphors for, 41–44
Society of Industrial Designers, 79
Speaking subject, designer as, 23
  balancing language with things in, 25–26
  concept of, 185–188, 237–238
  enigma of, 226–227
  political dimension of, 223–227
  programs created by, 210
  response-ability of, 244–245
Speculative Realism, 253n1
Speech prostheses, 229–230
Spinoza, Baruch, 153
Spuybroek, Lars, 7–8, 152–153
Star, Susan Leigh, 214
Stengers, Isabelle, 240
Stoner, Eugene, 25, 196, 207
Strong concepts, 54
Stubbornly realist attitude, 218–219, 240
Studio 65, 78
Subjectivity of humans, 101–102, 107, 143, 185–186, 188
Sub-lunar terrain, 255n1
Suchman, Lucy, 7, 67
Suharto (president of Indonesia), 221
Superarchitettura exhibition, 80, 81f
Superconsumption, 80
Superstudio, 78, 168. See also *Superarchitettura* exhibition; *Supersurface* (Superstudio)
Supersurface (Superstudio)
  description of, 24, 168–169, 169f, 170f
  designer as force in, 183–184
  intensities and origins in, 190
Surveillance capitalism, 209–210
Survival-with, 186
Sustainment, 6–7
Sylvie and Bruno (Carroll), 183
Symbiotic Process Laboratory, 132–133
Sympathy of things, 7, 152–153, 250
Sympathy of Things (Spuybroek), 7
Sympoiesis, 245

Table-non-table (Everyday Design Studio), 26–28, 27f
Tariff engineering, 80
Tatar, Deborah, 43–44
Taylor, Russell, 254n2
Technical artifacts, 106–107
Technical objects
  concretization of, 181–182, 188–190, 209
  milieu of, 181
Technical practices, 41–44
Technical rationality, shift away from, 36–37
Technicity, 11, 16–17, 95, 97–100, 182
Techno-fashion, 105–106. See also *Phototrope* (van Dongen)
Technological artifacts, 106–107
Technologically textured ecosystems, 16
Technological mediation, 11, 17, 95, 101, 253n2. See also Mediating technologies
Technology, philosophies of, 6–8. See also Slow technology
Technology-centered design, 37
Technology-in-practice, 67
"Ten principles for good design" (Rams), 60, 76, 109
Theoretical claims, embodiment in artifacts, 66, 68–70
Thermoplastic, 61
Into Thin Air (Krakauer et al.), 20
Thing-centeredness, 127, 149–150, 250, 253n2
Thingpolitics, 12, 24, 202, 205, 239. See also Constituencies
Things, 15. See also Mediating technologies
  artifacts compared to, 108–109
  balancing language with, 25–28
  conceptual understanding of, 106–107
  continuous reassembly of, 116–117
  definition of, 10–12, 236
  dual meaning of, 215

Index

embodiment of (*see* Embodiment of things)
as fluid assemblages, 8, 209
human relationship with, 9, 11–12, 16–18, 106–108
immediate nature of, 108, 109, 118
innocence and, 143, 159–160
intentionality of, 116–117
interconnectedness of (*see* Interconnectedness of humans/things)
matters of concern and care, 12, 22, 24, 202–204, 238
as means to reveal being, 6–7
multiplicity of, 159–160
non-neutrality of, 17, 104–105, 107, 109, 126, 141–142, 236–237
not-knowing, 245–250
ontology of, 7–8
in participatory design, 8
philosophical concepts behind, 10–12, 11f
political dimension of (*see* Politics of things)
relationality of (*see* Relationality of things)
sympathy of, 7, 152–153, 250
thing-centeredness, 127, 149–150, 250, 253n2
transformative nature of (*see* Transformative nature of things)
variantly embedded, 19
vitality of (*see* Vitality of things)
Things-before-things, 217, 228, 239
Thinking-with, 4, 13, 176, 245
Thousand Plateaus (Deleuze and Guattari), 50
3D printer deconstruction. See *Being the Machine* (Devendorf and Ryokai)
Three Paradigms of HCI, The (Harrison, Tatar, and Sengers), 43
Tilting Bowl (Wakkary et al.)
defamiliarizing/disidentification strategies in, 138–140

description of, 22, 121–123, 122f
designer as force in, 182
interpretive positions on, 136–141, 139f, 157
material speculation in, 146–147
matters of concern in, 215
scale of, 182
trajectory in, 157
Timbli, 198
Tinkering, 164
Toeters, Marina, 87. See also *Phototrope* (van Dongen)
Tracing, 250
Traffic system. See *+Lichtlijn* (HIG Traffic Systems)
Trajectory, 157, 179, 184, 237
Transcendental experiences, technology for. See *Prayer Companion* (Interaction Research Studio)
Transformative nature of things, 16–17, 100–106. *See also* Intentionality; Mediating technologies
Great Pacific Garbage Patch, 18, 87, 93, 93f, 116–117, 118, 205–206
+Lichtlijn project, 18, 87, 90, 91f, 110–113, 111f, 179, 188–189
natureculture, 11, 16–17, 95, 97–100, 182, 188, 253n2
New Faces, New Identities wearables, 89, 90f, 104–105, 108
Phototrope project, 18, 87–89, 88f, 89f, 102–104, 107–110, 118
Prayer Companion, 18, 87, 90–91, 92f, 113–116
summary of, 236
Transhumanism, 4
Transversals, practices as, 45, 49
Turner, Joseph, 76
Twin Towers, 215

UFO design studio, 78
Ulm School of Design, 60
"Ultimate particular," 10

Unawareness, 33–34
Underwater Table (Mineral Accretion Factory), 132–133, 158
Unformed particles, 153
Unintended consequences, inevitability of, 23, 116, 211, 216, 242, 245. *See also* Anti-biographies
Universalism, 54
Unpleasant design, 143
Usability analysis, 72
Use-before-use, 213, 217

Value sensitive design, 212, 255n4
van Abel, Bas, 57. See also *Fairphone*
van der Mark, Peter, 57. See also *Fairphone*
van Dongen, Pauline, 87–89, 102, 105. See also *Phototrope* (van Dongen)
van Doren, Harold, 79
Variances, cultural, 137
Variantly embedded things, 19
Verbeek, Peter-Paul
  on autopoeisis, 244–245
  on intentionality, 13, 20, 47, 100–101, 148–150
  on mediating technologies, 113, 243–244
  on philosophies of technology, 6
  postphenomenological understanding of technology, 102–103
Verburg, Pepijn, 33. See also *Olly* (Hol, Naus, and Verburg)
Virtual computing, materialities of, 108–109
Vitality of things, 19–20, 147–158. *See also* Agency and agentic capacities
  Burgundian Black Collaboratory, 121, 129–131, 131f, 154–156, 155f
  concept of, 148
  designing-with, 173
  Mineral Accretion Factory, 121, 132–133, 132f, 158
  Morse Things project, 22, 121, 126–129, 128f, 129f, 130f, 149–156, 160

Obscura 1C Digital Camera, 22, 121, 124–126, 126f, 127f, 145, 157–158, 179
  summary of, 236–237
  trajectory, 157
Vital materialism, 253n1. *See also* Agency and agentic capacities
  balancing language with things in, 25
  concept of, 8, 12, 20–21, 131, 135, 148, 153
  political goal of, 186
  speech as, 227
Vital matter, assemblies of, 12, 16, 136f, 203f, 236–237. *See also* Agency and agentic capacities; Multistability; Vitality of things
Vivino, 207

Wanderer/wayfarer, maker as, 191
Ways of knowing, 3, 9, 14, 37, 42, 49, 54
Wearables. See *Greenscreen Dress* (Mackey et al.); *New Faces, New Identities* (Baeza); *Phototrope* (van Dongen)
WeatherBug, 256n8
Weather Channel Weather App, 25, 196–197, 207–208
When Second Wave HCI Meets Third Wave Challenges (Bødker), 38–39
Whitehead, Alfred North, 8
Wildtech, 133. *See also* Mineral Accretion Factory
Williams, Thomas H. A., 255n6
Willis, Anne Marie, 6
Wiltse, Heather, 8, 208
Winograd, Terry, 103
Wolfe, Cary, 9, 96, 99
World-in-itself, 100

Yamasaki, Minoru, 215

Zoe-centered understanding, 176
Zuboff, Shoshana, 209